Popular Politics and the Quest for Justice in Contemporary China

The rise of popular politics is among one the most significant social and political developments the People's Republic of China has witnessed in the post-Mao era. People from all walks of life have responded to rising inequalities and the privatization of collective goods with a new quest for justice. Although China has remained a censorial society under the authoritarian rule of the Chinese Communist Party, state–society relations are being remade by interventions of emergent publics through word and action.

In this book, a group of anthropologists, specializing in Chinese society, examine various facets of popular politics, which are animated by the pursuit of justice, fairness and good government. The ethnographic chapters collectively analyse how 'the political' arises in particular judicial situations, provoking public judgements or other forms of critical engagement. Focusing on the interplay between private and public spaces, between morality and law and between speech and action, the contributors in this book explore how such engagements are changing Chinese society from the bottom-up.

As the first systematic exploration of the relationship between popular politics, emergent publics and notions of justice in contemporary China, this book will be useful for students of Chinese Studies, Politics and Anthropology.

Susanne Brandtstädter is Professor and Chair in the Anthropology of Globalization at the University of Cologne.

Hans Steinmüller is Assistant Professor in the Department of Anthropology at the London School of Economics.

Routledge Contemporary China

For our full list of available titles: https://www.routledge.com/Routledge-Contemporary-China-Series/book-series/SE0768

163 **Reconfiguring Class, Gender, Ethnicity and Ethics in Chinese Internet Culture**
Haomin Gong and Xin Yang

164 **Gender and Employment in Rural China**
Jing Song

165 **Migration in Post-Colonial Hong Kong**
Edited by Susanne Y P Choi and Eric Fong

166 **Popular Politics and the Quest for Justice in Contemporary China**
Edited by Susanne Brandtstädter and Hans Steinmüller

167 **Cyberdualism in China**
The Political Implications of Internet Exposure of Educated Youth
Shiru Wang

168 **Political Mobility of Chinese Regional Leaders**
Performance, Preference, Promotion
Liang Qiao

169 **Civilising Citizens in Post-Mao China**
Understanding the Rhetoric of Suzhi
Delia Lin

170 **China's Rise and the Chinese Overseas**
Bernard P. Wong and Tan Chee-Beng

171 **Competing Economic Paradigms in China**
The Co-Evolution of Economic Events, Economic Theory and Economics Education, 1976–2016
Steve Cohn

Popular Politics and the Quest for Justice in Contemporary China

Edited by
Susanne Brandtstädter and
Hans Steinmüller

Routledge
Taylor & Francis Group
LONDON AND NEW YORK

First published 2017 by Routledge

2 Park Square, Milton Park, Abingdon, Oxfordshire OX14 4RN
52 Vanderbilt Avenue, New York, NY 10017

Routledge is an imprint of the Taylor & Francis Group, an informa business

First issued in paperback 2018

British Library Cataloguing-in-Publication Data
A catalogue record for this book is available from the British Library

Library of Congress Cataloging-in-Publication Data
A catalog record for this book has been requested

ISBN: 978-1-138-22859-7 (hbk)
ISBN: 978-0-367-17265-7 (pbk)

Typeset in Times New Roman
by Apex CoVantage, LLC

Contents

Contributors

Susanne Brandtstädter is Professor of Anthropology at the University of Cologne. As a China anthropologist, her work has focused on issues of gender and kinship, moral economies, justice and value, and local responses to global capitalism. She is author of a recent book in Spanish (*Falsificaciones*, Fondo Cultura Economica, 2015) and co-editor of *Irony, Cynicism and the State* (with Hans Steinmüller, Routledge, 2016) and of *Rights, Cultures, Subjects and Citizens* (with Pete Wade and Kath Woodward, Routledge, 2013).

Chi-Pui Cheung is Assistant Professor in the Department of Anthropology and Ethnology at Xiamen University. He has conducted fieldwork in different parts of China, focusing on the politics of urbanized development in rural areas, rural land use, local policy implementation, and peasant resistance, and published on those topics that address the central issue of 'policy imagination'. He is working on a research project on local funeral and burial practices in response to the Chinese government's cremation policy.

Weishan Huang is a sociologist and Assistant Professor in the Department of Cultural and Religious Studies at Chinese University of Hong Kong. Her work mainly focuses on migration and religion, new religious movements, and urban gentrification and religion. She is the co-editor of the book *Ecology of Faith in New York City* (Indiana University Press, 2013). Her current research project is to examine the reconfiguration of two significant state-planned social phenomena, urbanization and religious revival, and its impacts on Mahayana Buddhist communities in contemporary Shanghai, China.

Ellen Hertz is Professor of Anthropology at the University of Neuchâtel. Her background in Chinese studies, law and anthropology has translated into a long-standing interest in the complex and ambiguous mechanisms of bureaucratization and marketization that characterize contemporary modernity, and on the place of gender in these configurations. She has published on diverse topics: financial markets, international organizations, intangible cultural heritage, sex work, corporate social responsibility and environmental anthropology.

Marylène Lieber is a sociologist and Associate Professor in the Department of Gender Studies at the University of Geneva. Her work has focused on gender violence in public places, Chinese migration and Chinese sex workers in Paris, and more recently on corporate social responsibility, with a research project on soft governance in the electronics industry in China. Her most recent publications include *Chinoises au XXIème siècle. Ruptures et continuités* (with T. Angeloff, Paris, La Découverte, 2012) and " Nouveaux instruments de justice sociale en Chine. Du droit du travail au développement personnel " (SociologieS [online], 2015)

Cuiming Pang received her PhD in digital media from the University of Oslo in 2012. Her research interests concern society and politics in China in general and digital media in particular. She writes about the Chinese internet and the emergence of internet communities.

Andrea E. Pia is a Fellow in the anthropology of China in the Department of Anthropology, London School of Economics. His research interests include the commons, sustainability, prefigurative grassroots politics, and the comparative study of human projects for the natural environment, with particular reference to the management of water in contemporary China and South-East Asia. His work is forthcoming in *PoLar: Journal of Political and Legal Anthropology Review* and in the *Journal of the Royal Anthropological Institute.*

Alan Smart is Professor at the Department of Anthropology and Archaeology, University of Calgary. His research has focused on urban issues, housing, foreign investment, social change, food safety, zoonotic diseases, and agriculture in Hong Kong, China, and Canada. He is author of "Making Room: Squatter Clearance in Hong Kong" (Hong Kong: Hong Kong University Press, 1992) "Petty capitalists and globalization" (co-edited with Josephine Smart, SUNY Press, 2005), "The Shek Kip Mei Myth: Squatters, fires and colonial rule in Hong Kong, 1950–1963" (Hong Kong University Press, 2006), and numerous articles in journals and edited volumes.

Josephine Smart is Professor of Anthropology in the Department of Anthropology and Archaeology, University of Calgary. Her research interests are social and economic development in post-1978 China, Chinese international migration, immigrant entrepreneurs, and the international mobility of capital and labour. She is a co-author of *Posthumanism – Anthropological Insights* (University of Toronto Press, 2017), co-editor of *Petty Capitalists and Globalization: Flexibility, Entrepreneurship and Economic Development* (SUNY, 2005), and sole author of *The Political Economy of Street Hawkers in Hong Kong* (University of Hong Kong Press, 1989).

Hans Steinmüller is Assistant Professor in the Department of Anthropology, London School of Economics. He is the author of *Communities of Complicity: Everyday Ethics in Rural China* (Berghahn 2013) and the editor (with Susanne Brandtstädter) of *Irony, Cynicism, and the Chinese State* (Routledge, 2016). His research interests include everyday ethics, family, ritual, gambling, and local governance. In his current research project, he deals with kinship and political authority in the borderlands of China and Burma.

Isabelle Thireau is Professor of Sociology at the Ecole des Hautes Etudes en Sciences Sociales (Paris) and Research Director at the Centre National de la Recherche Scientifique. Her interests include the sociology of norms, justice, and legitimacy in China. Her most recent publications are *Les Ruses de la démocratie. Protester en Chine contemporaine* (with Hua Linshan, Seuil, 2010); *De proche en proche. Ethnographie des formes d'association en Chine contemporaine* (Peter Lang, 2013); and "Contesting illegitimate situations, reassessing shared norms in contemporary China", *European Journal of Social Sciences* (2014, 52–2, pp 133–161).

Li Zhang is Professor of Anthropology and Vice Dean for Social Sciences at the University of California–Davis. Her research concerns the cultural, spatial, political, and psychological repercussions of market reforms and postsocialist transformations in China. She is the author of two award-winning books: *Strangers in the City* (Stanford, 2001) and *In Search of Paradise* (Cornell, 2010), and the co-editor of *Privatizing China, Socialism from Afar* (Cornell, 2008). Her current project explores an emerging psychological counseling movement and how it reshapes Chinese people's understandings of selfhood, well-being, and governing.

Acknowledgements

The main arguments of this book were first presented and discussed at the workshop "Justice, Popular Politics and the Chinese State" at the University of Oslo in June 2012. This workshop was funded by the Social Science Faculty of the University of Oslo, partially through a research grant to one of the editors (Susanne Brandtstädter), and partially through a special financial contribution that made the workshop possible. We gratefully acknowledge this financial support, as well as the administrative support we received at that time from the Department of Social Anthropology at UiO. We also gratefully acknowledge the contributions of paper givers and discussants at the conference who, for one reason or other, are not part of this volume, yet nevertheless with their ideas helped to shape it: Hu Zongze, Zhan Mei, Guo Yuhua, Chen Yifeng, Anna Lora-Wainwright, Adam Chau, Alpa Shah, Jean-Louis Rocca, and Don Kalb. We also thank Carmen Breuer at the University of Cologne for her support and accuracy in preparing the manuscripts.

Introduction

Judging the state

Emerging publics and the quest for justice in contemporary China

Susanne Brandtstädter

In contemporary China, people from all walks of life have become judges on the state of Chinese society and on the conditions under which it is governed. This critical engagement of common people for new public virtues and for public justice constitutes one of the most significant political developments the country has witnessed since the so-called Beijing Spring of 1989. So far, it has been the wave of rightful resistance in rural China (O'Brien and Li 2006), of new types of popular protests (O'Brien 2008) and of protest leaders (Brandtstädter 2011, 2016), of new dissident intellectuals and human rights activists (Béja, Fu and Pils 2012), together with the groundswell of new civil society initiatives (Hsing and Lee 2010) that has found much resonance in the literature. The everyday quest for justice and the critical judgements that ordinary people pass on Chinese society and its government, however, has by and large escaped the radar of social science research as it is expressed mostly on the level of personal narratives or enters 'ordinary ethics': in other words, it constitutes part of the stream of ordinary life. Yet, despite their personal nature, a striking feature of such judgements is both their ubiquity and standardized form. Today a visitor to China familiar with the language is confronted with an endless stream of critical statements about the country's remaining backwardness (*luohuo*) and chaos (*luan*), about the lack of quality (*suzhi*) or culture (*wenhua*) among its people, about rampant corruption (*fubai*) among government cadres, about an avalanche of fakes and fraudsters and about the general incivility, immorality and lack of trust that is blighting Chinese society.

In this volume, we take such ordinary acts of critical engagement, together with more collective, visible forms of protests, to be public judgements, calling on the state but also on a (real and imagined) audience of fellow citizens to make similar judgements. Public judgements imply a shared notion of justice or a shared standard of morality, and they seek, at the same time, to convince others to accept this as a valid basis on which to judge a particular situation. Especially as such situations are presented in a recognizable form that has resonance with others (e.g., 'corruption'), this volume suggests that public judgements play a central role in the creation of new publics, popular politics, and new subjects for politics in China. These subjects for politics are the product of a particular time and place in Chinese history, and the product of particular state–society relations, yet they also exist in friction with a newly privatized, civil and law-abiding citizen who is a state-product (see Keane 2001).

The chapters in this book analyze instances or situations where new publics come to the fore, where what counts as justice is being established, and where new political subjects emerge (or, vice versa, the processes that work against this) in a variety of cases from urban and rural, northern and southern China, and across many different social contexts. They focus, in particular, on the place of legal discourses and action, or of the new 'rule of law' (*fazhi*), in social imaginations and in popular struggles for justice in China. Finally, they explore the interplay between private and public spaces, between morality and law, and between 'front stage' and 'back stage,' to explore how the common quest for justice, which takes on state slogans but cannot be absorbed by state institutions, changes Chinese society from the bottom up by creating self-organized, and self-animated, new publics.

Judgement

Top-down attempts at ethical refashioning of the subject for politics in China have always involved actively establishing new parameters for public judgements. This was most obviously the case in the Maoist period, where participation in public criticism and struggle sessions sought as much to remake the subjectivity of the accused as that of those actively participating in, or witnessing, the rituals of public criticism or political judgements. In the post-Maoist period, in contrast, the main subject addressed by the state to exert public judgements became the private consumer, who was to learn "how to make money and how to spend it" (*nengzhen huihua*) and how to distinguish quality products from fake goods (see Hooper 2005). On the other hand, the so-called *pufa* campaigns, a number of five-year programs started in 1986 to promulgate knowledge about the law among the general population, aimed at creating the law-abiding rather than the rightful citizen, a subject who would know the law in order to follow it (Exner 1995: 78). This citizen would ensure the smooth progress of economic reforms, and develop new forms of self-management for a new type of socialist governing 'from afar' (see Ong and Zhang 2008, Murphy 2006). As an editorial in the *People's Daily*, the main press organ of the Party, made clear:

> Ruling the country according to law and running the country with morality are a closely integrated whole. The rule of law belongs to political construction and to political civilization; while rule by morality belongs to ideological construction and to advanced culture and ethics. They both have their respective positions and functions. [. . .] Socialist rule of law provides a legal guarantee for establishing, safeguarding and practicing socialist morality. Socialist rule of morality is to regulate the conduct of all social members with socialist ideology and morality and raise the moral level of the entire nation. Success in rule by morality makes it possible to administer the country according to law.
>
> (*People's Daily* Commentator 2001)

In the post-Tiananmen years, when these policies came to fully bear on Chinese society, a 'new social' emerged through the interplay between new institutional politics and a multitude of socially situated, yet largely self-interested actions of newly 'private' citizens (Zhang and Ong 2008: 4). Yet, as many recent studies suggest, China's new social is a deeply fragmented public space, riven apart by extreme levels of inequality, the unraveling of established social bonds, and administrative corruption; a situation that many Chinese perceive as a frightening growth of immorality and incivility in both society and state (see e.g., Yan 2009, 2011; Steinmüller and Fei 2011). To national audiences, this disturbing lack of public morality often presents itself in nationwide scandals as diverse as the baby milk scandal of 2008, where the sale of milk powder laced with melamine saw 54 000 infants hospitalized; the televised case of Yue-Yue in 2011, a two-year-old girl run over by a van in a Guangdong market and then left to die on the pavement by passing shoppers; or large corruption scandals surrounding public figures such as the former mayor of Shanghai, who was removed from office and tried for the disappearance of the city's welfare fund and for taking US $340 000 in personal bribes. Whereas official discourse has persistently judged an uncivil society in need of political guidance as the source of such immorality, the burgeoning corruption talk from below increasingly blames such ills on an immoral or uncivil state, threatening the legitimacy of the Party itself. The easy shading over of national disasters and scandals of immorality into scandals of corruption (*fubai*) and injustice reflects here a historical situation where the state has "been a far more conspicuous element in the constructions of the moral world in China than in the West" (Brook 1997: 20), amplified since 1949 by the claim of the Party to be the source of all progressive norms in society.

Judgement, as Michael Lambek has pointed out, is a central element of ethical practice; evaluations "with respect to situations, actions, and, cumulatively, actors, persons, or character" (Lambek 2010: 42) that are part of the stream of ordinary life but that, during periods of moral crisis or breakdown, seem to involve more conscious and more public forms of ethical deliberation (see Zigon 2007). Acts of judging are always reflective, situated and communicative, since they involve, as Hannah Arendt has pointed out (following Kant), an 'enlargement of the mind' that incorporates the standpoint of others. Judgements typically involve an indispensable element of publicity as they assert and seek to persuade, by reasoning from a common situation or a common sense (Hansen 1993: 210). Judging is thus not only an ethical but in essence a political act, even if not all judgements are by necessity political judgements (Hansen 1993: 212). Political judgements publicly denounce injustice, imagine how a just society should look or seek to determine the contours of a new public virtue. This is even clearer when in China popular protests denounce injustices committed by government officials, or the failure of political institutions to protect a public good. Judgements also become political acts when they lead to concrete action for a public good, as in the case of volunteer work or other forms of civic engagement.

Phenomena such as corruption talk and individual complaints; popular protests by legal and illegal, institutional and extra-institutional means; and civic engagements for a better society are typically bracketed under different rubrics, such as 'collective resistance', 'civil society' or 'moral complaints'. Here, we view them together as individual and collective acts of judgement, through word and deed, on the state of justice and on the conditions for living a good life in contemporary China – acts of judgement that address and seek to mobilize an audience and that also always involve the act of imagining how society should be (see Huang, this volume).

Publics

In the 1990s, many China scholars discussed possible historical roots for a Chinese civil society and debated the conditions for the rise of a liberal public sphere in China, as a motor for political reform after Maoism. During the Beijing Spring of 1989 and its demands for political democracy, a new civil society of the country's urban intellectual elites seemed to suddenly assert itself publicly, making demands on the state for democratic participation and political voice. On global TV screens, the Tiananmen events appeared as yet another showdown between politically awakened citizens and a post-totalitarian state, in this case between demonstrating students erecting a (Statue-of-Liberty lookalike) 'goddess of democracy' and a Politburo of mostly octogenarian Party leaders. When, however, on June 4, 1989, the student uprising for democracy was crushed by tanks of the People's Liberation Army, many observers attributed this "anticlimactic outcome" to the absence of civil society institutions that had helped to topple Communist regimes elsewhere (Wakeman 1993: 109). The most important theoretical model against which to gauge these historical developments became Jürgen Habermas' "The Structural Transformation of the Public Sphere" (1989), which made a direct links among the rise of civil society institutions; the emergence of a public sphere of free, rational citizen debate; and political democracy. For Habermas, it was the new split between a state public and a private public – a result of the growth of commerce and trade – that gave rise to a national public sphere: "The bourgeois public sphere may be conceived above all as the sphere of private people coming together as a public: they soon claimed the public sphere regulated from above against the public authorities themselves, to engage them in a debate over the general rules governing relations in the basically privatized but publically relevant sphere of commodity exchange and social labor" (Habermas 1989: 27; quoted in Huang 1993: 218). In Chinese intellectual circles, *Habeimasi*, in particular his writings on communicative rationality and the public sphere, became central to debates on China's modernization and democratization and helped to shape a perspective in which the Party was no longer the sole agent of social and political progress (Davies 2007).

Since the early 1990s, Chinese society has been reshaped profoundly by the forces of the global market, by urbanization, by mobility and new types of labour, by new media and by new forms of 'legalistic' governance known as *fazhi* ('governing through law', 'rule of/by law'). But instead of a Habermasian, deliberative public sphere ("Öffentlichkeit") representing the interests of civil society, it has been the rise of popular protests for justice that has significantly reshaped state–society relations in post-Tiananmen China (e.g., Perry and Selden 2000, O'Brien and Li 2006, O'Brien 2008, Hsing and Lee 2010). Habermas' rationalist utopia did not just face the obvious limitations of censorship in China, the concept itself cannot account for the moral underpinnings of public judgements and the passions mobilized through them. As Kevin O'Brien and Rachel Stern note in their introduction to *Popular Protests in China*, already in 1993 official Chinese statistics counted 8700 collective incidents (*quntixing shijian*), which included protests, demonstrations, sit-ins, marches and group complaints. By 2005, this number had grown to 87 000, or 250 'incidents' a day (2008: 12). This landscape of popular protests would look even more impressive if individual lawsuits against administrative malpractice, legally possible since 1989, were added to it, as well as complaints lodged at various Offices of Letters and Visits (*xingfangbu*), which have exploded in numbers since the 1990s, and transformed established spaces of governmental control into public spaces of appropriating a voice vis-à-vis the state (Thireau and Hua 2010). At the same time, protests for justice are complemented by new civic engagements for the common good – for example in the form of philanthropy and charity work, or in volunteer organizations and NGOs (see Hsing and Lee 2010). Public and private seem to exist here in a dynamic interface: in a context where the privatization of former public goods for the benefit of the few has become rampant (which is typically decried as corruption and injustice), the private challenge of remaking the moral person in a rapidly changing society (Kleinman et al. 2011) is increasingly turning 'outwards' into a popular politics of passing judgement on the moral quality of public life, on the parameters of public justice and the nature of public virtue. The growing number of studies on popular protests and other civic engagements in contemporary China underlines the relevance that scholars grant the increasingly vocal personal and collective quest for justice of large numbers of Chinese citizens as an important political, social as well as cultural phenomenon – as a form of action and a form of dialogue within society and with the state that seeks to address, and renegotiate, the fundamental parameters of social life and of public virtue.

Contemporary protests, although never reaching the scale of the democracy protests of 1989, address a wide diversity of injustices and involve people from all walks of life: urbanites and rural people, homeowners and workers, the old and the young, feminists and environmentalists, land losing peasants, religious groups, internet communities and users of new media. Using Habermas' terms, such protests aim to reshape the parameters of justice within life-worlds of communicative action after the partial withdrawal of the system in the Reform era. On the other hand, however, the various quests for justice described in this volume seem to more precisely reflect the *very fragmentation of life-worlds* after a century of top-down revolutions against pre-existing normative orders. Such fragmentation is also reflected in newer ethnographies on post-Maoist society: whereas Yan Yunxiang has emphasized the rise of a new individualism together with an egotistic culture in urban China (2013), and Xin Liu (2000) described a rural community totally lacking any authoritative ethical order, other anthropologists, like

Ellen Oxfeld (2010), have depicted how ordinary Chinese villagers still cherish traditional moral obligations that make up their local worlds. Closer to the subject of our edited volume, Isabelle Thireau and Wang Hansheng, together with the authors of their seminal volume *Disputes au Village Chinois* (2000) show that common disputes in Chinese villages reveal a plurality of normative frames that people draw on to evaluate each other's actions or to justify their own. As a result, even on the village level there is no longer any automatic agreement on the substantive meaning of fundamental terms such as 'fair' (*gongping*) or 'reasonable' (*you daoli*). Notions of justice are characterized by a high degree of uncertainty as people can invoke different normative orders for justifications, and the one eventually adopted can throw light on the emergence of a new order (2000: 163).

The articles in this edited volume demonstrate a similar plurality of notions of justice and of public virtue 'at play' behind the typical affirmation of 'the rule of law' (*fazhi*) or the increasingly popular use of the language of 'rights defense' (*weiquan*) in collective protests (see Pia, Steinmüller, this volume). Recent studies have analyzed these protests as either social, legal or political phenomena, which derive their meaning from their particular link with the 'system'. As contentious politics they exist within a sphere dominated by the state and institutional politics (O'Brien 2008); as a new type of social activism, together with the burgeoning number of new NGOs, they recapture society from the new market economy (Hsing and Lee 2010). Or, given the protests' focus on justice, frequent employment of the language of legality and rights and the growing involvement of lawyers and courts, they are "engaging the law in China" and form part of a new legal culture (Diamant, Lubman and O'Brien 2005). The 'conceptual void' or 'collective paradox' at the heart of the burgeoning landscape of justice protests in China has, as a phenomenon in its own right, in contrast received very little scholarly attention.

From an ethnographic perspective, what connects these diverse forms of civic engagements for justice despite obvious differences in meaning is their element of publicity, as they address others in a common situation and strife to work from, but also towards, a common sense. In other words, we emphasize the public-creating capacity of acts of judgement and of the quest for justice in contemporary China. Such 'justice publics' lack the disembodied, rationalist consensus of the Habermasian public sphere, yet are not *per definitionem* delimited by relations of descent, kinship or neighborhood as the classic *gong* or public of pre-modern China (see Rowe 1990). Rather, they are publics in Michael Warner's sense (2002) – products of social poetics and social imaginaries that are realized in and through the act of public address. They constitute "stranger-relationalities" rooted in the "resonance" of one's subjectivity with that of others; as Warner writes, they are "scenes of self-activity, of historical rather than timeless belonging, and of active participation rather than ascriptive belonging" (2002: 62). As the other of the modern state, their appeal is ideally universal, although they are practically bounded by the shared subjectivity they project. Such publics are self-organized entities but neither discursively nor culturally autonomous. Rather than being epiphenomena of institutional politics, law or market economics, Warner's publics are world-making entities, which constitute themselves in public discourse. Since they are connected to the 'national public' which, as Warner points out, is a state project, publics ordinarily include elements of state discourse in their own narratives.

What role does the quest for justice itself, which animates these forms of civic engagements, play in the formation of publics in China? If senses of justice are rooted in particular moralities or visions of self and society, how then can the quest for justice in a deeply fragmented society provide a universalizing idiom for the emergence of publics as 'stranger-relationalities'? What impact has the governing discourse of *fazhi*, the frequent appeal in collective protests to particular laws and policies (see Cheung, this volume), the discourse of 'rights defense' (*weiquan*) (see Zhang, and Hertz and Lieber, this volume) and the increasing involvement of lawyers, or various forms of law 'experts'? How do the shifting boundaries between the legal and the illegal shape particular publics, social practices and discourses on a social or common good? The latter question seems particularly relevant as many of the publics described in this paper exist in the shadow of, at best, semi-illegality. This is because they, as the religious associations described by Huang (this volume), are not 'licensed' by the state or because their activities are seen to threaten social stability (*shehui wending*) and thus become 'outlawed'.

In their introduction to "The Mirror of Justice", Goodale and Clarke focus on similar questions in the context of transnational justice and global human rights. Starting with the perennial problem of what justice *is*, they point to the continuous, empirical pluralizing of justice in a context of transnational movements: a pluralizing that affirms the context-dependency of justice and the emergence of justice concepts in particular fields defined by issues, actors, cultural idioms and historical situations. Although increasingly shaped by the universalizing human rights discourse, they argue that justice must be less understood as a "set of norms (however contested) that shapes social action but as a rationale for social action" (2009: 11): it functions both like an empty signifier and like a 'mirror' reflecting various combinations of political, moral and ideological imperatives from a particular angle. As an ideal, justice forever "shimmers [. . .] in the distance" (2009: 12), and thus can animate collective social action in an in-between space – somewhat similar to Zhang and Ong's 'new social' – where public values are being negotiated by various local and institutional (state and non-state) actors. Referring to processes of post-conflict resolution, Goodale and Clarke argue that justice outcomes cannot be determined in advance, and that it is the "invocation of justice itself" that creates meaning in what is essentially a political process (2009: 12).

The last point is particularly relevant to understand the circulation, the appeal to, and the idiosyncratic appropriation of elements of state discourse in public protests in contemporary China, but also in individual and collective forms of moral reasoning that express threats to moral order and dilemmas of public justice (see Pia, Steinmüller, this volume). In my own research on peasant law experts and resistance leaders, Maoist symbolism and language, together with the appropriation of new slogans such as "use the law as your weapon", became central means by which activists claimed a legitimate space of political agency and sought to mobilize 'peasant' publics (Brandtstädter 2011). As Thireau and Hua write in their article on labour protests:

> Mobilizing formal elements of the official discourse also entails resorting to state ideology and the government's professed objectives. In other words, official commitments made by the government, when popularized, provide a legitimate and shared language to express feelings of injustice. They originate from specific orientations towards public action concerning all citizens and encompass a given understanding of the 'common good,' whatever the nature of the policy implemented.
>
> (2005: 100)

For those who struggle for justice in China, the discourse of *fazhi* or the invocation of government policies and law thus provides an idiom of power, and a legitimizing language to become publicly active – or even to just voice personal reflections on the state of public morality in contemporary China. It also appears to provide the universalizing language necessary to create publics as stranger-relationalities, beyond social fragmentations and the plurality of particular justice meanings. This is particularly evident in the recent spread of the language of *weiquan*, commonly translated into English as 'rights defense', as the universalizing language for a large number of public protests against injustice. Yet, as Benney (2012) has shown, this term historically originated as part of a government discourse on the 'legitimate rights and benefits' (*hefa quanli*) of China's consumers and within China's state-sponsored 'Women's Federation' (*fulian*). It only developed its more recent, critical civic edge as part of a plethora of individual and collective actions against injustice, also through the involvement of a new type of public interest lawyer.

Yet, as we have seen, the practice of invoking *fazhi* or the *weiquan* discourse in itself does not seem to define, once and for all, what kind of citizen is speaking or what kind of public virtues are being invoked and defended. Rather, the language of *fazhi* is currently invoked by different types of local actors for widely divergent political and moral ends, entering a wide array of local disputes and conflict. Some scholars emphasize an incongruity especially in the countryside between the sphere of institutional politics, market and law and local worlds, between citizen rights and the valuing of human relations and interpersonal etiquette, between court procedures and a culture of mediation. To them, encounters between these two 'worlds' are necessarily shaped by negotiation, compromise, pragmatism and strategizing, and sometimes by manipulations, bluffing and outright disingenuity (see e.g., Zhao 2003; Zhu 2000). Those who have studied political or legal activists, in contrast, tend to argue, similar to what Sally Engle Merry postulates for processes of legal vernacularization (2006), that phrasing complaints in the language of law and rights has 'made a difference' in terms of personhood, citizenship and political awareness (e.g., Ying 2011; Brandtstädter 2011; Kleinman et al. 2011; Thireau and Hua 2010).

Such different interpretations are likely to also reflect the normative fragmentations of contemporary Chinese society. One generalizing statement might nevertheless be possible: the appropriation of policy slogans or government discourses from below, in the context of public judgement or action, always involves a change of perspective or authorship, because it is now no longer the state that acts on society, but self-organized others or 'world-making publics' who seek to universalize their vision of public virtue or a just society, and thereby rewrite to the social contract between self, society and state. In China's emergent new publics, furthermore, discourse and action, the two elements through which publics constitute themselves and which, according to Warner (2002: 68), define how close a public stands to politics, cannot usefully be separated – rather, in the Chinese political context, appropriating a public 'voice' (*shengyin*) without official invitation is in itself a fundamentally political act, while collective action typically provides the stage, or creates the space, for such voices to be heard as public voices.

Action

What are the material relations fostering these outbursts of public action, the collective and individual quest for making one's voice heard and for justice that China has witnessed since the 1990s? In other words, what are the relevant social, political and economic parameters that have given rise to these phenomena? In the introduction to the edited volume "Civil Society: Challenging Western Models", Chris Hann (1996: 4–6) argues that there have been two major strands in Western perspectives on the rise of civil society in modernity (both of which he finds wanting from an anthropological perspective): first, Marxian perspectives that saw in the freedoms of a new civil society nothing but a smoke screen hiding the powers of the ruling class cemented by capitalism, and instead emphasized the fragmentations of class society and the alienation of citizens from each other, their labor and their 'species-being'; and second, liberal accounts, going back to Tocqueville, where new forms of active citizenship were emerging from associations of private economic interests, developing into a civil society in opposition to the state and protected by the rise of a *Rechtsstaat*. For Hann, these are oppositional narratives which are nevertheless rooted in the same basic assumptions:

> Both identify civil society with realms outside the power of the state, and emphasize economic life as such a realm. Even more importantly, both strands assume the universality of modern Western notions of the person, what Seligman calls the 'autonomous agentic individual' [. . .]: the Marxist tradition merely allows these atoms to be aggregated to form social classes. [. . .] But none of these accounts leaves room for the exploration of alternative forms of social relationships to those assumed by liberal-individualism, of culturally specific patterns of generating trust in human communities that are growing ever more crowded and complex.
>
> (Hann 1996: 5)

Contemporary China seems to provide evidence for both Marxist and liberal accounts, for the fragmentations, dislocations and moral alienations of a new class society, and for the rise of a new, politically activated civil society that seeks to establish the contours of a new 'public morality', often in the name of 'the rule of law' (*fazhi*). At the same time, as some of the authors of this volume show, alternative forms of social relationships can be called upon in collective and individual struggles against injustice, and point to the continuing significance of other modalities of justice and perspectives on the moral person. Since protests against injustice in China are typically framed in the name of a particular common good, a more convincing perspective is to view these struggles as responses to the dispossession of common goods – which can account for new fragmentations, conflicts and divisions as well as for the wide variety of forms of public engagements and the plurality of notions of justice and the common good. The recent interest in dispossession as the common denominator behind various types of struggles around the world goes back to David Harvey's work (2004). Dispossession, in short, involves the coercive expropriation of means of production, subsistence, private or common goods in order to render them available for capital accumulation, a process that threatens existing livelihoods and that produces new outcasts and forms of precariousness. This process, according to Harvey, is not limited to a stage of 'primitive accumulation' but is an ongoing feature of global capitalism. The concept of dispossession allows Harvey (and others) to link the privatization of common resources, of land, water and public works, taking place in many countries, to diverse struggles against injustice: struggles of workers against plant closures, of peasants against land expropriation or of the urban poor against dislocation and the destruction of social welfare provisions (Kasmir and Carbonella 2008: 9).

Transformation of state–society relations in post-Tiananmen China, by many commentators described as an economic 'miracle', have been driven by dispossession of common goods on a mass scale. After Deng Xiaoping called for a deepening of economic reforms during his famous southern tour (*nanxun*) in early 1992, the rapid privatization of industry and services, the influx of international capital and fiscal reforms that forced local governments to generate more revenues culminated in a massive rollback of what had been regarded as central achievements of socialism – free health care and education, job security and the 'iron rice bowl', affordable housing and the rights of peasants to land and to social benefits distributed by their collectives. Whereas former state workers were forced by the closure of plants to 'dive into the sea' of private enterprise (*xia hai*), peasants were turned into a new proletariat by the massive state-led expropriation and sale of farmlands.

The chapters in this volume tell stories of dispossession of common or public goods of various types and on various scales. Often the ensuing struggles are framed in the language of *rights defense* (as in the chapters by Pang, Hertz and Lieber, Pia, Cheung and Zhang), yet the notion of *defense* implies, again, the threat of being dispossessed of existing rights (whether collective or individual), rather than the struggle for new rights. Common goods are also the goods in which particular social and moral 'worlds' are anchored. Struggles against dispossession or injustice are thus always struggles to retain or to recreate *this particular* public good, which also defines the moral vision or the idiom of justice they are framed in. The classic description of such struggles is E. P. Thompson's seminal article "The Moral Economy of the English Crowd in the 18th Century" (1971). Here, he develops the concept of a moral economy as linked to the values and relationships of a 'paternalistic economy' and its notions of economic justice. The concept of the moral economy was then popularized by Scott's study of peasant rebellions in Asia (1977) as a useful framework to understand rural protests. Most recently, Kevin O'Brien and Li Lijiang have referred to it in their study on "Rightful Resistance in Rural China" (2006). As Thompson writes in *Customs in Common*:

> It is possible to detect in almost every eighteenth-century crowd action some legitimizing notion. By the notion of legitimation I mean that the men and women in the crowd were informed by the belief that they were defending traditional rights or customs; and, in general, that they were supported by the wider consensus of the community. On occasion this popular consensus was endorsed by some measure of license afforded by the authorities. More commonly, the consensus was so strong that it overrode motives of fear or deference.
>
> (Thompson 1993: 188)

The burgeoning corruption talk in China that decries a new 'immoral economy' shows that there is no reason to limit the salience of the concept to either a pre-modern past, or to a traditional rural context. Also modern citizenship regulates access to public goods, whether this is the right to vote, the right to social welfare or the right to education and public health services. As Smart and Pia (both this volume) show, socialist peasant collectives were moral economic institutions that clearly distinguished between insiders and outsiders. All papers in this volume deal, in essence, with threats to public goods, and the negative consequences thereof in terms of private lives and public moralities. Yet the various "social imaginaries" (Huang, this volume) connected to public goods seem to vary widely – they can refer to a shared local tradition, to the history of Chinese socialism, to the country's constitution and the new discourse on *fazhi*, or to new transnational spaces. The striking coevality of apparently contradictory types of justice and concepts of the public good in contemporary China is clearly an epiphenomenon of modern Chinese history; not just a consequence of globalization but also the product of a history of top-down revolutions against the nation's various 'pasts'.

The relevance of public action for creating publicity, again in a certain parallel to the bread riots described by Thompson, lies in the fact that there is no permanent institutional 'slot' or space for oppositional voices in contemporary China; instead, this space needs to be created in and through action. Public action also typically seeks to de-localize a contentious issue, whereby what might otherwise be portrayed as local or parochial is turned into an issue of 'the people', the 'citizens', the 'masses' and so on (see Zhang, this volume). This has additional significance within two contexts. First, the dispossession of collective assets or common goods, and here of land in particular, is in China always legitimized by an overriding 'public interest' (*gongyi*), implying vice versa that resistance against this is likely to be for private or 'selfish' (*zisi*) reasons. As a result of the mass expropriation of collective lands, for example, peasants feel they are no longer part of the general public (Zhao 2009). Secondly, China's spatialized citizenship regime (Zhang 2002) also perceives of urban and rural in hierarchical terms as 'up' (*shang*) and 'down' (*xia*), whereby *shang* stands for more prestige, power and 'publicness'. *Shangfang*, to personally lodge a complaint at one of the Office of Letters and Visits (*xingfangbu*), thus typically involves travelling up in the administrative hierarchy often all the way to Beijing, where complainants not only expect to meet officials who are more just and public-minded than those working at lower levels but whereby an issue in itself is made to gain greater importance in relation to the general public. Likewise, the appropriation and circulation of policy documents promulgated by the central state as described by Cheung (this volume) can be seen as a de-localizing move by villagers, who seek to transform their local conflict into a public issue. Action in this double sense is thereby also creating an effective link between public goods or publics of different 'orders of worth'.

Disputes and justifications

I adopt the phrase 'order of worth' from Luc Boltanski's sociology of situated judgements as particular forms of public action (Boltanski and Thevenot 2006; Boltanski 2012). Based on research among French bureaucrats, Boltanski and Thevenot show that people seeking public agreement with their particular perspective or judgement of an unjust situation will always refer to common higher principles, or orders of worth. Boltanski and Thevenot speak of worth, rather than values, as worth always refers to a justifiable order, based on principles of equivalence whose validity transcends the particular situation (Boltanski 2012: 47–48) An order of worth is something like a particular grammar of justice, articulated around a definite form of a common good. In disputes or 'tests' (*epreuve*), people seek not just to establish the truth of a matter, but also establish which 'order of worth' is to be applied to a given situation. In contrast to those who assume that agreement on the principles of justice can only be available among people sharing the same values, or those who seek a minimal yet universal definition of justice as procedure, Boltanski and Thevenot argue that – at least in modern, differentiated societies – there are always several 'orders of worth' available for social actors in what he calls the philosophical background of society. For, it is the *situation*, rather than the individual or the social whole, that is the basic core of what could be called a 'social ontology' and that shapes the process of agreement on the principles of justice that should apply (Boltanski and Thevenot 2006; Boltanski 2012).

Boltanski's theory might usefully be applied to dispute situations in contemporary China, where different concepts of justice or 'orders of worth' are at hand in particular situations, or, as Zhao Xudong (2003) has argued in his study of village disputes, formal law serves as just one source of authority, next to local customs or other forms of local knowledge. But the different orders of worth or principles of justice villagers call upon must not emerge from different moral pasts or value systems, but rather from different interpretations of the particular situation at hand and therefore disagreements over which of the different 'orders of worth' available to actors in society is here the relevant one.

Boltanksi also argues that making successful complaints not just involves convincing relevant others of one's interpretation of a situation, but also arguments about the particular and the general. As their empirical research had shown, complainants had to convincingly de-singularize the injustice they had suffered in order to be 'heard', by generalizing it into an injustice against the common good or the interests of a relevant 'category' of people (such as the masses [*cunzhong*], peasants [*nongmin*] or citizens [*gongmin*]). If they failed to do so, complaints were unsuccessful and complainants often labeled as paranoid or as otherwise 'abnormal'. Successful denunciations followed the reverse pattern of highlighting the particular behind the general, the secret personal interests behind the generous gesture, and the particular ties behind the official relation. As he writes, "[a] scandal is thus always a conspiracy – that is a secret alliance in favor of a particular interest where there ought to be only the agreement of all for a common good" (Boltanski 2012: 13). Denunciations, as well as larger political scandals in China, often involving rumors spreading through the internet or social media – such as that engulfing the former mayor of Chongqing Bo Xilai in 2012 – follow precisely this pattern.

Conclusion

In sum, justice disputes that involve efforts to establish the concrete nature of the injustice seek to establish new parameters for public virtue or to 'defend the legitimate rights and benefits' (*weiquan*) of citizens and are also always moments to reaffirm or to redraw the line between the private and the public in China. This is demonstrated in Pang's chapter on the 'subpolitics' of new internet communities, where complaints or worries about issues of personal or private life quickly gather the support of similarly affected netizens and are then reformulated as political demands on the government or as issues of citizen rights defense. The internet, with its possibilities to generate audiences that valorize and thereby generalize complaints about particular injustices, as well as to create virtual spaces for the discussion of 'citizen issues', seems of particular importance in contemporary China for the creation of new publics as stranger-relationalities. Justice publics, beyond the case of the government-sponsored consumer movement, have no permanent or legitimate institutional 'space' in contemporary China and therefore exist, much as Hannah Arendt has argued for publics in general, in and through expansive action of word *and* deed. At the same time, emergent justice publics seem to be engaged in a permanent tug-of-war with the official public sphere dominated by government discourse over who represents and speaks for 'the people', 'the public good' or even '*fazhi*', and who represents, in contrast, selfish interests. Corruption discourses from below, if they focus on particular cases, tend to reveal the private or "singular person" (Boltanski 2012: 13) behind the official or representative. To protest in the name of *fazhi* against 'corrupt' members of the government is thus appropriating the authority to speak in the name of a general public interest against a privatized government. This borders on a revolutionary challenge and is thus relentlessly repressed when such accusations are directed against members of the Politburo, who, despite an ongoing process of 'legalization' (*falühua*), still embody the sovereign power of the Chinese state.

Finally, justice disputes typically involve narratives about critical events and personal experiences as well as forms of moral reasoning about the social good. Such narratives are aimed not only at convincing others, but even more so at creating 'resonance' in others, according to Warner (2002) a central condition for the emergence of publics in general. According to Jarrett Zigon, narratives, a fundamentally social form of speech, aim at creating forms of intersubjectivity based on empathy and charitable living-together. This becomes particularly evident in a context shaped by social and moral fragmentations and thus ripe with misunderstandings. In his perspective, narratives do not so much seek to create mutual meaningful understandings across such divides (which can still happen). Rather, they involve a "process of coming to an embodied agreement on how to live together. [. . .] [T]o understand and to live charitably with another is not to share meaning with others, but to assume one can live with others despite the uncertainty of any such sharedness" (2012: 205). Such a 'function' of public narratives is very far away from a Habermasian public sphere of rational (i.e. dispassionate and disembodied) deliberation and consensus seeking among structural equals. Yet, it is likely such embodied processes of making publics through empathy or resonance across the established divides and the new fragmentations of post-Maoist China that will prove to be politically and socially most significant in relation to the future of state–society relations in China.

References

Béja, Jean-Phillipe, Fu, Hualing and Pils, Eva, eds. 2012. *Liu Xiaobo, Charter 08 and the Challenges of Political Reform in China*. Hong Kong: Hong Kong University Press.

Benney, Jonathan. 2012. *Defending Rights in Contemporary China*. New York: Routledge.

Boltanski, Luc. 2012. *Love and Justice as Competences*. Cambridge: Polity Press.

Boltanski, Luc and Thévenot, Laurent. 2006. *On Justification: Economies of Worth*. Princeton, NJ: Princeton University Press.

Brandtstädter, Susanne. 2011. The Law Cuts Both Ways: Rural Legal Activism and Citizenship Struggles in Neosocialist China. *Economy and Society* 40(2), pp. 266–288.

Brandtstädter, Susanne. 2016. The Rebel as Trickster and the Ironies of Resisting in Contemporary China. In: Hans Steinmüller and Susanne Brandtstädter, eds. *Irony, Cynicism and the Chinese State*. London: Routledge, pp. 122–137.

Brook, Timothy. 1997. Auto-Organization in Chinese Society. In: Timothy Brook and B. Michael Frolic, eds. *Civil Society in China*. Armonk, NY: M.E. Sharpe, pp. 19–45.

Davies, Gloria. 2007. Habermas in China: Theory as Catalyst. *China Journal* 57, pp. 61–85.

Diamant, Neil J., Lubman, Stanley B. and O'Brien, Kevin J., eds. 2005. *Engaging the Law in China. State, Society, and Possibilities for Justice*. Stanford, CA: Stanford University Press.

Exner, Mechthild. 1995. The Convergence of Ideology and the Law: The Functions of the Legal Education Campaign in Building a Chinese Legal System. *Issues and Studies* 31(8), pp. 68–102.

Goodale, Marc and Clarke, Kamari. 2009. Introduction: Understanding the Multiplicities of Justice. In: Kamari Clarke and Marc Goodale, eds. *Mirrors of Justice: Law and Power in the Post-Cold War Era*. Cambridge: Cambridge University Press, pp. 1–26.

Habermas, Jürgen. 1989. *The Structural Transformation of the Public Sphere: An Inquiry Into a Category of Bourgeois Society*. Cambridge, MA: MIT Press.

Hann, Chris. 1996. Political Society and Civil Anthropology. In: Chris Hann and Elizabeth Dunn, eds. *Civil Society: Challenging Western Models*. London: Routledge, pp. 1–26.

Hansen, Philip. 1993. *Hannah Arendt: Politics, History and Citizenship*. Cambridge: Polity Press.

Harvey, David. 2004. The "New" Imperialism: Accumulation by Dispossession. *Socialist Register* 40, pp. 63–87.

Hooper, Beverley. 2005. *The Consumer Citizen in Modern China*. Working Paper No. 12. Centre for East and South-East Asian Studies, Lund University.

Hsing, You-Tien and and Kwam Lee, Ching, eds. 2010. *Reclaiming Chinese Society: The New Social Activism*. New York: Routledge.

Huang, Philip C. C. 1993. "Public Sphere"/"Civil Society" in China? The Third Realm Between State and Society. *Modern China* 19(2), pp. 216–240.

Kasmir, Sharryn and Carbonella, August. 2008. Dispossession and the Anthropology of Labor. *Critique of Anthropology* 28(1), pp. 5–25.

Keane, Michael. 2001. Redefining Chinese Citizenship. *Economy and Society* 30(1), pp. 1–17.

Kleinman, Arthur, Yunxiang Yan, Jing Jun, Sing Lee, Everett Zhang, Pan Tianshu, Wu Fei and Guo Jinhua, eds. 2011. *Deep China: The Moral Life of the Person*. Berkeley: University of California Press.

Lambek, Michael. 2010. Toward an Ethics of the Act. In: Michael Lambek, ed. *Ordinary Ethics: Anthropology, Language, and Action*. New York: Fordham University Press, pp. 39–63.

Liu, Xin. 2000. *In One's Own Shadow: An Ethnographic Account of the Condition of Post-modern Reform Rural China*. Berkeley: University of California Press.

Merry, Sally Engle. 2006. *Human Rights and Gender Violence: Translating International Law Into Local Justice*. Stanford: Stanford University Press.

Murphy, Rachel. 2006. Citizenship Education in Rural China: The Dispositional and Technical Training of Cadres and Farmers. In: Vanessa Fong and Rachel Murphy, eds. *Chinese Citizenship: Views From the Margins*. New York: Routledge, pp. 9–26.

O'Brien, Kevin J., ed. 2008. *Popular Protest in China*. Cambridge: Harvard University Press.

O'Brien, Kevin J. and Li, Lianjiang. 2006. *Rightful Resistance in Rural China*. Cambridge: Cambridge University Press.

O'Brien, Kevin J. and Stern, Rachel E. 2008. Introduction: Studying Contention in Contemporary China. In: Kevin J. O'Brien, ed. *Popular Protest in China*. Cambridge, MA: Harvard University Press, pp. 11–25.

Ong, Aihwa and Zhang, Li. 2008. Introduction: Privatizing China. Powers of the Self, Socialism From Afar. In: Li Zhang and Aihwa Ong, eds. *Privatizing China*. Ithaca, NY: Cornell University Press, pp. 1–19.

Oxfeld, Ellen. 2010. *Drink Water, But Remember the Source: Moral Discourse in a Chinese Village*. Berkeley: University of California Press.

People's Daily Commentator. 2001. Integrating Rule of Country by Law and by Morality. February 1, p. 1.

Perry, Elizabeth J. and Mark Selden, eds. 2000. *Chinese Society: Change, Conflict and Resistance*. London: Routledge.

Rowe, William. 1990. The Public Sphere in Modern China. *Modern China* 16(3), pp. 309–329.

Scott, James C. 1977. *The Moral Economy of the Peasant: Rebellion and Subsistence in Southeast Asia*. New Haven, CT: Yale University Press.

Steinmüller, Hans and Wu, Fei. 2011. School Killings in China: Society or Wilderness? *Anthropology Today* 27(1), pp. 10–13.

Thireau, Isabelle and Hansheng, Wang, eds. 2000. *Disputes au village chinois. Formes du juste et recompositions locales des espaces normatifs*. Paris: Editions de la Maison des sciences de l'homme.

Thireau, Isabelle and Linshan, Hua. 2005. One Law, Two Interpretations. Mobilizing the Labor Law in Arbitration Committees and in Letters and Visits Offices. In: Neil J. Diamant, Stanley B. Lubman and Kevin J. O'Brien, eds. *Engaging the Law in China. State, Society, and Possibilities for Justice*. Stanford: Stanford University Press, pp. 84–107.

Thireau, Isabelle and Linshan, Hua. 2010. *Les ruses de la démocratie: Protester en Chine*. Paris: Seuil.

Thompson, Edward P. 1971. The Moral Economy of the English Crowd in the 18th Century. *Past & Present* 50, pp. 76–136.

Thompson, Edward P. 1993. *Customs in Common: Studies in Traditional Popular Culture*. New York: New Press.

Wakeman, Frederic Jr. 1993. The Civil Society and Public Sphere Debate: Western Reflections on Chinese Political Culture. *Modern China* 19(2), pp. 108–138.

Warner, Michael. 2002: Publics and Counterpublics. *Public Culture* 14(1), pp. 49–90.

Yan, Yunxiang. 2009. The Good Samaritan's New Trouble: A Study of the Changing Moral Landscape in Contemporary China. *Social Anthropology/Anthropologie Sociale* 17(1), pp. 9–24.

Yan, Yunxiang. 2011. The Changing Moral Landscape. In: Arthur Kleinman, Yunxiang Yan, Jing Jun, Sing Lee, Everett Zhang, Pan Tianshu, Wu Fei and Guo Jinhua, eds. *Deep China: The Moral Life of the Person*. Berkeley: University of California Press, pp. 36–76.

Yan, Yunxiang. 2013: The Drive for Success and the Ethics of the Striving Individual. In: Charles Stafford, ed. *Ordinary Ethics in China*. London: Bloomsbury, pp. 263–291.

Ying, Xing. 2011. *Qi yu kangzhen zhengzhi: Dangdai zhongguo xiangxun shehui wending wenti yanjiu* [Emotions and Contentious Politics in Contemporary Rural China]. Beijing: Social Sciences Academic Press.

Zhang, Li. 2002. Spatiality and Urban Citizenship in Late Socialist China. *Public Culture* 14(2), pp. 311–334.

Zhang, Li and Ong, Aihwa, eds. 2008. *Privatizing China*. Ithaca, NY: Cornell University Press.

Zhao, Bo. 2009. Land Expropriation Protest, and Impunity in Rural China. *Focaal* 9(54), pp. 97–105.

Zhao, Xudong. 2003. *Quanli yu gongzheng: Xiangtu shehui de jiufen jiejue yu quanwei duoyuan* [Power and Justice: Conflict Resolution and the Plurality of Authority in Rural Society]. Tianjin: Tianjin Guji Chubanshe.
Zhu, Suli. 2000. *Song fa xia xiang: Zhongguo jiceng sifazhidu yanjiu* [Sending Law to the Countryside: Research on China's Basic-Level Judicial System]. Beijing: Zhongguo Zhengfa Daxue Chubanshe.
Zigon, Jarrett. 2007. Moral Breakdown and the Ethical Demand: A Theoretical Framework for an Anthropology of Moralities. *Anthropological Theory* 7(2), pp. 131–150.
Zigon, Jarrett. 2012. Narratives. In: Didier Fassin, ed. *A Companion to Moral Anthropology*. Chichester: John Wiley & Sons, pp. 204–220.

1 'Battles over green space'

Land disputes, rights activism, and emerging publics in urban China[1]

Li Zhang

Over the past two decades, the post-Mao urban reform, which centers on housing and real estate reform and the restructuring of the state-owned enterprises, has generated new forms of tensions and contradictions between different social sectors. The emerging struggles are often organized on specific principles and are articulated in distinct political idioms born out of the Chinese historical and social context. Thus, they cannot be adequately grasped through such general and familiar notions as citizenship and democracy (see Holston 2009). At the same time, these struggles have also engendered new forms of urban publics to address a set of particular problems brought by the urban reform. The newly reconfigured power relations and social fragmentation further challenge the conventional way of thinking about Chinese politics in terms of the state/society dichotomy, and complicate the public/private divide.

In this chapter, I focus on the widespread urban land disputes between developers and urban residents by examining what has been known as 'battles over green space' (*lüdi baoweizhan*). This specific form of spatial struggle, however, is an integral part of the broader rights protection movement, known as *weiquan yundong*, which is becoming a powerful force in reshaping popular politics in reform China. This movement includes a wide range of grassroots activism for diverse causes, but the two most prominent ones are mobilization to fight for property rights and consumer rights.[2] Rather than invoking the notion of citizen rights (*gongmin quan*), these two forms of urban activism draw specifically from two distinct and contested notions – 'property rights' and 'public common good', and are based on two popular subject positions – 'property owners' (*yezhu*) and 'the masses' or 'ordinary people' (*qunzhong*). *Yezhu* is a relatively new category that has emerged as a result of the housing reform and the enacting of the new Property Rights Law (2003). By contrast, *qunzhong* is a long-standing political category that gained its salience under socialism and continues to remain relevant and significant today.[3] At first glance, these two sets of notions seem to invoke two opposing ideas – private versus public, individual versus collective. Yet, as I will show, the two are in constant interface with one another to constitute the strategy of not only urban homeowners' quest for justice but also the *weiquan* movement in general (see also Brandtstädter's introduction of this volume).

My analysis draws from two high-profile cases in two different Chinese cities. The first one was in the Chaoyang District of Beijing and lasted for about a year and five months between 2003 and 2004. It was also known as the 'Maizidian Green Triangle Battle', widely reported in the national media and the internet. A special website was created to document and publicize the progress of this struggle through detailed accounts and numerous photos. The second one, 'Riverside Battle over Green Space,' took place in the city of Kunming, where I conducted long-term ethnographic fieldwork on the privatization of housing and the making of the new middle classes between 2000 and 2006. As I will show below, although both cases concerned how a particular piece of urban land should be used, and who had the right to make such decisions, the terms of their struggle and the strategies deployed were quite different. Nevertheless, both cases raise important questions regarding the nature of such emerging activism, the possibility for new publics, and the implications for re-conceptualizing the Chinese state, power relations, and popular politics under urban reform.

I will begin by briefly discussing the importance of attending to cultural and historical specificities of 'publics' and rights discourses in and beyond China. Then I will present a detailed account of the two cases to illustrate how Chinese urban residents utilize different subject positions and legal/political means to challenge powerful real estate developers and engage different sections of the state. I conclude this chapter by reflecting upon the distinct characters of new *weiquan* publics and their ambivalent relationships with the developers and the reform state. I will also consider how incessant land disputes and grassroots activism might disrupt and articulate with the political regime's call to strive for a harmonious society.

Other publics

In his seminal book, *The Structural Transformation of the Public Sphere* (1991), Jürgen Habermas investigates and reflects upon a distinct form of bourgeois public sphere that is discursive in nature and had emerged in liberal capitalist societies. Since its original 1962 publication and later translation into English, the two key notions, 'public sphere' and 'publics' have been widely applied and critiqued in diverse historical and cultural contexts (see Calhoun 1994). Scholars like Nancy Fraser have pointed out that "the problem is not only that Habermas idealized the liberal public sphere, but also that he fails to examine other, nonliberal, nonbourgeois, competing public spheres" (1994: 115). Rather than recognizing only a singular public sphere dominated by white, male bourgeoisies, Fraser calls for attention to a plurality of publics and counterpublics that together constitute the politics (see also Hirschkind 2009; Lee 1998). This insight has opened up new possibilities of conceptualizing publics in a culturally and historically specific way. It has important implications for thinking about emerging urban politics and collective cultures in postsocialist China (see also Brandtstädter, Wade, and Woodward 2011). Rather than asking whether Habermas' concept of 'the public sphere' fits the Chinese condition, I follow Mayfair Yang to propose that it is more useful to understand "how a modern global category would work itself out in the particular modernity of China" (1999: 17). As I will show in this chapter, the emerging new publics in urban China tend to take diverse forms (rather than a singular one) and often involve both discursive and nondiscursive practices. In the case of urban land disputes, a new form of public is engendered in the process of ordinary people defending communal green space through protests, petitions, grassroots activism, and debates in the traditional and new media. It has the characteristics of what one might call 'a plebeian public sphere' left outside Habermas' discussion.

Further, as Fraser points out, due to socioeconomic inequality in almost all contemporary societies, participatory parity essential to a democratic public sphere is often hindered or remains as an ideal only. The public sphere is thus always a contested and fragmented domain, in which what is considered 'private'/'inadmissible' or 'public'/'admissible' for public debate is not pre-given or self-evident. Dominant groups tend to have the control over the qualification of 'public matters' by relegating certain issues to the sphere of 'private interests' and thus excluding them from public discussions of political and social issues. For example, Chinese urban residents' battle against illicit land appropriation by powerful real estate developers can be easily defined as a matter of private ownership and thus pushed back to the domain of economic interests negotiation. Yet, Chinese homeowners and residents defy this artificial differentiation by demonstrating precisely the complex nature of their struggle – it is both public and private, political and economic. Their collective mobilization and effective engagement in the public space (both physical and discursive) suggest that a nascent form of *weiquan* based public is taking place in China. Further, the notion of 'common good' has become a central part of the *weiquan* politics in general. However, as I will also show later, this new formation, which we might call 'other public', has its own limits despite its potentials.

"Defend qunzhong's interests, return our common space"

Since the real estate reform, urban and suburban land value has skyrocketed over the past two decades. This is particularly true for major metropolitan areas such as Beijing, Shanghai, Guangzhou, Hangzhou, and so on. The revised 1998 Land Management Law has made it possible for the commercialization of land use rights even though the Chinese state retains the formal ownership of land. The early experiments with this new policy, however, had occurred much earlier in the late 1980s. With this fundamental shift, a new wave of land appropriation by developers has taken place through the frenzied and often corrupt redistribution or 'grabbing' of land use rights in Chinese cities (see Zhang 2010). Some firms or work units simply hold on to the land they have acquired for a long period of time and develop it later when land values increase dramatically. It was in this context that Maizidian's Green Triangle Battle took place.

In 1986, Dacheng Real Estate Development Company (Dacheng) obtained the use right to several pieces of land in Chaoyang District of Beijing. One of them was a triangle-shaped land that was originally scheduled for building a "Civic Foreign Cultural Exchange Center" and was later approved by the municipal planning bureau in 1997. But two years later, Dacheng changed the type of usage to that of residential housing development. In January 2003 the company managed to obtain the construction permit for a housing project named "Haiyue Mingmen" (meaning "Pleasant Ocean Manors") – an upscale, commercial housing complex. In May 2003, the early phase of the project involved the building of walls enclosing the triangle and the cutting down of trees on site. The formal groundbreaking ceremony took place on June 27, but residents who lived in the surrounding areas protested and interrupted the ceremony. Local district government ordered a temporary halt of the construction due to this unpleasant clash. But Dacheng moved on anyway by putting up several construction sheds on site in preparation for the full-scale construction. This action further infuriated the residents. What was the root cause of this confrontation? Why did the residents oppose the new housing construction? What was the motivation and logic behind their action? To answer these questions, we must examine several social, legal, and ecological factors.

The space in dispute was not very large, about 1,800 square meters. It was called 'green space' or 'green field' (*ludi*) because it was an outdoor area covered by more than twenty large, decades-old trees and some three hundred smaller pine trees planted by the local government in recent years. Back in the early 1990s, residents who bought their apartments in the surrounding areas were told that this place would be developed into a street park with a senior center. Therefore, this green triangle site had become a de facto public space and the only one in this area for the tens of thousands of nearby residents to come to stroll, exercise, breathe in fresh air, and engage in communal activities. The significance of this space was expressed by local residents dubbing it the 'green lung' for the community that consisted of some 20,000 residents residing in the sixty-two residential buildings. Given the rapidly expanding real estate development, public green space was shrinking significantly in Beijing, leaving residents with limited open, outdoor places to go.

Another important event further heightened popular awareness of the importance of maintaining a sound eco-system in safeguarding public health in overcrowded urban areas. In 2003, China encountered an unprecedented national public health crisis – the outbreak of SARS (severe acute respiratory syndrome) (see Kleinman and Watson 2005). Beijing was one of the hardest hit areas and many were in panic. Maizidian residents quickly linked their effort to fight for green space to the government's call to fight SARS. In June, some 700 residents mobilized and signed an appeal letter addressed to the developer and the general public. Titled, "Fight Against the SARS, Protect the Ecology, Return Our Green Space," it made an explicit connection between the national crisis and their spatial struggle. Their goal was to gain further legitimacy and wider public recognition of their crusade. The logic could be summarized as follows: The overcrowded living condition and the lack of communal parks in metropolitan areas might have worsened the spread of SARS. Green space in local communities was thus critical for public health because it provided people with space for exercising and getting fresh air. Therefore, the struggle for public green space was also a struggle to defend public health and the common interests of the people. This was an effective strategy Chinese people frequently adopt – making connections between their localized struggles to a nationally recognized cause or re-articulating their struggle through the officially approved language. Several major newspapers and television stations quickly reported the Maizidian conflict, linking it to the widespread urban movement to protect green communal space and calling it a crucial moment of "the awakening of green space consciousness by SARS."

The nature of the Maizidian clash was complex. It was not only about property rights but also about the contested notion of 'public common good'. There were at least three major challenges brought by the protesting residents. The first was a legal contestation over use-right. The residents did not own any property on the disputed land; rather the developer (Dacheng) was the holder of the use-right of this land regardless of how it managed to obtain it. However, the residents claimed that because Dacheng had not engaged in any development on this site for the past eighteen years, it had in effect lost its use-right. According to China's Urban Real Estate Management Law, holding on to land for a long period of time without developing it is considered an illegal practice, called *tunji tudi* ('hoarding land'). The second contestation was over the usage type of the land. Residents claimed that the triangle was originally planned as *lüdi* (green space) and it was illegal to alter its use to commercial housing development according to the Beijing Municipal Green Regulations. The third contestation involved a social and moral argument. Residents reasoned that since this land had been customarily used as a common communal space by tens of thousands of people over the years, the broader public interest it served should outweigh the private interests of a few. It was immoral to take away public common good in the interest of capital. Protesters thus drew a sharp contrast between the interests of *qunzhong* (the masses/ordinary folks) and the profits of the greedy developer.

The pivot of the Maizidian clash was on the removal of several temporary construction shacks put up by the developer in May 2003 in preparation for the forthcoming housing construction. Residents declared these structures illegal and demanded that they be demolished immediately because they were not properly authorized by relevant government agencies. Their ultimate aim was to demonstrate to the developer and local government their determination to halt the entire construction project. Both sides understood the significance of this initial showdown regarding the temporary shacks. Since the developer ignored the residents' demand and refused to back down, some resident representatives began to visit the Maizidian streetship committee (the lowest level of urban government bureaucracy) and urged the government to intervene. The party secretary, Mr. Yang, listened to them sympathetically and then replied: "We [local government] too would want to get back the green space! But the construction project was approved by the city government. Thus we have no authority to question and intervene. Go to plead to those who approved the project."

The residents subsequently made their case to the higher-level authorities including the municipal government and the city-planning bureau. They charged

Dacheng with using illicit means of obtaining approval for the housing project while putting up unauthorized sheds. The district planning bureau authority eventually admitted that the land where the construction sheds were built was indeed planned to be used as a street park and thus should be returned to the public. Having heard this decision from above, Mr. Yang changed his attitude and promised the protesting residents: "Since Dacheng did not get a proper permit and started the construction of sheds, these are illegal structures that must be removed without any hesitation!" But nothing happened in the following month. Dacheng not only did not tear down the sheds, but moved on with the full-scale housing construction. This act further infuriated the residents. The district government's "urban management division" (*chengguan dadui*) was supposed to be in charge of clearing illegal constructions. In this case, if the developer refused to follow the official order, this division had the authority to carry out forced demolition and impose fines. But it did not do so; instead it kept delaying its action, citing various excuses. Residents grew angry and claimed that the division was corrupt and must have received a bribe from the developer.

In the midst of this land dispute, residents waged another symbolic or discursive, yet highly effective battle. After the developer built up walls to enclose the triangle space, it covered the walls with large advertising banners, which typically included such information as the name of the property in Chinese and English, the types and sizes of the apartments to be developed, the sales office's phone numbers, and some alluring images and slogans that sought to portray the new development as an upscale domestic 'paradise'. Residents soon mobilized and covered these banners with their own defiant slogans – for example, "Return My Green Space," "Demolish the Illegal Construction Sheds and Walls According to the Law," and "Protect Qunzhong's Interests." Several days later, these slogans made of used newspapers were torn into pieces. No one was certain who did it, but many speculated that it was done by the developer's hired men. The residents then used big Chinese ink brushes to paint their slogans on the wall space not covered by any banners. They also tore down and cut the advertising banners. These spontaneous skirmishes were known as 'the slogan battle', which was driven by the struggle for space on the level of symbols. Since these walls were located along major public streets, such symbolic clashes gained high visibility and caught the attention of the local and city governments.

In addition to these various forms of everyday activism (petitions, protests, visits, and slogan fights), there appeared another creative engagement, marking the emergence of a nascent public in reform China. Maizidian residents were not only to invoke the law and rally the intervention of their local district and municipal governments, but were also able to create a parallel discursive arena, a website called *Chengshi Ludi Wang* ("Urban Green Land Network") for broader collective mobilization and public support across Chinese cities. Many of the residents were white-collar professionals with the capacity to create and maintain a sophisticated webpage. This discursive space kept track of all the important encounters and struggles surrounding Maizidian, published numerous social commentaries, and posted relevant legal documents that Chinese urban residents could utilize to defend their rights and interests.[4] It also uploaded over one hundred pictures showing the destruction of the green field, the construction of a luxury apartment complex (with units selling at the extremely high price of eighty-eight hundred yuan per square meter), and the defacing of massive advertisement banners for the new complex by activists.

One of the posted open letters signed by Maizidian residents made a powerful statement. Titled "Who Is the Law Enforcement Agent? *Qunzhong* Are Protecting the Dignity of the Law," it evoked government urban planning rulings to demonstrate the illegality of the new construction. It asserted that "the battle over the green land by the masses is not only to protect our own interests but also to protect the dignity of law, the image of the party, and the legal system." The letter strongly urged the Beijing municipal government to step forward to protect the interests of "the people" by calling off the construction and returning the land to its rightful collective holders – the residents or *qunzhong*. As this letter indicates, a focal point of the contestation was on the question of what should be counted as "common matters" or "public interests." Clearly Maizidian residents sought to present this dispute as a matter of harming or protecting public interests rather than a matter of private ownership rights. They spoke from a superior and specific subject position of *qunzhong* that was historically formed in the milieu of Chinese political culture.

By spreading their struggle to the larger public beyond their locality and beyond Beijing, this website served as a new public arena for those engaged in similar spatial struggles to come together and share information and tactics. Updated daily by activists, this webpage had a total of nearly five thousand hits and played a significant role of articulating the cause and logic of the green space battle. Under the mounting pressure from the residents, the Beijing Municipal Government ruled in 2004 that the construction must stop and wait for further investigation and consultation with the residents. Dacheng eventually tore down the temporary sheds and spared the green triangle from its housing development. Once the residents claimed the victory, they made a public announcement and soon closed down the special website: "In the triumphant sound of laughers, the Urban Green Land Network has fulfilled its mission. Thus, we are closing the website and will use the domain name for other purposes." This act revealed the limitations of the nascent publics in urban China, namely they tend to be issue based and short lived. Once the pressing concerns are addressed, the mobilized public engagement tends to dissipate.

"Stop selling land twice"

There exists another kind of fierce battle over the appropriation of communal space within the new private residential compounds. In order to maximize profits, some developers attempt to construct additional commodity housing buildings on the common land within a *xiaoqu*. The existing families believe that such an act is a breach of the contract they signed with the developer and thus a violation of their property rights and their entitlement to the communal space they commonly hold. Therefore, they come together to challenge the predatory developers by engaging in protests, legal action, and other oppositional behaviors to block what they see as an illicit appropriation of their land. Unlike the Maizidian case, the residents involved in this situation do not speak so much as *qunzhong*, but more often as rightful *yezhu* (private property owners). Both developers and residents enter actual legal battles in courts. Sometimes, the confrontation turns violent when outraged homeowners clash with the illicit forces deployed by developers. The case I present below provides a glimpse into this form of conflict and the complexity of the social forces involved. It further illuminates a major problem that comes with "governing at a distance" (Rose 1999) in that the struggle for property rights and social justice can be easily tampered with by powerful real estate authorities.

I first heard about the 'Riverside *weiquan* incident' or the 'Riverside Battle over Green Space' in Kunming from a casual conversation with a friend in August 2004. I soon located reports from five major local newspapers from June 2004. Three of them stated that the development firm had just filed a lawsuit against several resident activists. I called one of the reporters and found out the names of the two lawyers working on behalf of the activists. When I contacted them and told them about my research, they agreed to meet with me and introduce me to some of the residents involved. At a meeting in the law office to discuss their next move, I met the two lawyers and four homeowners, two women and two men.

Riverside Garden was developed by the Dragon Development Company in Guandu District of Kunming. The focal point of conflict was the use of communal space already designated as the green space within the community. In 1997, before the housing construction was finished, the apartments were already on the market for sale at a price of about twenty-one hundred yuan per square meter. At that time, this property was considered upper-middle-level housing. One of the factors that attracted many buyers was the developer's promise that nearly half of the development was committed to green communal space – a number much higher than most of the existing residential communities in the city. The developer promised to create a dreamlike living environment with ample lawns, trees, flowers, and strolling areas. Ms. Liu Jin told me how appealing this feature was to her: "The developer purposely used this green space as the selling point to allure us. If I knew that the green coverage would be significantly reduced and there would be high-rises built on our property later, I would not have bought my two units. But they lied to us." According to several newspaper reports and my own interviews, the sales agents indeed verbally promised all the buyers that there would be a large, open green space in their community, but this was not clearly written in the contract. Liu Jin, who planned to buy two apartments there, wanted to make sure that the promise was real. She called the municipal planning office and they assured her that no construction of any high-rises within the community would be approved. The residential units there were sold quickly within a year.

For the first five years, the residents enjoyed the large green space in their community, which had become a popular space for kids to play, the elderly to gather, and others to stroll and exercise. But the situation suddenly began to change in late May 2005. One day a group of construction workers arrived at Riverside Garden and started to cut down trees and remove light posts and benches. The noise of big trucks hauling away things disturbed the residents. They initially thought that perhaps the developer wanted to do some new landscaping work but then found it suspicious because they were not notified about it. Soon they discovered that this green field of twenty *mu* (about 1.33 hectares) would no longer belong to them and two new high-rises would be built on the site. The residents became furious at the developer. On June 2, they launched the "battle to defend the green field" (*lüdi baohuzhan*). Here is a brief account of the incident by Liu Jin:

> On the evening of June 1st, the road to our *xiaoqu* was blocked by dozens of homeowners because they heard that heavy construction machinery was about to move in. Initially we were told that the top leaders of the real estate firm would come to have a dialog with us. So we waited there. But no one showed up to meet with us. On June 2nd, when I came back from work at noon, I saw some five hundred men hired by the developer forming a circle hand by hand around the green space to prohibit anyone from entering. There were still a few elderly people taking a walk within who refused to leave. They were simply carried out forcefully by the hired men. At that moment, a bulldozer was moving in. I jumped out and tried to stop them, but the driver would not listen to me. As some of the residents pushed into the green space, their men began to beat us. Many residents were injured and eight of them with more serious injuries were sent to the hospital. We have video to prove all this.

According to several newspaper reports, angry residents also injured several construction workers and broke the windows of the trucks and bulldozers. That afternoon, three to four hundred infuriated residents marched to the street and blocked traffic on the busy second ring road. They held large banners with such slogans as "Return Our Garden, Return Our Green Space," "The Dragon Real Estate Firm Is a Swindler," and "Riverside Garden Property Owners' Interests Cannot Be Violated." Local government officials and the police came out to persuade the protestors to return home. After a couple of hours, they finally left the street and decided to hang the banners from their home windows. To gain wider public attention, a group of activists printed and posted flyers about their struggle throughout the streets in the nearby area and asked residents in the community to display the slogans on their car windows.

The violent confrontation and protest temporarily halted the construction. The developer began to use other means to terrorize the residents. Mr. Ma, a middle-aged man whom I met at the meeting, gave me the following account of a mysterious incident:

> On June 11 an attempted homicide occurred. A female homeowner who was an activist drove to a nearby supermarket. When she stopped at a red light, two strangers suddenly came up and broke her car window and tried to stab

> her. She quickly jumped to the other seat and the knife cut her leg. The men vanished into the crowd. Luckily the injury was not life-threatening, but the incident terrified Riverside's residents. For a while our community was in the shadow of "dark terror," as some people phrased it. Since that incident, I have been afraid to go out alone at night. The management also installed seven surveillance cameras around the green field, not to protect us but to watch our activities. It also replaced all the security guards with a new crew we did not know. We think they are their thugs. They even followed some of our leaders. We can no longer feel safe at home even if the green field is saved. The developer has connections with the underworld and can hire thugs to bully us while denying any involvement. The police will not come to defend us either because they are bribed by the developer.

Even though the residents could not prove that the man who stabbed the woman was hired by the developer, they believed that it was not accidental and that she was clearly targeted, not for her money but to intimidate her. The timing of the incident was also telling, as it occurred during the height of the conflict. I visited Riverside in July and the green space was almost destroyed but no construction was going on. When I took out my camera to take pictures of the site, a man who appeared to be a private security guard ran toward me and questioned why I was there and what the pictures were for. I said I was visiting a friend. He told me that no photography was allowed because this was private property, and that if I did not leave immediately, I might be detained.

The developer later told some newspaper reporters that they regretted not having communicated better with the residents and understood their emotional reaction, but they could not forgive the damage inflicted on the company's reputation by their protest. As a result, the firm filed a lawsuit against six activists at the local district court on June 10 and demanded that the defendants immediately "stop all the destructive action," clear the negative influence by making a public apology, and each pay two hundred thousand yuan for damage to the firm's reputation. The six residents simply could not believe that the firm had turned things upside down. As Liu Jin put it, "It was the firm that broke the contract, cheated on us, and exercised violence on us. But now it acts as if the developer is the victim demanding justice. Unbelievable!" Even though the defendants had photos, videos, and eyewitness accounts of the violence imposed on them during the encounter, they had little confidence in the legal system and were deeply worried about their fate. Individuals fighting against a powerful developer rarely had a positive outcome. According to Mr. Ma, when the incident had just taken place, the developer had already leaked word that if the residents dared to hire any lawyers to file charges against the firm, his people would make sure that the lawyers would face serious trouble. Then, on the first day of the hearing, the representatives of the firm made some threatening remarks, saying that if the defendants won, they would use their clout to make sure that the judge in the case would lose his job in the near future. "They act as if they rule this district. They do not even take the judge seriously. How can they take us ordinary citizens seriously?" said Ma.

The homeowners who were dragged into this litigation finally found two lawyers who were willing to take their case. I asked why they accepted the case even when they knew it was an uphill battle, and I wanted to know whether they were concerned for their safety. They told me that the foremost reason they took the case was that several residents living there were their friends who pleaded for help. Second, after studying the case, they felt strongly that the residents were mistreated and that it was their professional responsibility to help the weak seek justice. Third, the residents preserved ample evidence of the developer's wrongdoing, which could be used in their defense. The case was widely reported by major local newspapers, except for one whose major advertiser was Dragon Real Estate (and thus a main source of income). "We could in turn file a lawsuit against the developer, charging him with breaching the contract and the illegal use of violence. If they dare to touch us, their involvement will be too obvious and draw attention from higher authorities beyond their district. Chinese people's awareness of rights protection is increasing greatly. Hopefully we will get support from the media, the public, and higher-level officials who are not directly tied to the developer," explained one lawyer. Another reason they took the case, which they did not mention, was the legal fee they charged, eighteen thousand yuan, which was not a small amount.

In the law office I was allowed to read a set of litigation documents including the contract of purchase and four pages of detailed arguments repudiating the charges. They asked whether I had any connection with major foreign news agencies and hoped I could perhaps write a report on this case. Exposure in the international press is usually beneficial to the weak and powerless in such battles. When I told them that I had no such connections and could only document this case in my own publications later, they were a bit disappointed, but they were still pleased by my attention to their struggle. Curious about the role of the government in this clash, I asked whether they had considered seeking help from the district or city government. One of the women replied quickly:

> Yes, we did pay a collective visit to the city government, but [it was] no use. One hundred to two hundred of us showed up at the city government building, but we were blocked by some ten security guards. None of the top officials came out to meet with us. Only a lower-level cadre from the Bureau of Popular Appeals came to talk to us briefly and dismissed us. We initially thought that the government would speak for justice on behalf of ordinary people because our rights were obviously violated. But that turned out to be an illusion. We are on our own.

Their situation is not a unique one. Local governments tend to take a hands-off approach by staying out of a dispute unless the situation gets out of control. The official rhetoric today is to let citizens seek justice from the legal system. This system is supposed to be relatively independent from politics, but in reality it is heavily permeated by political and corporate power. I heard an anecdote that encapsulates this troubling condition. A young reporter asked the head of the planning division of Dragon Real Estate: "Do you think in our country today it is *quan* [political power] that rules over the law or vice versa?" The director replied: "None of these. I tell you that it is money that rules over everything today."

Although the lawyers were somewhat confident about winning the case, the defendants were still deeply concerned because after all they were fighting against a powerful corporation. The two hundred thousand yuan suit against them each was not a small amount. Meanwhile, they were worried about the safety of their families as they were followed and watched by thugs sent by the developer. One of them said: "We sometimes feel like members of an underground party since we have to change our meeting places all the time. We cannot meet at home within the compound as it is under surveillance. We cannot call each other from home as we believe that our phones are tapped." Despite the obstacles, Riverside residents eventually won the green land battle on two fronts. First, the developer eventually withdrew the litigation after two rounds of court hearings due to lack of evidence. This was a big relief for the six charged residents. Second, over three hundred Riverside homeowners collectively filed a lawsuit at the municipal middle court in mid-August of the same year against the city planning bureau for wrongly issuing Dragon Real Estate a license to develop commodity housing on the green space. They claimed that this common space belonged to them collectively according to the newly passed Property Management Law. They demanded that the city government cancel the land development license and formally transfer use rights to the disputed land to the residents. Two weeks later, the municipal planning bureau announced that it would withdraw its approval for housing development on the disputed site and put this land under the category of "public green project" (*gonggong lühuadi*). It was speculated that the city government was under pressure from higher authorities to prevent this highly publicized conflict from escalating into larger civil unrest. On the evening of August 24, several hundred Riverside residents gathered in the communal garden and celebrated their victory with firecrackers and fireworks. In an interview with a newspaper reporter, a female resident exclaimed: "This decision is great news to our property owners. We believed that the government would eventually stand up for the people and protect the interests and rights of the masses." Her words can be interpreted as a plea for greater government intervention in residents' battles against corporate infringement on their rights.

What are the social, political, and psychological impacts of the surging rights protection mobilization in urban areas? On the individual level, those who engage in *weiquan* pay a heavy price. Many property owners reported that during the several months of intense conflict they could not focus on their work or business, and thus suffered varying degrees of financial loss. For instance, Ms. Liu from Riverside Garden told me that ever since she was drawn into the lawsuit she had spent most of her time reading relevant legal documents, meeting with lawyers and other affected residents, and attending court hearings. As a result, she had to close down her hair salon for two months. Further, the value of their property was dropping due to the widely publicized confrontation. Some homeowners within the compound no longer felt safe and wanted to sell their homes at half the price they had paid so as to move to another community. But few people were willing to buy the property and move into this troubled place. Perhaps the greater loss was to their emotional and psychological well-being. One male resident in Riverside made a suicide threat, claiming that he would jump off his residential building to protest the developer's action and social injustice. Distressed residents often used such bleak images as 'prison' and 'surveillance camp' to describe their own community. When the homeowners could not feel relaxed and peaceful in their own residential community, they felt that their houses were no longer homes. Ms. Liu articulated the impact on her family this way:

> Ever since June 2, I asked my husband and my son to live outside [Riverside Garden] temporarily and not return home because I was actively involved. I stayed home because I had to fight. I am especially worried about our child because he was not aware of the potential danger. If they hurt me, I could handle it. But I could not let that happen to my child. We have been living apart for over two months. I feel exhausted now. Look at the financial and psychological damage they [the developer and his thugs] have done to us!

On the collective level, *weiquan* has brought about several positive changes. The actual participation in collective activism brought previously isolated individuals closer and resulted in a stronger sense of group solidarity. As Ms. Liu pointed out:

> Prior to this incident everyone in the neighborhood seemed to be busy with his or her own things. We rushed out to work and rushed back home, hiding in our own private space and not wanting to talk to each other. I did not know my neighbors after living there for six years. But now because of the incident we all know each other and have more interaction. This is a good thing. This Autumn Festival the residents in our compound have decided to celebrate together by each contributing a moon cake. This is unprecedented.

Weiquan struggles also motivate homeowners to get organized on a more permanent basis. For example, during the months of confrontation Riverside residents began to discuss how to formally establish their own property owners' association and keep it as a permanent part of communal life. They hope that eventually they would be able to fire the current management company supplied by the developer. The experience of collective action has also enhanced the rights consciousness among the residents directly involved as well as other citizens who are the spectators of such events. The mass media and new information technologies provide a broader stage for such social dramas to unfold publicly. The residents in other communities I spoke to followed these events and lawsuits on the internet and in newspapers. They applauded the actions of those who dared to defy the developers. Finally, property-based middle-class activism has become a driving force for important legal changes. As I have shown, the root cause of the 'green land battles' is the greed of real estate developers who want to use land twice over for enormously lucrative new construction. The developers dare to do so because of the ambiguous and weak legal regime concerning property and the pervasive power of real estate firms. It is in this context of increasing property conflicts that the new property law was enacted. Yet it is far from certain whether and how the new law will make a significant difference in the near future in Chinese homeowners' quest for property rights and social justice.

The ambivalent relations

Disputes and conflicts over the use of communal space for new construction are widespread across Chinese cities today. To defend their rights and interests and challenge the encroachment of corporate interests, urban residents are compelled to come together and engage in collective mobilization and activism. This situation provides a useful opportunity for us to reflect upon the complex dynamics among developers, government agencies, residents, and the media, as well as ponder the nature of emerging publics in the Chinese context. As the two cases I present show, the state–society relations model can no longer sufficiently help us grasp the shifting reality of China as the myriad forms of articulation and confrontation among different social and political elements are taking place (see also Pieke 1995; Rofel 2007; Tomba 2014; Zhang and Ong 2008). In this context, the role and nature of emerging publics are quite different from what Habermas envisioned for liberal European bourgeois societies. The key to Habermas' conception of the public sphere is that private people come together to form a public and legitimate its public authority in front of public opinion (1991: 25–26). And this arena is conceptually distinct from the state and in principle critical of the state; it is also distinct from the economy or market relations (see Fraser 1994:110–111). Yet, the kind of new publics forming in contemporary China complicates a number of divisions: the state and the market, the public and the private spheres, the discursive and the nondiscursive, the individual and the collective in the following ways:

First, the nascent forms of publics in China tend to be issues based and form in the process of fighting for a common and concrete cause – i.e. environmental protection (Weller 2006), consumer rights protection, land disputes, property rights protection, advocacy for people with AIDS (French 2006) and so on. Thus, the idea of 'common good' as manifested in different forms is critical to *weiquan* movements, which often take on both discursive and nondiscursive forms. Second, the new publics are not necessarily critical of the state per se, but are antagonistic towards those perceived as predatory or destructive forces to the life of the ordinary people, or *qunzhong*. In some cases, the antagonism is directed primarily at local governments (Brandtstädter 2011; O'Brien and Li 2006); in other cases, it is directed at both corporate entities and elements of local governments (Zhang 2010; Hsing 2010). But in any case, a distinct milieu of public debates and civic engagements is emerging, in which private individuals come to assume a collective and public presence. In the case of urban housing, 'homeowners' become 'the willful masses' seeking justice and protection of their collective space. The press and new media play an increasingly important part in connecting discrete social groups together and rendering their existence visible. Third, when the government is called into question, the popular rhetoric is rarely directed at the state as such but is rather carefully crafted to challenge certain elements of the government while seeking support and sympathy from other government elements. In the case of urban land disputes, rightful residents generally demand the intervention of higher level state authorities to counter what they see as corrupt local bureaucratic entities that have formed entrenched alliances with developers. Thus, unraveling this ambivalent relationship between the reform state, commercial entities, and citizens engaged in civic activism is a critical step toward a deeper understanding of popular politics in postsocialist China.

Finally, I would like to consider the political implication of endless land disputes and nascent *weiquan* publics for the Chinese regime's endeavor to build a 'harmonious society'. On one level, land battles and spatial struggles have no doubt posed a threat to the effort to achieve social harmony. The *weiquan* movement of all kinds has become arguably the largest and most active civic engagement and manifestation of social discord in urban China. It contests the utopian vision of a harmonious society at a time when income inequality is soaring, rights consciousness is rising, and business profits trump concerns of sociality and morality. On another level, rights-protection publics do not reject but actively appropriate the official language of socialist harmony and public good. They claim that their struggles are a necessary component in constructing a truly harmonious society because a harmonious society must first be a just society, in which ordinary people's rights, interests, and place are recognized and defended.

Notes

1 An early version of this paper was presented at the workshop on "Justice, Popular Politics and the Chinese State" at the University of Oslo, the Public Space Working Group of the Humanities Center at the CUNY-Graduate Center, and the Center for Global Metropolitan Studies at UC Berkeley. I thank all the participants at these events, especially Susanne Brandtstädter, for their comments and insights. Parts of the ethnographic material are adapted from the author's book *In Search of Paradise: Middle-Class Living in a Chinese Metropolis* (Cornell University Press, 2010), with the permission of the publisher, Cornell University Press.

2 For the struggles over land and property rights related to the real estate developments, see Hsing (2010) and Shao (2010). For consumer rights movements, see Rofel (2007) and Latham et al. (2006). In my book *In Search of Paradise* (2010), I also offer accounts of another activism among property owners based on the conflicts with property management agencies over community service and regulation fees.

3 The notion of "qunzhong" or "the people" has its socialist origin and a strong moral connotation. It has been frequently deployed by those engaged in battles against various forms of social injustice and exploitation (see Shao 2010; Lee 2007; Cho 2013).

4 The website, www.yiyitong.com, lasted for a year and five months, and was removed after the developer abandoned the new construction plan.

References

Brandtstädter, Susanne. 2011. The Law Cuts Both Ways: Rural Legal Activism and Citizenship Struggles in Neosocialist China. *Economy and Society* 40(2), pp. 266–288.

Brandtstädter, Susanne, Wade, Peter and Woodward, Kath. 2011. Introduction: Rights, Cultures, Subjects and Citizens. *Economy and Society* 40(2), pp. 167–183.
Calhoun, Craig, ed. 1994. *Habermas and the Public Sphere*. Cambridge, MA: MIT Press.
Cho, Mun Young. 2013. *The Specter of "the People"*. Ithaca, NY: Cornell University Press.
Fraser, Nancy. 1994. Rethinking the Public Sphere: A Contribution to the Critique of Actually Existing Democracy. In: Craig Calhoun, ed. *Habermas and the Public Sphere*. Cambridge, MA: MIT Press, pp. 518–536.
French, Howard. 2006. Chinese Turn to Civic Power as a New Tool. *The New York Times*, April 11.
Habermas, Jürgen. 1991. *The Structural Transformation of the Public Sphere: An Inquiry Into a Category of Bourgeois Society*. Cambridge, MA: MIT Press.
Hirschkind, Charles. 2009. *The Ethical Soundscape: Cassette Sermons and Islamic Counterpublics*. New York: Columbia University Press.
Holston, James. 2009. *Insurgent Citizenship: Disjunctions of Democracy and Modernity in Brazil*. Princeton, NJ: Princeton University Press.
Hsing, You-Tien. 2010. *The Great Urban Transformation: Politics of Land and Property in China*. Oxford: Oxford University Press.
Kleinman, Arthur and Watson, James. 2005. *SARS in China: Prelude to Pandemic?* Stanford: Stanford University Press.
Latham, Kevin, Stuart, Thompson and Jakob, Klein. 2006. *Consuming China: Approaches to Cultural Change in Contemporary China*. Abingdon, UK: Routledge.
Lee, Benjamin. 1998. Peoples and Publics. *Public Culture* 10(2), pp. 371–394.
Lee, Ching Kwan. 2007. *Against the Law: Labour Protests in China's Rustbelt and Sunbelt*. Berkeley, University of California Press.
O'Brien, Kevin and Li, Lianjiang. 2006. *Rightful Resistance in Rural China*. Cambridge: Cambridge University Press.
Pieke, Frank N. 1995. Bureaucracy, Friends, and Money: The Growth of Capital Socialism in China. *Comparative Study of Society and History* 37(3), pp. 494–518.
Rofel, Lisa. 2007. *Desiring China: Experiments in Neoliberalism, Sexuality, and Public Culture*. Durham, NC: Duke University Press.
Rose, Nikolas. 1999. *Power of Freedom: Reframing Political Thought*. Cambridge: Cambridge University Press.
Shao, Qin. 2010. Waving the Red Flag: Cultural Memory and Grass-Roots Protest in Housing Disputes in China. *Modern Chinese Literature and Culture* 22(1), pp. 197–232.
Tomba, Luigi. 2014. *The Government Next Door: Neighborhood Politics in Urban China*. Ithaca, NY: Cornell University Press.
Weller, Robert. 2006. *Discovering Nature: Globalization and Environmental Culture in China and Taiwan*. Cambridge: Cambridge University Press.
Yang, Mayfair. 1999. Introduction. In: Mayfair Yang, ed. *Spaces of Their Own: Women's Public Sphere in Transnational China*. Minneapolis: University of Minnesota Press, pp. 1–31.
Zhang, Li. 2010. *In Search of Paradise: Middle-Class Living in a Chinese Metropolis*. Ithaca, NY: Cornell University Press.
Zhang, Li and Ong, Aihwa, eds. 2008. *Privatizing China, Socialism from Afar*. Ithaca, NY: Cornell University Press.

2 Making personal life political

Political trajectories of everyday conversations in China's online communities

Cuiming Pang

There is a widespread belief among observers of the Chinese internet that its netizens are more inclined to pursue personal interests rather than to inform themselves about and voice their opinions on national politics (e.g., Damm 2007; Leibold 2011; Liu 2009: 52–54). Typical online activities, such as documenting one's everyday life in blogs and microblogs, chatting on instant messaging services, making friends through social networking sites, and exchanging personal opinions in discussion forums, are regarded as indications for internet users' general political indifference. This characterization of Chinese netizens corresponds to the portrayal of contemporary Chinese society as de-politicised. It is widely believed that in the Reform era, Chinese society became dominated by a consumer culture and that especially since the 1990s Chinese people have retreated from political participation and involved themselves in the private realm to seek self-fulfillment.

Evidence from an online community, in which I conducted ethnographic research between 2007 and 2014,[1] supports the view that Chinese netizens use the internet primarily for realizing interests of a personal nature. It does not, however, support the assumption that this pursuit of personal interests is fundamentally apolitical. The chosen community, which I call Tan Street,[2] was established in late 2005. By late 2014 it had more than fifty thousand registered members. Most of its members grew up in the same county (Wen County), but later came to live elsewhere in China and even overseas. Tan Street's founder created the site in order to provide a platform where the county's emigrants could communicate with each other. As with other online communities, Tan Street has a discussion forum focusing on various topics, such as photography, bicycling, music and movies, investment, literature, and so on. None seemed to have a connection with politics. Nevertheless, a closer look at the detailed content of each thread and individual post revealed that the boundary between the political and the personal was not rigid. Discussions derived from personal life often touched upon governmental practices and frequently evolved into political discussions. A number of scholars have pointed out that conversations about politics are not necessarily distinct from, but instead are part of ordinary conversations of daily life (see e.g., Lichterman 1999; Walsh 2004). In the same vein, scholars like Graham have begun to focus on online everyday conversations. As is the case in Tan Street, they could show that often conversations about personal life and entertainment bring on political debates and that thereby they have a political function (Graham 2012; Wu 2011). These studies have proven that the political and the personal are interconnected; however, the question of how these interlinkages emerge and how they evolve has not been satisfactorily answered.

In this paper, I shall present some of the Tan Street participants' apparently mundane online conversations in order to analyse the processes and framings through which personal conversation turns into political 'talk' and engagements. Inspired by Alfred Schütz and Thomas Luckmann's social phenomenology (1973), I argue that it is through processes of typification that personal situations become linked to political issues. When Tan Street participants talk about their own experiences, they do not divulge much information about these, but rather interpret them by situating them within a broader political and social context. A personal experience is thereby typified as an 'issue', rather than treated as a unique and particular instance. I also find that participants often relate personal experiences to state practices, a framing by which their experiences may appear as political issues. As Brandtstädter points out in her introduction, it is in everyday judgements of the state that ordinary people in China understand, interpret, and participate in social and political situations. Moreover, actively seeking out audiences to discuss issues, share opinions, and arrive at a common view on particular issues is itself a public-making practice with effects on state–society relations in China.

In the following, I will first discuss propositions in the literature that, under the influence of both globalization and individualization, conventional political participation has been in retreat and individual-initiated and individual-centered subpolitical engagement on the rise. I then give a brief summary of the rise of subpolitics in China. The main part of the text will focus on the features of online subpolitics. Based on a detailed reading and coding of 111 everyday political threads from Tan Street, it analyses the mechanisms that make personal talk political. In the last section, I focus on the relation between internet censorship and online subpolitics in China.

The end of politics?

The decline of the political and its public effects have first been described for Western societies. For instance, in the book *The End of Politics: Corporate Power and the Decline of the Public Sphere*, Carl Boggs (2002) laments the loss of political and civic participation in the United States. He argues that the shrinking of political space is a consequence of economic globalization and corporate colonization. As the globalization of the market empowers corporations to penetrate every realm of people's lives, economic interests and private consumption become paramount, and people are being pulled from the public sphere into the private realm. As a consequence, civic engagements decline and political participation suffers. Although Boggs is aware of the existence of social movements, he argues that these movements are typically driven by an interest to improve individual life quality and not by genuine, liberal-democratic citizenship ideals. In other words, contemporary social movements favor the personal over the political (ibid.).

Boggs rightly points out that globalization is impelling people to focus more on their personal well-being. However, he oversimplifies the connection between personal fulfillment and political involvement. His conclusion – the end of politics – is based on a normative judgement on what political involvement looks like. For him, politics equates with the state and the political system, and political involvement or public action presupposes a public sphere of a conventional, Habermasian type, where people gather to debate and rationally decide on issues related to the conduct of the state. This political landscape Boggs portrays as an idealized and nostalgic landscape. It needs to be redrawn to capture the new features of globalizing and individualizing societies. When the concept of politics is broadened, as has been suggested by Ulrich Beck, to include what he calls "subpolitics", it becomes evident that political action is not so much on the decline but rather being "reinvented" (Beck 1997).

Beck has coined the term "subpolitics" to describe a new kind of politics designed by citizens to secure their personal and their family's well-being. To him, the emergence of subpolitics has largely resulted from the inability of the state to deal with the risks brought about by industrialization and globalization. States have thus outsourced some of their responsibilities to formally "private" actors, such as non-governmental organizations, private corporations, and individual citizens. As a result, citizens are being forced to make informed choices and take more initiative to counter threats to their well-being and more generally their livelihoods. Under such circumstances, they may raise personal issues with the public and require the government to adjust its policies to meet their personal demands.

Political consumerism is a typical arena where the phenomenon of subpolitics becomes manifest. Following Beck's argument of the predicament of the state, Michele Micheletti (2003) has argued that the state's inadequacy in regulating markets and corporate behavior compels consumers to purchase as citizens. They choose products on the basis of political values and ethics. Their choices reflect a private interest in personal and familial well-being, as well as broader issues of justice and equality. These political consumers often make ethical judgements about corporations and government practices and use tools such as boycotts to engage in political struggle. Former divisions between political and the personal spheres are thus being erased.

The concept of subpolitics is helpful for understanding political participation in an era when individuals are forced by modern institutions to take charge of their own lives. This concept captures two main features of the political scene in the current global age. First, politics is decentralized. The state is no longer the only actor in politics. Individuals and societal collectives also become political actors, and often deal with political problems directly instead of relying on the mediation of politicians and political parties. Second, the boundary between political and personal has become fuzzy. Political campaigns frequently focus on issues of private life, such as abortion and gay marriage. Citizens voice their private problems and worries by appealing to the public, and demand that the government adapt policies to personal demands. It is impossible to distinguish whether their acts are personal or political, more related to the private sphere than to the public. In sum, the pursuit of personal fulfillment does not imply a privatized retreat from politics. Rather, the new 'fuzziness' signifies a shift from state-oriented conventional politics to alternative and individualized subpolitics, pursued by citizens having personal concerns.

The changing nature of political participation

This rise of subpolitics manifests itself also in Chinese society. Since the introduction of market reforms in the late 1970s, China has experienced a transition from state-enforced mass political participation to individual-initiated and individual-centered subpolitics. During the Mao era, state-enforced mass political participation was a distinctive feature of the Chinese political scene. Through a series of national campaigns, Chinese people were mobilized to break away from traditional family, kinship, and community institutions and were assigned to work and live in state-organized collectives. These collectives, known as rural communes and urban work units, took on economic, social, and political functions. They provided members with material resources while delivering political order, and they mobilized members to demonstrate political loyalty to the party-state. Political study became part of people's everyday lives. Ideological slogans and images of political role models were spread throughout the nation. Rewards and sanctions were implemented by Party leaders to encourage politically acceptable behavior.[3]

People also engaged in mass politics in the interest of private aims and personal needs. However, disclosing this motivation was politically dangerous, and it therefore had to be hidden behind a mask of 'altruistic' political engagement. Andrew Walder, for instance, describes how workers in socialist factories developed various strategies to build personal connections with factory officials, who controlled access to benefits such as material goods, welfare services, and career opportunities. These could include an active display of political loyalty, such as the expression of obedience to and support for Party leaders and Party policies during political campaigns and meetings. Workers sought to make a positive impression on officials in order to receive better evaluations. Their chances of being promoted, receiving better housing, or reaching other instrumental goals were thereby enhanced (Walder 1986).

In the post-Mao era, the pursuit of personal interests is no longer an underground activity. On the contrary, it has been officially acknowledged and socially accepted as a valid and valuable endeavour. In the course of the country's 'opening up' to global markets, the state launched a series of top-down reform programs that disbanded rural communes, privatized state enterprises, cancelled job assignments, and led to the emergence of markets in housing, education, and medical care. The explicit political goal of these measures has been to decrease the dependence of Chinese citizens on state provisions. People have been encouraged to seek private employment and become entrepreneurs, rendering the pursuit of 'private' goals, including personal wealth and well-being, morally acceptable. Even though different generations of Party leadership have continued to launch propaganda campaigns to strengthen ideological control, participation in such campaigns has become rare and typically limited to groups such as Party members, students, and the armed forces (Brady 2008:12). Ordinary Chinese are no longer forced to involve themselves in politics.

Yet while state-enforced political participation has declined, individual-initiated and -centered subpolitics have been on the increase. Collective protests are on the rise and initiated by citizens from all walks of life. They are triggered by various, yet recurrent issues. For example, workers who lost their jobs during the process of privatizing state enterprises collectively demand that the government provide better welfare protection. Peasants whose land was requisitioned by the state seek more compensation. New house owners protest against real estate developers, who deliver substandard buildings or breach contracts, and against the local governments apparently protecting them. Fake commercial products mobilize consumer protection movements. Such protests are initiated by citizens driven by the need to protect personal livelihoods and well-being, as well as by the hope to obtain justice in the face of an uncaring state. Chinese people have thus re-entered the political field (see e.g., Cai 2010; O'Brien 2008; Brandtstädter 2011; Zhang and Cheung, both this volume), but this time not through conventional political channels but as part of turning personal concerns and struggles into public issues.

Subpolitics in Chinese cyberspace

Subpolitics began to emerge in China in the early 1980s and became normalized with the deepening of market transformations. It was the popularization of the internet in the late 1990s that turned it into a mass phenomenon. internet penetration rates in China are still low in comparison with so-called developed countries. Nevertheless, there is no doubt that the internet affects the everyday lives of Chinese people from all walks of life. As with internet users elsewhere, Chinese netizens engage each other in many different ways. They might pursue personal interests and projects – for example, by seeking information, purchasing commercial products, sharing personal stories and opinions, or simply looking for sociability. Passing judgements on current policies and seeking political support for one's views is also a common behavior.

There are two common types of political activity in Chinese cyberspace. The first is protesting. For instance, in 2003, a migrant worker named Sun Zhigang was sent to the Custody and Repatriation Center in Guangzhou because he did not have his identity card and temporary residence permit with him. He was subsequently beaten to death in custody. When Sun's death was revealed online, it immediately ignited a public protest against the government's unjust migration policy and inhuman treatment of vagrants. In 2009, online protests started as Deng Yujiao, a 21-year-old hotel waitress, was charged with deliberate homicide after killing a local government official who had tried to rape her. After a huge wave of protests against this judgement, however, she was released from prison and the charges were dropped. The internet and mobile phone network also play an important role in environmental protests. Initiated by Xiamen residents in

2007 and Maoming residents in 2014, such protests prevented the construction of chemical factories that were perceived as health hazards and their construction permits as resulting from corruption. The phenomenon of online protests has been widely discussed by China scholars (see e.g., Yang 2009).

The second type of online political activity emerges from everyday conversations. The often political nature of such conversations has been overlooked by observers of the Chinese internet, who claim that political activity comprises only a small part of Chinese netizens' online lives (e.g., Damm 2007; Leibold 2011; Liu 2009: 52–54). James Leibold enlists as evidence of Chinese netizens' political indifference that more results on China's leading search engine relate to famous actresses than to political leaders, that millions of posts in a fan community address a particular singer, or that blogs by stock experts are among the most popular on the net (2011: 5). Moreover, a national survey report on online activities, released by the Chinese Academy of Social Science (CASS) in 2007, concludes that the internet in China is mainly a medium for entertainment.

Based on my in-depth observation of the Tan Street community, however, I contend that the above studies fail to notice the many practices through which personal issues are being politicized on the net. Activities such as listening to music, watching movies, playing games, and browsing the web, as listed in the CASS report, become political if netizens use music or videos to convey their anger about the government. Fans of the actress, the singer, or the stock expert mentioned by Leibold can easily become involved in political discussion if their idols publicly express political views. A conclusion that Chinese netizens are more interested in personal life or entertainment than politics is thus premature. To understand the subpolitics of the Chinese internet, that is, the interlacing between the personal and the political in a censorial society, a more detailed scrutiny of netizens' online lives is needed.

Identifying political conversations in Tan Street

In Tan Street Online Community, we frequently find this interlacing of personal and political issues when we follow the trajectory of conversations on certain topics. Everyday political conversations are informal and non-purposive conversations that connect personal life with general public and political issues. This definition stresses two points: first, everyday political conversations do not serve a specific purpose. They do not primarily serve activities such as protesting, but rather occur spontaneously and informally in everyday settings. Second, when everyday political conversations touch on governmental practices, the issues debated are derived from personal life, or they use life experiences to make sense of formal political issues.

I made a list of all the political topics discussed by Tan Street participants in a board entitled "Random Talk" within a two-month period. Topics were considered political when participants' conversations either focused directly on conventional politics or framed personal life experience by reference to national policies. This board itself did not define particular topics for discussion, but rather allowed participants to discuss various topics of their own choosing, thereby making it a perfect place to observe everyday discussions among Tan Street participants.

There were in total 395 threads published on the board within the two-month period; among these, 111 threads could be classified as 'political'. Of these, 50 threads discussed conventional political topics, while 61 discussed personal life issues that had political implications. The former focused on political parties, politicians, governmental policies, and foreign affairs. The latter centered on work, education, migration, health, housing, daily consumption, media, sports, and charity. Yet even conventional political topics were debated by relating state practices to personal lives, or by linking them with life experiences. For instance, discussions about political parties often centered on the civil war between the Chinese Communist Party and the Nationalist Party during the 1940s. Participants in the thread would publicly defend their viewpoints by citing history textbooks they had read in school and documentaries they had seen on TV, or by retelling stories of veteran soldiers they had known. When discussing the issue of political corruption, contributors would relate stories about particular politicians' abuse of their positions for personal desires, such as gaining business opportunities, maintaining luxurious lifestyles, or finding young lovers. General discussions about governmental policies would focus on policies related to real estate, household registration, rural construction, vehicle tax, and social welfare – all of which are issues affecting personal lives. In these threads, participants often shared their own experiences and knowledge of these policies. Finally, the main focus of discussions on foreign affairs was China's strained relationship with Japan. Debates often linked national policies to personal consumption practices by debating, for example, whether or not, or how, to boycott Japanese products.

Other conversations originated in shared personal concerns but developed into comments on state practices. For instance, discussions about work often criticized the political treatment of laid-off workers or of teachers who are not civil servants. Discussions about education, migration, health, and housing issues stressed weaknesses of related policies and the negative impact these have on society. Discussions about consumption practices complained of the lack of political supervision over the food industry. Discussions about media use touched upon state censorship. Discussions around sports life mentioned the involvement of politicians in sports associations and the corruption resulting therefrom. Discussions around organizing donation drives complained of the difficulties in running grassroots charities in the Chinese political context.

Typifying personal life

How is the personal and the political systematically being connected in Tan Street participants' online conversations? Jürgen Habermas, in his study of communicative action, has argued that it is through rational debate that people transform personal concerns to public concerns (Habermas 1984). While pointing out the importance of communication, his notion of the public sphere has limited application to Chinese online communities. In Habermas' definition, the public sphere is shaped by citizens' free exchange of opinion and by rational debates, conducted with the aim of arriving at rational agreements. It is through this particular process that private interests become public issues. Tan Street participants often engage in heated debates on issues of mutual concern, where they evaluate the opinions of others and try to convince them of their own particular perspective. In other cases, they acknowledge fundamental differences of opinion and are open to accept alternative points of view on particular topics. Yet, in all cases it is possible to identify a mechanism through which personal concerns are transformed into public concern, which in itself is independent of whether agreements are reached or whether the debate itself adheres to the principles of communicative rationality.

This mechanism can be called "typification," a concept developed by the social phenomenologist Alfred Schütz (Schütz and Luckman 1973). According to Schütz, as members of a society we tend to assume that others experience this society in the same way as we do. Yet, it is de facto intersubjective processes of typification through which we conceptualise the world around us which both allow for social predictability of individual behavior and make common or collective experiences possible. In these processes, the objects, persons, events, actions, motivations and even feelings that we encounter in real life are clustered into types – linguistic, political, cultural, social and other types. For instance, although every book is different, a book also exists as an object 'type'; although teachers are unique individuals, we call them 'teachers'; and we all experience 'happiness', although the catalyst for such a feeling varies from case to case. In this way, we conceptualise what we have experienced and take this stock of knowledge with us when we enter a situation. Our action in every commonplace situation is guided by a typified stock of knowledge. For example, when we want to send a letter, we buy an envelope and stamp(s), write down a destination address on the envelope, put on the stamp(s), place the letter in a mailbox, and expect the letter to be picked up by postal workers and delivered to its destination. Although the activity of sending a letter is an individual activity, we conduct the activity based on a typified knowledge that is common in our society.

In Tan Street's everyday online conversations, members not only used typified knowledge for successful communication, but they frequently communicated in a way that allowed personal issues to be typified as public concerns. Two examples shall illustrate this process. The first comes from a discussion thread about the dispute between two of China's IT giants, Tencent and Qihoo. Tencent runs China's most popular instant messaging service, QQ. Qihoo provides one of China's leading anti-virus products, 360 Safeguard. The dispute started when Qihoo alleged that QQ scans the private data of its users, and claimed that by updating its 360 Safeguard, QQ users could block pop-up ads and avoid privacy leaks. Tencent denied the allegation and sent a notification to its users that the company will stop running QQ on computers that have installed 360 Safeguard. As a result, users were forced to 'choose sides' and to uninstall either QQ or 360. The second example comes from a thread about a nationwide measles vaccination campaign initiated by the Ministry of Health (MoH). The MoH required all Chinese children between the ages of eight months and four years to be vaccinated within ten days, regardless of whether or not they had been vaccinated against measles before.

Both of the two cases had direct impact on Tan Street participants' personal lives, and participants exchanged personal experiences and concerns during their online conversations. In the first thread, participants mainly expressed their own feelings regarding Tencent's decision, and explained their decision about which 'side' they had chosen. In the thread on the vaccination campaign, participants expressed worries about potentially serious side effects, and their uncertainties as to whether or not to comply with the vaccine drive. In both cases, participants talked not simply in a factual manner about personal experiences or presented personal opinions. Rather, they presented their interpretations of the cases at hand by typifying them in a particular way.

These typification processes include three different but interrelated practices: contextualisation, orientation, and naming. Contextualisation refers to the practice of situating an instance in a broad social, political, and cultural context. It is a subjective process of framing that reflects how people understand a particular instance. Every person has different views regarding which contexts can be linked to an instance. Whenever people contextualise an instance, they are also giving it an orientation towards particular 'issues'. In addition, as part of the work of contextualisation and orientation, people always give a name to their typified categories. By naming an instance and placing it in a particular category, they can easily connect it to similar instances, and thereby de-singularise it.

In the conversation about the dispute between Tencent and 360, participants contextualised and oriented the case to the issue of rights violations and the narrative of "rights defense" (*weiquan*). They called or 'named' Tencent's response – which forced users to choose 'a side' – a "violation of privacy" and a "violation of the right to choose". The following were rather typical comments: "I have never updated my QQ software, neither have I changed the version of my QQ. How will QQ find out whether or not I have 360 in my computer? If QQ can discover this, it shows that QQ is supervising my computer, and thus is violating my privacy." "It is our right to choose Tencent or 360. Tencent has no right to deprive us of our right to choose." "Has McDonald's ever forbidden its customers to buy Kentucky Fried Chicken? Has Canon ever forbidden its customers to buy Nikon? Has Apple ever forbidden its computer users to use the Windows system? This is my computer! Mine! It is not up to you, Tencent, to decide which software I use or don't use!" By typifying Tencent's act as an act of rights violation, participants oriented a specific instance to a public issue and gave the instance a more political interpretation.

In the thread discussing the MoH's measles vaccination drive, too, participants did not orient it primarily to health issues, but to issues of power exertion and rights violations. The campaign was commonly typified as an example of "coercive behavior" that the government uses against the people. This typification process is apparent in a post written by a father, who expressed his personal feelings in relation to the campaign and linked these with a political statement on government behavior and his own lack of rights. As he wrote:

> Unlike non-Chinese parents who can have two or even more children, I am only allowed to have one child. I cherish my only child. I want to protect her, so I am concerned about all the possible harm the world may bring to her. [. . .] In fact, I have no choice but to accept the government's coercive behavior. I have no courage to oppose state policies, because I don't want to be fired. I have to keep my job, so that I can afford my daughter's education.

Also other participants in this conversation harboured misgivings about the government's "coercive behavior". Some demanded from the government to publicize where the vaccine was produced as well as information about potential side effects, and that it publicly state its reasons for enforcing the vaccination of children (even of those who had been vaccinated before). The phrase "right to know" (*zhiqingquan*) was often included in the posts: "I hope that the government will reveal the truth immediately. We demand the truth! We protest against this mysterious vaccination. Please give people back the right to know." "My daughter is two years old. Should I have her vaccinated or not? What is the truth? Where is my right to know?" Similar to the case involving personal computer software, participants in the thread gave the vaccination drive a larger political significance when orienting it towards the field of politics and naming it state coercion and rights violation. In discussion forums, the vaccination drive was no longer an isolated event or a 'mere' health issue, but it evolved into an issue of wider public and political concern.

Typifying the state

The above conversations show how Tan Street participants typify encounters and instances from everyday life. They also show how participants, as part of online conversations, come to typify and judge the Chinese state. In fact, all the threads that I consider 'political' included judgements of the state. The dispute between Tencent and 360, for instance, was related by many participants to government practices. As one participant wrote, "In the real world, we are deprived of almost all individual rights. Will we lose the rights we have in the virtual world too?" Other participants related the case to state censorship. One poster wrote, "The conflict between these two companies shows that they still have some freedom. They are lucky that they have not been yet 'invited to drink tea'. Let us wait and see which company will be harmonized in the end."[4]

Another conversation focused on the Chinese government's 'hidden' motivation for encouraging private consumption, namely enhancing national economic development. Participants posted comments such as: "The government needs people to consume, even if there isn't sufficient social welfare to secure our educational and medical expenses. The government encourages excessive consumption." "The government is bluffing." "We, the ordinary Chinese people, can never live life simply following our own wishes." The comments typified Chinese people's daily consumption as excessive, and considered this to be the negative result of central policies. The "government" (*zhengfu*) and the "ordinary people" (*laobaixing*) were treated as two entities with opposing interests. These threads display a common tendency in typifying the Chinese state, namely as a unitary and monolithic entity. Participants' everyday problems were often treated as the outcome of general state practice and central policies, and not caused by a specific local government, department, or government official. Similarly, whenever discussions turned on a particular official or officials of a specific department, these were depicted as members of the larger group of Chinese "officials" (*guan*). Moreover, in these political threads participants always identified and typified themselves as "ordinary people", and not by their occupation, gender, age, or place of origin. They made themselves, the "ordinary people", into the other of the Chinese "state" (*guojia*) and "government"(*zhengfu*), the "party" (*dang*), and its "officials" (*guan*).

One political thread was of particular interest. This thread posted an existing petition of laid-off workers to an "Office of Letters and Visits" (*xingfang ju*) in Wen County online, and collected Tan Street participants' comments on it. Both the petition and the comments contained people's judgements of the Chinese state, but the framing of the judgements was different. A comparison between both highlights the particular ways by which Chinese netizens typify the state.

The petition deals with the fate of a group of laid-off workers, originally employed by a state-owned factory for thirty years, who, so it claims, had been betrayed by Wen County government (as the original owner). In 1996, Wen government had privatized the factory and many of the formerly state-employed workers had signed labour contracts with the factory's new owners. Those eventually laid off, in contrast, received a certain amount of compensation for the cancellation of their employment contract and their pension relations with the local government. Yet, only five years later, the Wen County government determined that this agreement had no legality anymore and declared it null and void. Replacing the contract was then a ruling that required the workers to return their original compensation to the local government, in exchange for being allocated new jobs and having their basic pension needs met. However, according to the petitioners, although the money had been returned, the government would not honour its part of the deal by providing new employment and a new pension deal.

The petition named specific bureaucratic departments and concrete officials. It made a difference between the central, provincial and county levels of the government, between previous and current local governments and between various bureaucratic departments. It argued that "certain officials at Wen County's Personnel and Labor Security Bureau" were guilty of "ignoring state policy and provincial leaders' guidance", and mentioned critically a specific official "who was responsible for social security issues and who had worked at the Personnel and Labor Security Bureau for about twenty years". The petition ended with a statement that "many current government officials have already criticized certain previous officials at the Personnel and Labor Security Bureau" and asked the "current government leaders" to "follow state policy to correct the mistake made by previous officials". It did so by clearly distinguishing between the state in general and particular representatives of it on the local level.

In online debates, the opposite was the case. Netizens always took administrative malpractice as representative of political problems on the most general level. Even where discussions would single out particular officials or government departments, these were always perceived as representative of the Chinese government or Chinese policies as a whole. For instance, in a conversation about a local government that had approved the arrest of local teachers petitioning in Beijing, most comments lamented that such injustice happened everywhere in China, and blamed it on China's system of governance. In another conversation, participants discussed the fact that various local civil affairs bureaus allocated social security subsidies to citizens who did not meet the criteria. Rather than being concerned with these bureaus in particular, participants perceived the case to have "typical Chinese characteristics", because "the Chinese political system has no supervision". In contrast to the petition, which called this incident "a particular and rare case", those who commented in the case online perceived it to be "common" in China. One post, for example, situated the case in China's historical and political transformation process: "In China, every state-initiated movement, including the release of new major policies, causes significant changes in the society. The reform of state-owned enterprises is just one example." Instead of merely commenting on this specific case, many participants used it to express their general perspective on the Chinese political system, bureaucracy and administration. As one participant posted: "The biggest problem in China is that it is still ruled by people (*renzhi*) instead of being ruled by law (*fazhi*)." In two further posts, more attention was paid to government officials: "The government advocates a harmonious society. Officials are required to 'serve the people' (*wei renmin fuwu*). However, I never feel that I am served by them." "Officials say one thing and do another. They treasure power and money but shirk responsibility. What can we do about it?!"

In sum, whereas the original petition had 'unpacked the state' by distinguishing between different administrative levels, departments and officials, online comments ended in creating the picture of a unified state that is opposed to its people. It is a picture in which the state is a powerful, irresponsible and non-democratic entity, and the people powerless and without rights.

One important reason for this difference is that the petition was written as an appeal to Wen local government to redress grievances derived from official malpractice – it was a purposeful and strategic act, not a result of everyday undirected political conversation. Petitioners would therefore neither directly criticise the government as a whole nor question the political system in general. Tan Street members who commented on the case did not face these limitations or wanted a particular claim to be answered. Rather, they were interested in the political dimension of the particular case and were willing to share their own understandings and interpretations. Moreover, the relative anonymity of their communicative environment – the internet – allowed them to speak more freely. They could more easily disclose deep-seated values and political judgements and express more freely the emotions linked to them.

The paradox of internet censorship

What is the relation between these particular "subpolitical" features of Chinese online communications and China's well-known internet censorship? China operates the most extensive and sophisticated internet filtering system in the world. This system comprises legislative, administrative, and technological measures. Many rules and regulations are directed at internet service and content providers, internet café operators, and individual users. Several government agencies, such as the Public Security Agency and the Industry and Information Technology Agency, are involved in the administration and implementation of internet regulations at the national, provincial, and municipal level. Various types of technological filtering mechanisms have been implemented to block access to websites and content that are deemed by the party-state to be illegal. In addition to legal, administrative, and technical means of regulation, the Chinese propaganda system has continued to be employed as an important strategic tool to guide internet use in the way that is favored by the party-state.

How does the censorship impact netizens' everyday political conversations? I found several threads in Tan Street where members discussed and responded to internet censorship as part of their online conversations.

In one of them, a member of Tan Street wrote a post entitled "Questioning the People's Government of Wen County". This post revealed that the local government had allowed the construction of a factory building in a residential area, and criticized the government for ignoring the health risks for local residents. When the founder of the online community discovered that the author had repeatedly commented on her own post in order to attract others' attention, he locked the thread to prevent follow-up responses. His treatment of this post irritated not simply the original author, but also other members, who then entered the debate. The conversation between the community founder, the author of the post, and other participants in the debate, which I reproduce here in its entirety, well demonstrate the 'paradoxical' impact of internet censorship. (*A* refers in the following to the original post author; *B*, *C*, *D*, *E*, *F*, *G* to other participants).[5]

A:	Why was the thread "Questioning the People's Government of Wen County" locked?! Who locked it? I strongly protest!!!!!!
The founder:	Sorry, I locked the thread. One reason for this is that everybody knows who is right and who is wrong with regard to this issue. It is meaningless to repeat it. The other reason is that I want to avoid trouble. It is very difficult for ordinary people to establish discussion forums. Hope for your understanding and forgiveness!
B:	I support the threadopener! Who pushed the administrator to lock the thread?
C:	I support the threadopener.

The founder: Let me explain again. Nobody pushed me to lock the thread. A few days ago, one of the discussion boards in another online forum in Wen County was forced to close down. I do not want to have the same problem. Hope everybody can understand.

A: Locking the thread is not convincing, you will lose the support of the people. [. . .] Since this issue has happened, why should we hide it? What's wrong with letting the victims voice their claims [. . .]. The disadvantaged group voices their claim because their livelihoods and their health is threatened. The only thing the other party could possibly lose are their official careers. [. . .] The disadvantaged group comes here to seek support. Even this is not allowed?!

D: If people from ZF [the government] come here to express their opinions, will they be prohibited to do so? No!

E: I personally think it makes no difference whether or not the thread is locked. It is useless to complain. We've offered suggestions before, but we don't see anybody putting them into practice. There are two ways to choose: either act or wait!

F: I support the above poster.

G: In my opinion, members of this forum have provided many suggestions. It is up to the litigants themselves to solve this problem. [. . .] However, if our public servants can restrain their interest in fame and gain, and are aware of what they should and should not do, why should they be afraid of grumbling netizens?!

H: Is a forum a place for people to write and respond to posts, or a tool for the government to keep up appearances? If this place does not allow people to express themselves freely, can it be called a discussion forum?

I: For a nation, if there is no freedom, there is nothing else. [. . .] Freedom of speech is what human beings long for. However, it must not remain a dream. To transform an undemocratic political environment into a democracy is the goal that a nation should continually struggle for.

The founder: Hehe, I give up! I have already unlocked the thread. But I hope everyone will be careful about which words to choose. Please do not use extreme expressions. I believe that you also don't want this website to be closed down. Thank you!

D: Thank you!

Here, outrage over the community founder's treatment of a particular post has developed into a critical debate in which eventually 'the people' demand clean government and publicly criticise China's political system. In the course of this debate, commentators emphasise the importance of freedom of speech for a community and a nation, with one commentator directly linking it to the ideal of political democracy. When the founder emphasised the difficulties of running an online community in China, he also highlighted that Chinese online communities suffer from state censorship. While the founder locked A's post in order to prevent further political discussion about the government, this decision caused yet another political discussion with a focus on governmental censorship.

In Tan Street as well as in other Chinese online communities, it is common that members use satire – for example, ironic metaphors, jokes, images, videos, and songs – as a vehicle for the public expression of political criticism (e.g., Esarey and Xiao 2008; Yu 2007; Yang 2009). A typical example is the word "harmony" (*hexie*). This word has been used in official propaganda since 2004 when it appeared in the political slogan "building a harmonious society" proclaimed by former president Hu Jintao. As with many other political slogans, Chinese netizens satirized this phrase to criticize governmental practices such as internet censorship. Yet when the ironic or cynical use of words like harmonious, harmonise, or harmonisation started to be politically censored, commentators increasingly turned to homophones – characters or sets of characters that have different meanings but are pronounced similarly – to express public criticism. Such tactics are widespread in China. For instance, when one of Tan Street's QQ chat groups was temporarily closed down by the company that provides the chat service, a member wrote a post entitled "Tan Street is being harmonised". Some respondents replaced the characters for "harmony" with the characters for "river crab" – a homophone – to say "Tan Street is being river crabbed". Some used the phrase "river crab society" to replace "harmonious society", while others simply posted the image of a crab as a response. Besides being a homophone for "harmony" in Mandarin, river crab is also often used as a metaphor for a bully. The use of the term 'river crab', or the picture of a river crab to stand for "harmony/harmonious/harmonise" in contemporary Chinese cyberspace thus signifies not just netizens' evasion of state censorship, but also a political critique towards a state that bullies its netizens. Also here, practices related to state censorship become a trigger for netizens' political debates.

Netizens' response to internet censorship is thus another example of how the personal becomes the political, or of the rise of subpolitics. In China the rise, and particular shape, of subpolitics is the result of the dialectics between control and freedom embedded in what Yan Yunxiang has called "state-managed individualization" (Yan 2009: xxvii). In order to ensure both economic growth and political stability, the Chinese state has provided citizens with a greater level of personal freedom to design their own life projects, while at the same time retaining a high level of political control over the public sphere. Netizens' everyday political engagements with the Chinese state are inevitable responses to the (negative) interference of the state in areas significant to personal lives where Chinese citizens are today "free" to carry own responsibility, such as work, education, and housing. State censorship of netizens' online complaints about this state interference then results in another round of political response in Chinese cyberspace. The relationship between state interference and citizens' political participation can thus be compared to a pendulum. The state interferes in citizens' personal lives in order to prevent their political participation. This, however, results in a situation where citizens engage in political participation in order to retain a certain minimum of control over their own lives and to keep an intrusive state at bay.

Concluding remarks

This article has taken issue with the notion that Chinese netizens are apolitical, because they are primarily interested in pursuing personal lives and seldom use the internet to engage with party politics. Rather, by drawing on Beck's concept of subpolitics and Alfred Schütz's work on social types, it has tried to demonstrate various ways in which debates about personal issues not just become politicized but create an arena for emergent publics around shared concerns. Both Beck and Schütz's theories describe mechanisms and patterns of de-singularising personal experiences and of turning personal issues into public concerns, i.e. mechanisms and patterns of making personal experiences available for popular politics. The economic reforms and the onset of state-controlled individualisation, in the highly controlled political environment of contemporary China, including internet censorship, has not just given rise to subpolitics in Beck's sense (as a response to living in a 'risk' society and a replacement of the formal, state-focused politics of an earlier age). As a detailed examination of the political trajectories of everyday conversations among Tan Street participants could show, the dearth of legitimate avenues of political participation in China made the personal a preferred place from which to reason about the state of the state in China. This is accomplished by forms of generalization, or typifications in Schütz's sense, that resonate with the experiences and concerns of distant others and allow emergent netizen publics to turn personal, particular experiences into exemplary political issues, or issues of political justice. Such communicative work, through which new publics emerge focusing on issues of justice, can in the Chinese context be deemed political (or politically subversive) in itself. It is also a channel through which the state can be imagined and judged and where a new divide between 'the people' and 'the state' takes shape in communicative practice, affecting state–society relations. The work of de-singularisation of personal experiences through typification finds its correspondence in a re-assembling of the state as a unitary entity opposed to ordinary people (*laobaixing*).

I would like to conclude my chapter with some reflections on how these processes, observed on the Chinese internet, might relate to 'offline' communicative and political practices. The judgement of the state made by Chinese people on the internet is likely the same as in their offline daily conversations. On the other hand, as I have shown, there is an important difference between opinions expressed online and those expressed offline. The difference lies in the way opinions are communicated and the social space within which they are circulated. In offline conversations, personal opinions are for the most part circulated within the group of people who are physically present in the conversations. It is only through traditional media such as posters, television, radio, and newspapers that opinions can be spread to the public. Traditional media are tightly controlled also by their 'producers'. The internet, in contrast, gives everyone the opportunity to be a producer rather than merely an audience, and to render personal views public.

The internet thus changes the way knowledge is produced and circulated. The production of knowledge is no longer connected with power in any simple sense, but rather its collective and divergent origins are being emphasized. Largely due to the internet, there is no longer simply 'one' public discourse but many versions thereof, and authoritative statements are often questioned and challenged by common citizens. These have been forced, increasingly, by the post-Maoist state to take charge of their own lives, and as a result have turned personal interests and concerns into issues with public and potentially political dimensions. The new visibility of an alternative, 'grassroots' discourse on the Chinese internet provides emergent publics with another framework for understanding and judging social reality. The internet has much facilitated the public resonance of private concerns and issues across people from various walks of life, and thus the emergence of new publics (as stranger-relationalities in Michael Warner's sense; see Warner 2002). Participation in the production of a 'grassroots' discourse here creates a collective consciousness of mutual political recognition and identity. It also helps to create a collective political response to the contemporary Chinese state's interference in personal lives.

Notes

1 My ethnographic fieldwork included both online and offline sites. I read messages posted on discussion forums and joined in conversations in chat groups. I also conducted face-to-face interviews with the online community's participants and joined their offline collective activities. The combination of online and offline fieldwork helped me to develop a full picture of the practices of the community and its participants.
2 The name of this community, as well that of the participants' home county, has been altered to protect participants' anonymity.
3 For a detailed description of Chinese people's political lives during the Mao era, see for example: Madsen 1984; Walder 1986.
4 'To be invited to drink tea' here means to be taken in for police interrogation. 'To be harmonised' means to be censored.
5 It is also possible that some of the 'other' participants were actually aliases of the original post author. *A* may have created other nicknames to support his or her case.

References

Beck, Ulrich. 1997. *The Reinvention of Politics: Rethinking Modernity in the Global Social Order*. Cambridge: Polity Press.

Boggs, Carl. 2002. *The End of Politics: Corporate Power and the Decline of the Public Sphere*. New York: The Guilford Press.

Brady, Anne-Marie. 2008. *Marketing Dictatorship: Propaganda and Thought Work in Contemporary China*. Lanham, MD: Rowman & Littlefield.

Brandtstädter, Susanne. 2011. The Law Cuts Both Ways: Rural Legal Activism and Citizenship Struggles in Neosocialist China. *Economy and Society* 40(2), pp. 266–288.

Cai, Yongshun. 2010. *Collective Resistance in China: Why Popular Protests Succeed or Fail*. Stanford, CA: Stanford University Press.

CASS. 2007. *Surveing Internet Usage and Its Impact in Seven Chinese Cities*. Beijing: Center for Social Development, Chinese Academy of Social Sciences. Online at www.policyarchive.org/handle/10207/bitstreams/16013.pdf, accessed November 17, 2008.

Damm, Jens. 2007. The Internet and the Fragmentation of Chinese Society. *Critical Asian Studies* 39(2), pp. 273–294.

Esarey, Ashley and Qiang, Xiao. 2008. Political Expression in the Chinese Blogosphere: Below the Radar. *Asian Survey* 48(5), pp. 752–772.

Graham, Todd. 2012. Beyond Political Communicative Spaces: Talking Politics on the Wife Swap Discussion Forum. *Journal of Information Technology & Politics* 9(1), pp. 31–45.

Habermas, Jürgen. 1984. *Theory of Communicative Action Volume One: Reason and the Rationalization of Society*. Boston: Beacon Press.

Leibold, James. 2011. Blogging Alone: China, the Internet, and the Democratic Illusion? *The Journal of Asian Studies* 70(4), pp. 1023–1041.

Lichterman, Paul. 1999. Talking Identity in the Public Sphere: Broad Visions and Small Spaces in Sexual Identity Politics. *Theory and Society* 28, pp. 101–141.

Liu, Fengshu. 2009. *Urban Youth in China: Modernity, the Internet and the Self*. London: Routledge.

Madsen, Richard. 1984. *Morality and Power in a Chinese Village*. California: University of California Press.

Micheletti, Michele. 2003. *Political Virtue and Shopping: Individuals, Consumerism, and Collective Action*. New York: Palgrave Macmillan.

O'Brien, Kevin, ed. 2008. *Popular Protest in China*. Cambridge, MA: Harvard University Press.

Schütz, Alfred and Thomas, Luckmann. 1973. *The Structures of the Life-World*. Evanston, IL: Northwestern University Press.

Walder, Andrew G. 1986. *Communist Neo-Traditionalism: Work and Authority in Chinese Industry*. Berkeley: University of California Press.

Walsh, Katherine Cramer. 2004. *Talking About Politics: Informal Groups and Social Identity in American Life*. Chicago: University of Chicago Press.

Warner, Michael. 2002. *Publics and Counterpublics*. New York: Zone Books.

Wu, Jingsi. 2011. Enlightenment or Entertainment: The Nurturance of an Aesthetic Public Sphere Through a Popular Talent Show in China. *The Communication Review* 14(1), pp. 46–47.

Yan, Yunxiang. 2009. *The Individualization of Chinese Society*. Oxford: Oxford University Press.

Yang, Guobin. 2009. *The Power of the Internet in China: Citizen Activism Online*. New York: Columbia University Press.

Yu, Haiqing. 2007. Blogging Everyday Life in Chinese Internet Culture. *Asian Studies Review* 31(4), pp. 423–433.

3 Marginalizing the law

Corporate social responsibility, worker hotlines and the shifting grounds of rights consciousness in contemporary China

Ellen Hertz and Marylène Lieber

In contemporary China, law and legal action have become increasingly central in popular struggles for social justice, as demonstrated by a number of chapters in this volume. However, as these contributions also demonstrate, this discursive centrality is accompanied by growing social fragmentation, diversification and contestation, with different collectivities appropriating the rhetoric and mechanics of the law for different purposes (Thireau and Hua 2001; Brandtstädter 2011; Froissart 2011). In this paper, we would like to complicate this picture one step further. We argue that transnational corporate discourse and practice must be more clearly factored into our understanding of Chinese approaches to law and social justice, following the forms of "legal transplant" (Lin 2009) currently taking place within global supply chains. When these influences are taken into account, we suggest, a contrary movement can be identified, away from the law and imaginaries of the public good, and towards an "ethics" of "responsibility" and "personal development" that cuts in a different, even opposing, direction.

There are many forces behind and ramifications of the rhetoric of "responsibility" in contemporary China (see e.g., Newendorp 2006; Chu 2006; Chahoud 2011; Weikert 2011; Yin and Zhang 2012), and we cannot do justice to this vast and productive semantic field here. What we propose to follow in this chapter are the entanglements of local terms such as "rights", "responsibility" and "citizenship" with the rise of the corporate social responsibility (CSR) paradigm in international arenas, a paradigm that has paradoxical consequences for the status and social uses of the law. Including CSR narratives and programs within our scope of inquiry broadens our perspective on civil society, drawing attention to the fragmentation of the NGO landscape in contemporary China (Lau 2009), to the rise of corporate-sponsored organizations working in the area of rights and social justice (Hsia and White 2002; Zajak 2013) and hence to the variety of economies, publics and norms involved in determining what is just and what is unjust, what are the causes of these injustices and what should be done about them. It also sheds light on a specific normative effect of this discourse: the tendency to marginalize the state and the legal apparatus, to the benefit of corporate and "civil society" actors (Kamat 2004).

Our argument is based on two years of multi-sited field research on the implementation and effects of CSR policies for regulating labor conditions in the electronics industry in China.* Drawing on participant observation and interviews carried out between 2010 and 2012 with corporate CSR officers, social entrepreneurs and white-collar workers in Chinese and international NGOs, located principally in the Pearl River Delta, in Hong Kong and in Taiwan, we highlight the role of corporate-based private governance and its various "soft law" instruments (Rodriguez-Garavito 2005) in framing the question of the rights and responsibilities of blue-collar workers. We adopt an "assemblage" approach (Ong and Collier 2008), in which we link transnational flows of ideas, norms and technologies of governance with local settings, without attempting to apportion the varying degrees of "Chineseness" that this concatenation implies. Clearly, the shifting, diverse and contradictory nature of the law as a tool for promoting social justice is in no sense unique to China; anthropologists have pointed to similar developments in Latin America (Nader 1991; Goodale 2009) and in Africa (Comaroff and Comaroff 2006), drawing attention to the global dynamics that generate these shifts (Griffiths, von Benda-Beckmann and von Benda-Beckmann 2005, 2009a, 2009b). In this chapter, we highlight one particular coming-together of these flows and shifts, in which socio-technologies employed under the rubric of "capacity building" for corporate social responsibility actually work to marginalize the law as an instrument for the pursuit of social justice in the area of working conditions in China.

A socio-technological approach to rights consciousness – the hotline

To give ethnographic depth and grain to our inquiry, we focus on a specific material-semiotic tool (Law 2008) – worker hotlines – that imposed itself upon us as a discreet but omnipresent actor in our encounters with the field. Our analysis of this actor builds on scholarship on governance and policymaking (Wedel, Shore, Feldman and Lathrop 2005) that directs our attention away from the explicit, formalized logics of institutions and towards their informal workings and effects, and particularly to those seemingly neutral black boxes that are its instruments (Lascoumes and Le Galès 2005). The hotline was born in the 1950s as a material expression of, and solution to, Cold War nuclear tensions (Keating 2009: 12). Hotlines today function as "dedicated channel[s] of communication" (Oxford English Dictionary) in all manner of settings, a standard element of marketing, management and oversight toolkits worldwide (Calderon-Cuadrado et al. 2009; Bidet and Le Méner 2014). In theory, they imply a dyadic relationship between caller and receiver (the "line"), in which presence (real-time oral communication) and engagement (courteous, helpful or sympathetic reception) are thought be the appropriate responses to the forms of urgency or sensitivity (the "hot") that service providers confront (Seeley 1998). In practice, however, hotlines are complex socio-technological networks: they require instruments, they mobilize multiparty interactions and they involve scripts that go well beyond an anonymous conversation between caller and called (Erwin 2000; Le Méner 2011). Their use is often related to notions of "participation" and "ownership" that are now omnipresent in administrative, development and governance discourse; they are thought to give "voice" or to "empower" stigmatized categories of social actors and to provide channels for reporting in contexts in which information does not flow freely.

Hotlines became a commonplace feature of urban life in China in the 1990s, as a combined result of the introduction of new communication technologies and of the reconfiguration of private space under the Reform and Opening policies of the Deng Xiaoping era (Erwin 2000). First employed by municipalities for suicide prevention and crisis intervention (ibid.: 150), they were rapidly taken up by talk radio, attracting large audiences with programs focusing on the newly public problems of romantic involvement, sexual health and changing roles and expectations within the family. Hotlines are currently employed in areas as diverse as rights counseling for women (Off Our Backs 1993; Cornue 1999) and gays and lesbians (Cao and Lu 2014), reporting of intellectual property violations (Choukroune 2009) and environmental complaints (Economy 2007) and public debate over regional identity and heritage in a context of rapid urban transformation (Zhang 2006). According to Cheng, Ngok and Zhuang, the first labor rights legal advice hotline in China, the *Shandong Qingdao Xiao Chen Rexian* (Shandong Qingdao Mr. Chen Hotline), was created in 2000 by migrant worker Chen Mingyu as a way to offer "services for young migrant workers via legal consultations as well as in exchanges of cultural and life experiences" (2010: 1086–1087).

The diversity of areas in which hotlines are employed is a first hint as to the multiplicity of their objectives and effects. An ethnographic analysis of hotlines, however, goes beyond the question of thematic diversity to focus micro-sociologically on the particular technologies at work (what kinds of telephones, what kinds of receiving and recording devices?), on the social practices surrounding the use of the hotline (what degree of intimacy, what role for face-to-face encounters, with whom, where, when?) and on the structural characteristics of the organizations that run them (institutional form, funding sources, number and socio-professional background of employees, etc.). The worker hotlines we will be examining in this chapter are all motivated by a desire to assist workers in understanding and asserting their rights, and yet they mobilize a wide variety of explicit and implicit norms and practices. As such, they represent a particularly telling locus for examining the "everyday processes" (Ong 1996) of asserting rights and pursuing justice or, in other terms, of making and perceiving of oneself as a citizen, both in relation to working conditions and in relation to broader issues of belonging, modernity and the good life. Thus, at the most general level our fieldwork corroborates and even expands on one of the principal observations of this volume, as developed in Susanne Brandtstädter's nimble introduction: "the language of *fazhi* is currently invoked by different types of local actors for widely divergent political and moral ends, entering a wide array of local disputes and conflict". Like Brandtstädter, we emphasize the very different "orders of worth" (Boltanski and Thevenot 2006; Boltanski 2012), or as we prefer, "*registres du juste*" ("registers of justice"; Thireau and Hua 2001), that distinguish hotlines operating in the area of workers' rights and working conditions.

Drawing on our study of seven different worker hotlines, we have identified three ideal types, each of which presupposes a different conception of what is a "right", what is a "condition", who is the "public", in sum, whom should be mobilized and how in order to improve working conditions for factory production in China.[1] The first of these is collectivist in orientation and draws on a Marxist-socialist conception of industrial relations and of the place of worker contestation in the pursuit of social justice that resonates with the "humanist/Communist" argumentative strategies examined by Hua and Thireau in their seminal study of worker complaints to the Shenzhen City Office of Letters and Visits (*Xinfangke*) (2001: 1297–1305). The second centers on the concept of rights and exemplifies a worldview that has much in common both with the law-based argumentative strategies examined by Hua and Thireau (ibid.: 1306–1311) and with many of the other sites of legal activism examined in this volume. The third hotline we examine is the one we wish to emphasize most, for it highlights the presence in China of a set of CSR discourses and practices that divert questions of social justice and rights consciousness away from the law and towards a nebulous ideal of "responsibility". We will demonstrate how these transnational discourses of "responsibility" converge with local discourses that mobilize notions of "new citizenship" (*xin shimin*) and "quality" (*suzhi*), sinicizing a potent global paradigm in particular ways.

PRD workers' counseling centre – a socialist-moralist hotline

We visited the Pearl River Delta Workers Counseling Center (PRD WCC) in the summer of 2012. PRD WCC is housed in an almost invisible office on the outskirts of an industrial zone of Zhuhai; no sign or nameplate at the street or apartment level indicates its location, and during our visit, no workers stopped by. We were warmly received by the founder-director, a vigorous woman in her early 50s and one-time migrant worker from Sichuan province, who described her organization, founded in the early 2000s, as one of the older labor NGOs in the area. Installed in a two-bedroom apartment, PRD WCC's offices consist of a front room which seats two people (two desks, one computer, one telephone) and a back room that serves as the director's office (two chairs for visitors, a couch, a desk, some books in a run-down bookcase, calendars and newspaper papering the walls). PRD WCC employs three young staff members with tertiary education, possibly in social work, and benefits from the services of a number of volunteers, including local workers.

Our visit lasted two hours and consisted almost entirely of a monologue by the director herself, during which she exposed with great verve and an apparent absence of self-censorship her personal vision of socialism, her critique of the poor choices made by the Chinese Communist Party over the course of its history, her conception of the value of her organization and some aspects of PRD WCC's concrete everyday activities. Clearly, the director made virtually no distinction between her personal engagement for and conception of labor rights and the organization itself, with the uncomfortable consequence that it was never clear whom the "we" in her discourse actually referred to. (The two young staff members who were present during the interview had virtually no opportunity to speak, and did not seem to find this situation unusual.) Furthermore, despite this warm welcome, certain aspects of the organization's operations remained opaque throughout the interview; notably, it was difficult to get a clear sense of how PRD WCC was financed, but it seems that it received modest fees from the workers whom it assisted, and also received payment for services (such as worker trainings) from other NGOs working in the area of labor rights in the Pearl River Delta, as well as from companies. The director had not registered the organization in any way, fearing the complications that this would create: thus PRD WCC was listed neither as a business, nor as a non-profit enterprise, nor as a "social organization", nor as a "foundation", the options generally open to NGOs working in the non-profit sector in China today.[2]

In contrast to the apparently marginal status of PRD WCC, however, was the director's rather impressive international network; indeed, the very first thing she told us was that she had just returned from a visit to Indonesia, invited by a number of Asian labor unions to discuss the future of labor rights in China. Highly critical of the institutionalized labor movement in much of Europe and even more so of that in the United States, she nonetheless clearly benefited from her international contacts with these entities. And despite its modest size, PRD WCC was, in the words of its director, "terribly busy". The Center engaged in worker education and training, and though the director is not a lawyer, she frequently accompanied workers to court; indeed, during our interview, she clearly took pride in telling us how she harangued local judges with socialist rhetoric, mobilizing a language of honesty in the face of hypocrisy, and seeking to make them lose face. As to the organization's political orientation, their main emphasis, in the words of the director once again, was on bringing workers together (*tuanjie*), on helping them become conscious of their rights (*tigao quanli yishi*), and on giving them whatever other forms of assistance they might need.

Perhaps as a reaction to our status as university-based social scientists, the director spent considerable time explaining to us how she understood the message of genuine socialism. Over the course of our discussion, it became clear that she took considerable political risks in her work. Not only does the organization advise individual workers about their rights, they also encourage them to form in-house workers associations and to mobilize collectively. The hotline, while providing a means for confidential contact with workers, was clearly not at the center of her understanding of her mission. Rather, PRD WCC informs workers of its existence through pamphlets and brochures, as well as by driving a small car through the main streets where factories are located, announcing its services by megaphone or stopping outside factory gates to distribute information. Workers who call are questioned as to the nature of their legal situation and are encouraged to meet with staff face-to-face, in the office or at an outside location. During these meetings, they are advised of their rights and on the procedures they must follow to enforce them.

According to the director, their hotline received twenty to thirty calls a day that entered on a single non-dedicated landline. The young employees receive the calls and keep a simple registry of contact names and numbers, the time of the call and a brief description of the problem. The director emphasized the fact that no information is entered into their computers, for she worries that they could be stolen or hacked, disclosing sensitive information to the police. (Not incidentally, the organization has no website.) Furthermore, they discourage the use of e-mail and QQ[3] for communication with workers, and no statistics are kept of the nature of calls received, the names of problem companies or the social or legal status of the callers. While they are not against giving psychological advice to callers, they do not emphasize this aspect of their work, for they believe that psychological problems are the reflection of social problems and are produced by them. Rather they concentrate on legal advice, actively contacting workers to make sure that their cases are advancing.

Despite the director's emphasis on worker autonomy and self-respect, the stories she told about the workers she assists are strikingly paternalistic in tone, as this excerpt from our fieldnotes demonstrates:

> She gives an example of how they give legal advice to a worker who has been hurt on the job. She says often workers don't know anything about the law, and she has to walk them through each step very concretely. For example, she first asks the worker how s/he is going to prove that s/he really worked for that factory. Does s/he have a contract or any kind of official paper proving that? If s/he doesn't, then she asks – "well what else can you think of that proves you worked at that factory?" "How about my uniform?", asks the worker. "No good (*buxing*)" says the director. "Anyone can put your uniform on, that's not good proof, keep thinking! How about a fellow worker? Can one of them testify for you?" "No", says the worker, "because they will be afraid of retribution from the factory." "Keep thinking!" And so she keeps working with the worker until they find something that can prove that s/he worked at that factory. And she tells them: "don't blindly believe in the government, you need to learn to fight for your rights yourself!"
>
> (fieldnotes, summer 2012)

As the interview progressed, the director became more and more brash, and seemed to take inspiration from the early heroes of the Communist movement, those who were not afraid to die for their ideas. Indeed, her organization's philosophy was, in her words: "ignore wealth, resist evil, fear not death, and love humanity" (*buzai cai, juxie, bupa si, er ai ren*). She believes in the utility of moral persuasion and moral condemnation for raising worker consciousness, as this second incident suggests:

> She gives an example from the previous day where she accompanied a worker to court for an incident involving a deposit that the factory had taken from him and not returned. She got into an argument with the guy from the

> department of Human Resources and accused him of not doing his job. At some point, the judge said to her: "You cannot insult him in the courtroom," to which she answered. "I'm not insulting him, I'm just telling it like it is." (*shishi zaizai di shuo*). For her, the important element in this story is that the worker could witness this exchange, could learn that he was a citizen with rights, that he can stand up for his rights, that one can talk back to government officials who don't do their job.
>
> (fieldnotes, summer 2012)

Welcome – a hotline for the promotion of the law

Welcome is a small but well-established operation run almost entirely by volunteer lawyers. The organization registered in 2004 as a non-profit company (*minban feiqiye danwei*), a form of registration, explains the director, that allows for more flexibility because it is not necessary to ask for sponsorship by a government administration, and censorship is less direct. Situated in the maze-like basement of a Guangzhou hotel, the office consists of a big room entirely occupied by an imposing conference table, and two small offices, one for an old black phone dedicated to the hotline, the other for the director. At the time of our first visit, a young woman was typing on a computer, while a volunteer lawyer sitting in one of the small attending offices was uploading photos of their activities on their website.

Workers are informed of Welcome's existence by word-of-mouth and through brochures, distributed by volunteers (often other workers) who station themselves in factory areas and at the entry gates to plants. The hotline is open during regular working hours, and according to the director, receives fifteen to twenty calls a day. Volunteer lawyers answer the phone and proceed with an initial interview in "intake" format, gathering the necessary information to know whether and what kinds of legal provisions apply. Workers whose complaints are legal in nature are then encouraged to come into their offices to discuss the proper course of action. This often requires that workers better document their complaint and find the proper door on which to knock in order to lodge it. Volunteer lawyers strictly restrict their advice to the legal aspects of the worker's situation. During one call we could observe, the lawyer specifically insisted that they were only there to help with legal demands. Most of these legal demands, as revealed by the organization's archives located in one of the corners of the main room, are related to the absence of work contracts or unpaid wages. The staff helps workers throughout the procedure, representing them in court as *pro bono* lawyers when necessary, but more frequently acting simply as informal mediators between workers and their bosses.

As the director explained, their mission is to protect workers by "informing them and defending their rights". They have no contract with any factory or brand, in part because companies are reluctant to let them in, but mostly because of their desire to maintain independence. However, they are funded by a non-Chinese government agency, as is often the case with such NGOs. As our field journal states:

> I asked him if they have good collaborations with corporations or plants working in the area of CSR. He told me that it is not the case, that most companies do not really want their workers to be trained about their rights. [. . .] For him, hotlines are a good method because there is no written record. Furthermore, people have become accustomed to hotlines because the government uses them a lot. He does not think that QQ is a good tool because people cannot say the same things.
>
> (fieldnotes, spring 2012)

Welcome's orientation corresponds to a form of legal activism and legal consciousness-raising that has been largely described in the literature (Gallagher 2006; Brandtstädter 2011). Welcome takes the government's resolution to move China from the "rule of men" to the "rule of law" at its word. In line with government programs designed to promote the spread of legal education (*pufa*), Welcome remains strictly within the parameters set by the state. Thus, as many chapters in this volume point out, their conception of the law and the language of "rights protection" (*weiquan*) differs in significant ways from the liberal view of right-bearing citizens common in Western political theory. Rather, promoting the law and protecting workers' rights is viewed as a way to participate in the "development" and "modernization" of China, to the benefit of its citizens, and not as a basic challenge to the Party's authoritarian rule. Ho (2008) has called this form of legal advocacy "embedded activism", emphasizing its largely conciliatory and palliative attitude towards the injustices produced by the Chinese Party-State. Furthermore, as Lora-Wainwright, Zhang, Wu and Van Rooij (2012) have pointed out, while this kind of activism often takes legal form, it is fundamentally based on local repertoires and experiences, that is, on tacit normative codes that allow parties to negotiate solutions for particular problems without the forms of generalization and abstraction that leverage legal compromises into binding legal principles.

Our observations and interviews with Welcome staff confirm the informal nature of the solutions that Welcome negotiates for aggrieved workers, all the while mobilizing the formal vocabulary of law and rights. Most frequently, the lawyers at Welcome do not go to court, and may not even file legal documents; rather they help industrial workers recuperate unpaid wages and right other workplace wrongs simply by accompanying them to the company and exposing the worker's problem to management using the language of the law. One of the volunteers we talked with, for example, showed us a picture of an event that Welcome had organized a few days earlier: in the photo, the unhappy boss of a local factory appears trapped in his own office by a number of workers and the volunteer lawyer herself. While law and lawyers are the props for this theatrical event, clearly it is not the law's formal, binding properties that are appealed to here but rather its legitimacy, in reference to the government's push for socialist morality under law. Singular in its temporality and limited by its own particularism, this event is not intended to promote the development of workers' collective consciousness, as in the cases mentioned by the director of PRD WCC, and even less the creation of independent workers' associations or unions, a point of immense political sensitivity.

Importantly, the volunteers we talked with all downplayed the political aspects of their work and emphasized their formal training and their interest in providing legal advice and education for the largely migrant populations who consulted them. In their account, legal aid can help migrant workers, all too frequently discriminated against on the job, to share in the benefits of socialist modernization and to overcome the stigmas of poverty and backwardness with which they are afflicted. As mentioned in our field journal:

> The association takes care of *mingong*. Its aim is to spread a better understanding of the *mingong*'s situation and to help them, for example by recovering wages. (. . .) The organization's original purpose was mutual help – it organized meetings for *mingong* who felt alone. In the words of the director: "People come from remote provinces and they are very isolated, they do not know anyone in town, do not know what to do or how to find work. The idea is to help them. We organize activities during the weekend; we go and see elder migrants." Today, while they still promote this kind of activity, they mostly act as a legal aid clinic.
>
> (fieldnotes, spring 2012)

Moral suasion under the law – the rights-based approach to worker hotlines

As these brief descriptions demonstrate, Welcome and PRD WCC share certain characteristics, while differing with respect to others. One clear difference is their respective sociopolitical statuses: while Welcome is officially registered, staffed by trained lawyers and operates with a certain visibility, PRD WCC exists on the margins of a constantly shifting "forbidden zone" (Stern and O'Brien 2012), neither registered, nor professional, nor, they hope, visible to snooping government eyes. Mirroring these different postures, Welcome limits itself rather strictly to legal information and advice, while PRD WCC clearly puts more emphasis on consciousness-raising in all forms, both individual and collective, through highly dramatic interventions in court and information campaigns in factory areas. The volunteers at Welcome saw themselves as moving China slowly towards a system governed by the rule of law, that is, a conception of government in which law and rights served as the basis for the apportioning of power between government and the people. The director of PRD WCC, on the other hand, believed that law was meaningless without collective organization and true workplace democracy; without workers' organizations capable of articulating collective concerns and raising worker consciousness, the law could only lead to the resolution of individual disputes and never strike at the fundamental causes of the production of injustice.

Despite the different emphases and strategies employed by these two organizations to advance the cause of labor justice, they nonetheless shared a vision distinctly grounded in the law, viewed as a system of norms promulgated by the government that legitimized workers' complaints and bolstered their claims to a fair workplace environment. And not coincidentally, in our view, for both of these NGOs the hotline was a mere tool, its use strictly limited to initial contact and the providing of information. Workers were not encouraged to call for personal reasons, and though they were not discouraged from talking about their daily lives, "real" cases clearly represented cases in which a worker's legal rights had been infringed. In sum, both NGOs used the telephone as a simple instrument for establishing contact, not as their primary means of communication with workers.

The third hotline we will examine takes us out of the realm of law-oriented Chinese labor NGOs and into the burgeoning field of NGOs, domestic and foreign, operating within the private regulatory regime established by transnational firms in the form of CSR programs and policies. Our findings echo Zajak's observation that the field of corporate governance in the area of labor rights is increasingly occupied by "labour-support organizations backed by and cooperating with transnational private regulatory initiatives [that] are entering and shaping the Chinese field of industrial relations" (2013: 181). Before going into the details of our example, a few words are necessary to introduce the historical origins and the organizational and conceptual framework underlying the CSR programs of foreign firms operating in China.

Private regulation, soft law and the "ethical reconstruction" of global capitalism

The complex nature of contemporary global production has given rise to an active transnational anti-sweatshop movement that, since the 1980s, has criticized global outsourcing, pointing out that it is a way to avoid strict labor regimes in industrialized states (Rodriguez-Garavito 2005). The anti-sweatshop movement has gained visibility through actions such as "naming and blaming" campaigns, and its presence on the international scene has significantly reshaped the discourse and practices of contemporary capitalism; indeed, in response to public pressure, over the past twenty-plus years we have witnessed transnational firms adopting positions that were unthinkable even a generation ago, seemingly embracing the ideals of "responsible capitalism" (see generally Dolan and Rajak 2016). High-profile brands have ceded to consumer and NGO pressure by agreeing, at least on paper, that they should be held responsible for production conditions "throughout their supply chains", thereby tacitly acknowledging that their purchasing and pricing decisions have a direct influence on the conditions under which supplier firms, often located in the "South", produce for the global market (Gereffi, Humphrey and Sturgeon 2005; Locke and Romis 2007). Furthermore, to demonstrate their willingness to "walk the walk", many have signed on to voluntary corporate codes of conduct intended to impose international norms of human, environmental and labor rights on their suppliers, and have made efforts to guarantee that these norms are enforced through auditing and monitoring procedures, a process that Pun Ngai calls the "ethical reconstruction" of labor relations under global capitalism (Pun 2005b).

China has proved a particularly fruitful terrain both for denouncing inhumane working conditions and for experimenting with CSR programs designed to combat them (Pun 2005a, 2008; Hui 2011). NGOs such as China Labor Watch and Students and Scholars Against Corporate Misbehaviour (SACOM), unions (both national[4] and international[5]), international organizations such as the International Labour Organization[6] and journalists (Chang 2008) have all drawn public attention to the immoral and/or illegal conditions under which most industrial production takes place in "the world's factory". It is now an open secret that workers regularly work longer hours than those specified in the Chinese Labor Contract Law or in ILO documents; that they are frequently not paid on time or at proper overtime rates; that they encounter all sorts of bureaucratic problems (identity papers withheld, resignations denied, deposits and other entitlements confiscated, etc.); that factory health and safety conditions are not up to domestic or international standards; and that child and/or forced labor can be found in some sectors (Chan 2001; Lee 2007a, 2007b; Chan 2009; Chen and Chan 2010; Pun, Chan and Selden 2016).

In theory, application of industry-wide codes of conduct and monitoring of their implementation in supplier firms should already have brought production processes in China into increasing conformity with the law, but experience shows that such a perspective is illusory. Indeed, in our discussions with the CSR officers of transnational brands, they confirmed that they were well aware of the ineffectiveness of the expensive and time-consuming procedures for auditing and monitoring their supply chains that they themselves had put in place. The World Bank, in its first evaluative document on the question of CSR, came to a similar conclusion, citing problems of inefficiency, confusion and "audit fatigue" that discouraged "supplier engagement", along with insufficient understanding on the part of suppliers about the business benefits ensuing from compliance (World Bank 2003). As a consequence, at the time of our fieldwork and still today, the trend was to go "beyond monitoring", seen as a limited and overly disciplinary approach to governance, and towards "capacity building", in order to encourage more voluntary forms of compliance with international standards, through "engagement" and "ownership" on the part of Chinese firms and indeed Chinese workers as a whole.

Industry-sponsored "capacity building programs" in the area of labor standards can take many forms. Some firms organize workshops to inform management and line supervisors in their supplier firms of the basics of labor rights and to train them in Western-style management procedures. Others extend these training sessions to workers themselves, hiring mainland or Hong Kong-based NGOs to give day-long classes to workers on what their legal rights are and how to exercise them (SACOM 2009). As an alternative or addition to these rights-awareness training sessions, other firms have developed programs that involve a combination of consciousness-raising and confidence-building. This too can take many forms, including programs that take us quite a distance from the question of labor rights as such, as with the creation of community centers or drop-ins, places where workers can come to relax, inform themselves, receive various forms of counseling and meet other workers.[7]

It is in this context that worker hotlines, often operating in conjunction with workers' rights training sessions, have emerged as one of the key tools enabling brands indirectly to monitor labor conditions within their supplier firms. The business-based hotline scene is populated by quite a diverse set of "civil society" actors, many of whom we have visited. In some cases, hotlines are run by brands in-house, through dedicated lines available to workers without cost. These solutions are often criticized as ineffective for reporting serious grievances, and few firms we talked with relied exclusively on their own hotline services. Rather, they hired Western or Chinese based NGOs to operate what are qualified as "independent" hotlines for them, giving them various degrees of freedom (and financing) to support their operations. The example we present here represents one of the most professionalized of the NGOs we encountered, and thus serves as an ideal type for understanding the process of "consultantization" (Zajak 2013: 187) of labor NGOs entangled within the transnational CSR paradigm.

Outreach – a hotline for China's "new citizens"

Outreach was created in 2007 in response to a call-for-projects organized by a transnational consultancy firm specializing in the area of CSR. The consultancy was looking to set up hotline services at the request of many of its members: large international brands seeking new ideas for "capacity-building" programs for their suppliers in China (and their corporate reports back home). Outreach won the bid in large part because of its director, a young Chinese woman trained in business management with experience abroad, and Outreach began operations with initial funding from the consultancy firm.

Our visit to the hotline began with a long discussion with the director. She was loquacious, apparently quite proud of her operation, and explained to us in perfect English that in order to "do good work", she had willingly given up a potential career in business, including a large office through the windows of which she could see "the lights of the city at her feet". She believed that her business training abroad helped her in running the association and in marketing its services because she had a more creative approach to service providing than many of her counterparts trained in social work or law. For example, during promotional activities offered by supplier firms, Outreach organizes festivities, contests and entertainment and distributes flyers and gadgets centering on "fun" which, she emphasized, attracts more workers than dull and complicated explanations of their rights.

The organization is registered with the local authorities under a number of names and organizational forms, which allows it a certain room for maneuver.

Each of the names corresponds to a different type of activity, but by and large the same employees are involved in all facets of the NGO's work. The hotline itself operates under a separate name from that of the NGO created some years ago, but is located in the same office space, a decent but distinctly nondescript building far from the luxurious offices that are available in Shenzhen. Approximately ten young employees, men and women with various university diplomas (international trade, social work, English) work in the room dedicated to the hotline, each with his or her own computer allowing reception and sending of messages via the Chinese QQ system, which links portable phone messages directly to each work station.

The hotline works with a series of dedicated phone numbers that are centralized at the call center. Staff respond to these demands by providing information, but they are also encouraged to take a more proactive relation to workers, mixing information with expressions of friendship or encouragement. The following description, taken from our field notes, provides an example:

> X contacts various workers whom she sees online and who have not contacted her for a while. Her messages are short, cheerful and filled with emoticons, as if she were writing to a friend. Like her colleague yesterday, she explains that she feels that she is somehow close to some of the workers who contact her: they have developed a relationship, they know some of the same people. . . . To one worker, she sends a coffee cup emoticon with the message "What's the weather like in Shanghai? Are you very busy these days?" But she also sends more practical information, like "tomorrow we're coming to your factory, I hope you'll come and see me." When a new person contacts her, she uses not her own name but that of the association and asks how she can be of service. If she knows who's calling, she'll say "long time no see, how have you been recently?" She also keeps a list of her "buddies'" birthdays, and regularly wishes people well on their "special day".
>
> (fieldnotes, spring 2012)

In sum, these employees spend much of their time in a multi-party chat with other people approximately their own age who work in the nearby factories of the PRD and, in some cases, as far away as Shanghai. This generational proximity is not a coincidence; the director explained to us that, in her view, it is important that workers be put in contact with people their own age, and she deliberately hires young people to staff her organization. It should be added that these positions generally require some form of tertiary education and are thus attractive mainly to new graduates willing to work for a smaller salary (approximately 1,800 RMB per month in 2012) than they could get in foreign-run businesses.

Over the course of our observation, Outreach employees were involved in many conversations, involving a number of topics simultaneously. In the same room, other employees were occupied filling out activity forms. Each call is first registered on a chart, and then classified in one of three categories: green, yellow or red. These colors represent a scale of urgency, with green signifying light cases;

yellow, potential problems; and red, urgent problems that require that the management of the factory, or the brand, be notified immediately. One of the employees explained to us that red would be used for suicide threats or potential strikes. Reports on green incidents are sent to the factory or the brand once a month, on yellow incidents once a week and on red incidents within the hour of the phone call.[8] Over the course of our two days of observation, the vast majority of calls were classified as green.

Moving from their categories to our own, how can we classify the different kinds of calls that we observed? In line with the rights-consciousness focus of other capacity building programs, a certain number of callers raised questions concerning applicable law and regulations (social security benefits, how to terminate a contract, how salaries were to be distributed before the Chinese New Year, etc.). These calls were handled in a way that was at once professional and intimate. The counselors were both willing and able to provide the requested information, often through an exchange that involved clarifying the specific situation that the worker was in. However, this information was generally accompanied by small signs of friendliness – a smiley here, a more casual remark there – making the tone of the overall interaction more private than public. Interestingly, however, workers were not invited into the office to discuss their cases in person; rather, advice was given through a series of QQ or e-mail exchanges without obligatory face-to-face contact.

As mentioned, however, a large number of calls concerned what we would classify as strictly personal affairs. Workers logged on to ask advice on romantic matters, as well as simply to chat. Many of these conversations were quite moving, providing a glimpse into the grinding world of factory work. Clearly, the young men and women working for Outreach were also moved by these exchanges, and many of them told us that chatting with these workers and trying to cheer them up lent meaning to their jobs and even beyond. The compassion they expressed for workers' situations was often mixed with a sense of outrage that seemingly respectable Western brands should be associated with such exploitative and harsh working conditions.

In discussions with the director, it became clear that the charitable or social nature of the exchanges with workers was not an incidental part of the work being carried out, but rather its defining quality. She repeatedly emphasized the fact that most workers were of rural origins, having migrated to the city to earn money in factories to help support their families back home. Because of (well-documented) discrimination against the rural population in China, these workers were, in her words, looked down upon and therefore lacked confidence. It was Outreach's job to help them build up this confidence so that they could confront the challenges of city life. At the most general level, she saw her job as making competent "new citizens" (*xin shimin*) out of implicitly incompetent peasants. Rights consciousness in and of itself was, in her view, a narrow and "legalistic" way of seeing what was a much broader problem: peasants" unfortunate backwardness and low quality (*suzhi*). Similarly, she characterized other "law-oriented" NGOs" focus on wages and overtime as "economistic", arguing that Outreach took into account "the whole person", going beyond economics to ask what makes for a genuinely happy life in today's world. Thus, a paternalistic "civilizing" discourse overrode the more rights-based framework within which her NGO had been founded and which remained the explicit justification for the recourse to hotline services by brands and their Chinese suppliers.

Outreach's civilizing mission was even more evident in the case of another hotline that they had set up, with the help of a select group of brands, to help migrant parents communicate with the children they had left back in their villages to be looked after by relatives. In association with a professor of psychology from a local university, they had designed their hotline so as to train parents in better listening techniques. As the director explained, most parents have an "old-fashioned" way of thinking about communication, limited to scolding their children for not working hard enough and pushing them to work harder. As a result, the children "left at home" (*liushou haizi*) felt not only abandoned but also misunderstood, leading to even less communication and a vicious cycle in which both parents and children suffered. Training workers to use more "modern" styles of parenting was part of training them to be proper citizens, in her view, and was far more important to the overall happiness of these migrant workers than technical advice about their rights under the law. Indeed, throughout our discussions, the rights-based orientation was characterized as "narrow" and "inappropriate" to real workers' "mentalities", while her more broadly psychological approach was portrayed as more in touch with what workers "really need".

In sum, in the case of Outreach we see that the intimate, communication-based approach to workers' rights as embodied in hotline technologies produces overflow effects that go far beyond building the "capacity" of workers to exercise their rights under Chinese labor law. The hotline format privatized (in both material and moral terms) workers' problems or complaints, shifting their attention away from collective or legal concerns to questions of individual happiness and well-being. For transnational corporations and well-meaning Chinese urbanites alike, operations such as Outreach seem to hold out the promise of taking us "beyond legality", to a world in which the happiness of workers and management alike are attained through proper forms of communication, in the context of an idealized project in which working conditions and productivity could be improved simultaneously.[9] Under this worldview, promulgated by the some of the CSR professionals we interviewed and replayed in a local idiom by NGOs like Outreach, a focus on law and rights is portrayed as "bureaucratic" or "legalistic". In what resembles a cynical replay of the Confucianization of the law under the Han, players "at all levels of the supply chain" (including workers!) are encouraged to interiorize the norms of responsible capitalism rather than to rely on the external forces of the law. Hotlines of this sort are the concrete sites where this personalized relation to norms takes place, where the cold language of rights and duties is translated into the smiley-filled discourse of engagement and well-being.

From labor rights to personal development – marginalizing the law

Clearly, worker hotlines are hybrid instruments that can be adapted to a variety of frameworks for aspiration and action in the area of social justice. We have approached this variety "from the bottom", through an ethnographic description of how ordinary and seemingly innocuous operational tools frame the larger questions of what is a right, what is a wrong, what is a worker, in sum, whom should be mobilized and how in order to improve working conditions for factory production in China. Examined through the lens of Susanne Brandtstädter's introduction to this volume, we demonstrate that different hotline technologies appeal to different figures of the *public*, call for different repertoires of *action* and disseminate different *judgements and narratives* about social justice in industrial production. PRD WCC's ideal public is the courtroom, a place where moral suasion and authority can be brought to bear on companies and government alike, through theatrical performances of the law that seek to raise workers' collective consciousness of the injustices they suffer under the state-sponsored capitalist mode of production. Welcome also draws on the tools of moral suasion and theatralisation, but in a semi-private sphere, that of the enterprise itself, where management is confronted with the individual or collective complaints of its workers and shamed into taking reparatory action through appeal to the discourse of "ruling the country through law" (*yifa zhiguo*). Finally, Outreach's use of its technologically sophisticated hotline reflects a worldview in which workers' complaints must be handled through one-to-one counseling, taking into account their "whole person" and their desire and need to incorporate the norms of "new citizenship"; in this paradigm, accountability to corporate sponsors is the only form of "publicity" that is given to their action.[10]

As the example of Outreach demonstrates, this shift from law-based to "responsibility"-based modes of governance in the area of workers rights and working conditions can be read as a calculated move by corporate leadership located in the global North, part of a long-term strategy to avoid regulation and to profit from low-cost, low-enforcement production environments around the world (see Pun 2005a, for a persuasive argument in this direction). The role assigned to the Chinese state in transnational CSR discourse and practice is particularly revealing in this regard. In our interviews with "global professionals" active in the area of CSR, we found that their projects for promoting responsible capitalism through "multi-stakeholder dialogue" and "capacity building" for the most part simply ignored Chinese government actors. When we asked whether they included local or provincial officials in their meetings, talks and workshops, they tossed off our question dismissively, referring to common knowledge about the omnipresence of legal violations within China and to a general consensus that the state was both unwilling and unable to do anything about them.[11] Needless to say, this discursive framing of the problem of the "irresponsible" Chinese state forecloses certain solutions while encouraging others. Notably, it has rendered virtually unthinkable a solution that would consist in global brands insisting that they will not invest in or buy from production facilities located in China unless they can receive government guarantees that relevant laws and regulations will be applied. Rather than calling for Chinese enforcement of Chinese laws and regulations – a "solution" that, under any objective analysis of transnational corporate interests, looks an awful lot like a problem – they set out to establish their own, privately enforced normative framework based on managerial notions of "responsibility", "self-development" and "the unique individual" (Mercure 2013).

However, what goes on in an organization like Outreach cannot be fully explained by reference to the machinations of global capital. Rather, the social and economic transformations that have led to the emergence of "responsibility-based" as opposed to "law-based"[12] NGOs must be understood as an encounter between the transnational CSR paradigm and local frameworks for imagining China's participation in global modernity. In this "structure of conjuncture" (Sahlins 1985), the notions of "ownership" and "engagement", omnipresent in global discussions of the need for private regulation through soft law, are appropriated and transformed into state-sponsored and popular Chinese discourses about citizenship (Ong and Zhang 2008), individualism (Yan 2011), responsible subjects (Guiheux 2007) and the low quality (*suzhi*) of Chinese migrant workers (Anagnost 2004; Kipnis 2006; Jacka 2009). In sum, "corporate social responsibility" in China is a global assemblage that brings the rhetoric of capitalism's "ethical reconstruction" into contact with popular and government conceptions of citizenship, population quality, socialist morality and state power. In so doing, it has the potential to undercut, contradict and profoundly alter the notions of rights, obligations and rules that move Chinese citizens to "engage the law" (Diamant, Lubman and O'Brien 2005) in their everyday struggles for social justice. As scholars and citizens of the world, we would do well to "learn from our foreign friends", taking inspiration from these struggles to examine how this same assemblage, in different guises, is modifying conceptions of rights, justice and access to the law in contemporary societies throughout the globe, including our own.

Notes

* This article is based on research financed by the Swiss Network for International Studies (SNIS) for the period from 2010–12 (see http://www2.unine.ch/files/content/sites/maps/files/ shared/documents/Hertz_SNIS_summary-FR.pdf.). We extend our heartfelt thanks to the SNIS for their support.

1 In order to disguise identities, we have chosen to create composites rather than to describe the precise organizations we visited. In some cases, we have altered the location of the organization or the sex of an interlocutor, and we have combined details found in different organizations within a type. However, each of the details we report was actually observed in the context of the ideal type we are describing. This precaution seems all the more necessary as the current regime consolidates its crackdown on NGO activities, for both foreign and domestic NGOs (see e.g. www.taipeitimes.com / News/editorials/archives/2016/04/30/2003645137, accessed May 20, 2016). Indeed, some of the NGOs we interviewed for this study no longer exist. For more information, please contact the authors.

2 We do not review here the large body of literature on the formal requirements and organizational characteristics of Chinese NGOs (but see Hsia and White 2002; Lau

2009; International Center for Not-for-Profit Law 2012; Cheng et al. 2010), which differ from those of government-organized NGOs (GONGOs) (Spires 2011). It should be noted, however, that the use of this term in the literature does not always correspond to its occurrence in China, where many organizations that qualify under a functional definition as NGOs in fact register as businesses under Chinese law to avoid cumbersome and intrusive relations with the local government.

3 QQ is the most widely used chat system in China. It can be used between computers and cell phones.

4 In this article, we do not discuss the All China Federation of Trade Unions, as the ACFTU played no role in the hotlines we examine here. Unions" place in the overall landscape of industrial relations in China is examined in other work by members of our research team (see e.g., Liu 2010); see generally "Labor rights in China", online at www.aflcio.org/Issues/Trade/China/Labor-Rights-in-China, accessed May 20, 2016.

5 For a general introduction by the International Trade Union Confederation (ITUC), see "Internationally recognised core labour standards in the People's Republic of China", available online at http://www.ituc-csi.org/IMG/pdf/Chinal_Final-2.pdf, accessed May 20, 2016.

6 See Zeng Xiangquan, Lu Liang, Idris Sa'ad Umar, 2005 "Working time in transition: The dual task of standardization and flexibilization in China", ILO – Conditions of Work and Employment Series, no 11, available online at http://www.ituc-csi.org/IMG/pdf/Chinal_Final-2.pdf, accessed May 20, 2016.

7 The economic promise of this new market for "capacity-building" service provision has been sketched out by Zajak (2013) and is one of the questions we raise in our ongoing research on CSR in the electronics industry in China.

8 The control function of worker hotlines, which provide brands with immediate access to information about what is going on inside their supplier firms, may help to explain their popularity and brands" willingness to fund them, an issue that is explored in *L'écho de l'éthique* (2005) and Dolan and Rajak (2016).

9 The consensus-based model at the heart of CSR is discussed in Dolan and Rajak (2016: 21).

10 See also Zajak (2013: 189), who observes that "business-oriented" labor NGOs are often expressly forbidden from going public with the information about labor conditions that they collect within their clients" factories.

11 The statement of a director of the "human rights department" of a US-based transnational corporation, quoted in Pun (2005a: 103), is typical of the attitude we encountered in 2012: "The government is useless here; no labor law is actually enforced. We take up its role to provide labor protections" (*sic*).

12 The main problem with dichotomies is that they are too dichotomous. Specifically, dividing NGOs into "law-based" and "responsibility-based" orientations does not do justice to the time, energy and conviction that these NGOs invest in debating, both within and between organizations, correct strategies for advancing the cause of workers rights. We thus disagree with Zajak (2013: 187) when she argues that business-oriented NGOs do not have contacts with labor-oriented NGOs. Our fieldwork suggests, to the contrary, that NGOs communicate amongst themselves and via their academic sponsors, and are both savvy and critical about the merits and limits of their respective approaches and about the competition that structures their field.

References

Anagnost, Ann. 2004. The Corporeal Politics of Quality (*Suzhi*). *Public Culture* 16(2), pp. 189–208.

Bidet, Aexandra and Le Méner, Erwan. 2014. Les ressorts collectifs des signalements de sans-abri au 115: Appel politisé, voisinage troublé et geste citoyen en milieu urbain démocratique. In: Marion Carrel and Catherine Neveu, eds. *Citoyennetés ordinaires: Pour une approche renouvelée des pratiques citoyennes*. Paris: Karthala, pp. 101–130.

Boltanski, Luc. 2012 [1990]. *Love and Justice as Competences*. Cambridge: Polity Press.

Boltanski, Luc and Laurent, Thévenot. 2006 [1991]. *On Justification: Economies of Worth*. Princeton: Princeton University Press.

Brandtstädter, Susanne. 2011. The Law Cuts Both Ways: Rural Legal Activism and Citizenship Struggle in Neosocialist China. *Economy and Society* 40(2), pp. 266–288.

Calderon-Cuadrado, Reyes, José Luis, Alvarez-Arce, Isabel, Rodriguez-Tejedo and Stella Salvatierra. 2009. "Ethics Hotlines" in Transnational Companies: A Comparative Study. *Journal of Business Ethics* 88, pp. 199–210.

Cao, Jin and Xinlei, Lu. 2014. A Preliminary Exploration of the Gay Movement in Mainland China: Legacy, Transition, Opportunity, and the New Media. *Signs* 39(4), pp. 840–848.

Chahoud, Tatjana. 2011. Policies on Corporate Social Responsibility. In: Christoph Scherrer, ed. *China's Labor Question*. Mering: Rainer Hampp Verlag, pp. 158–181.

Chan, Anita. 2001. *China's Workers Under Assault: The Exploitation of Labor in a Globalizing Economy*. Armonk, NY: M.E. Sharpe.

Chan, Jenny. 2009. Meaningful Progress or Illusory Reform? Analyzing China's Labor Contract Law. *New Labor Forum* 18(2), pp. 43–51.

Chang, Leslie. 2008. *Factory Girls: From Village to City in a Changing China*. New York: Spiegel & Grau.

Chen, Mee-Shia and Chan, Anita. 2010. Occupational Health and Safety in China. The Case of State-Managed Entreprises. *International Journal of Health Services* 40(1), pp. 43–60.

Cheng, Joseph Y. S., Kinglun, Ngok and Wenjia, Zhuang. 2010. The Survival and Development Space for China's Labor NGOs: Informal Politics and Its Uncertainty. *Asian Survey* 50(6), pp. 1082–1106.

Choukroune, Leïla. 2009. Harmonious Norms for Global Marketing the Chinese Way. *Journal of Business Ethics* 88(3), pp. 411–432.

Chu, Yingchi. 2006. Legal Report: Citizenship Education Through a Television Documentary. In: Vanessa L. Fong and Rachel Murphy, eds. *Chinese Citizenship: Views From the Margins*. London and New York: Routledge, pp. 68–95.

Comaroff, Jean and Comaroff, John L. 2006. *Law and Disorder in the Postcolony*. Chicago: Chicago University Press.

Cornue, Virginia. 1999. Practicing NGOness and Relating Women's Space Publicly: The Women's Hotline and the State. In: Mayfair Meihui Yang, ed. *Spaces of Their Own: Women's Public Sphere in Transnational China*. Minneapolis: University of Minnesota Press, pp. 68–91.

Diamant, Neil J., Lubman, Stanley B. and O'Brien, Kevin J., eds. 2005. *Engaging the Law in China: State, Society, and Possibilities for Justice*. Stanford: Stanford University Press.

Dolan, Catherine and Rajak, Dinah, eds. 2016. *The Anthropology of Corporate Social Responsibility*. Oxford: Berghahn Books.

Economy, Elizabeth C. 2007. The Great Leap Backwards? The Costs of China's Environmental Crisis. *Foreign Affairs* 86(5), pp. 38–59.

Erwin, Kathleen. 2000. Heart-to-Heart, Phone-to-Phone: Family Values, Sexuality, and the Politics of Shanghai's Advice Hotlines. In: Deborah Davis, ed. *The Consumer Revolution in Urban China*. Berkeley: University of California Press, pp. 145–170.

Froissart, Chloé. 2011. Les "ONG" de defense des travailleurs migrants: Des organisations proto-syndicales qui contribuent à la stabilité dynamique du régime. *Perspectives chinoises* 2, pp. 20–28.

Gallagher, Mary. 2006. Mobilizing the Law in China: "Informed Disenchantment" and the Rising of Legal Consciousness. *Law & Society Review* 40(4), pp. 783–816.
Gereffi, Garry, John, Humphrey and Timothy, Sturgeon. 2005. The Governance of Global Value Chains. *Review of Political Economy* 12(1), pp. 78–104.
Goodale, Mark. 2009. *Dilemmas of Modernity. Bolivian Encounters with Law and Liberalism*. Stanford, CA: Stanford University Press.
Griffiths, Anne, Benda-Beckmann, Franz von and Benda-Beckmann, Keebet, von. 2005. *Mobile People, Mobile Law: Expanding Legal Relations in a Contracting World*. Surrey and Burlington: Ashgate.
Griffiths, Anne, Benda-Beckmann, Franz von and Benda-Beckmann, Keebet von. 2009a. *The Power of Law in a Transnational World: Anthropological Enquiries*. New York: Berghahn Books.
Griffiths, Anne, Benda-Beckmann, Franz von and Benda-Beckmann, Keebet von. 2009b. *Spatializing Law: An Anthropological Geography of Law in Society*. Surrey and Burlington: Ashgate.
Guiheux, Gilles. 2007. The Promotion of a New Calculating Chinese Subject: The Case of Laid-off Workers Turning into Entrepreneurs. *Journal of Contemporary China* 16(5), pp. 149–171.
Ho, Peter. 2008. Introduction: Embedded Activism and Political Change in a Semi-authoritarian Context. In: Peter Ho and Louis E. Richard, eds. *China's Embedded Activism: Opportunities and Constraints of a Social Movement*. London: Routledge, pp. 1–19.
Hsia, Renee and White, Lynn. 2002. Working Amid Corporatism and Confusion: Foreign NGOs in China. *Nonprofit and Voluntary Sector Quarterly* 33, pp. 329–351.
Hui, Elaine Sio-ieng. 2011. *Corporate Social Responsibility Revisited: Can It Address Chinese Workers' Needs in a Changing Socio-Economic Context?* CSR Research Paper Series, 1. Online at www.amrc.org.hk/node/1205, accessed July 2014.
International Center for Not-for-Profit Law [ICNL]. 2012. *NGO Monitor: China*. Online at: www.icnl.org/research/monitor/china.html, accessed October 5, 2012.
Jacka, Tamara. 2009. Cultivating Citizens: *Suzhi* (Quality) Discourse in the PRC. *Positions: East Asia Culture Critique* 17(3), pp. 523–535.
Kamat, Sangeeta. 2004. The Privatization of Public Interest: Theorizing NGO Discourse in the Neoliberal Era. *Review of International Political Economy* 11(1), pp. 155–176.
Keating, Joshua E. 2009. The Stories You Missed in 2009. *Foreign Policy* 176, pp. 10–16, 18.
Kipnis, Andrew. 2006. *Suzhi*: A Keyword Approach. *The China Quarterly* 186, pp. 295–313.
Lascoumes, Pierre and Le Galès, Patrick. 2005. *Gouverner par les instruments*. Paris: Presses de Sciencespo.
Lau, Clement Chu S. 2009. The Role of NGOs in China. *Quarterly Journal of Ideology* 31, p. 18.
Law, John. 2008. Actor-Network Theory and Material Semiotics. In: Bryan S. Turner, ed. *The New Blackwell Companion to Social Theory* (3rd edition). Oxford: Blackwell, pp. 141–158.
L'écho de l'éthique. 2005. "Ethical Hotlines": Instrument de Confiance ou Management Par Délation? *Finance & Bien Commun* 23(3), pp. 20–22.
Lee, Ching Kwan. 2007a. *Against the Law: Labor Protests in China's Rustbelt and Sunbelt*. Berkeley: University of California Press.
Lee, Ching Kwan, ed. 2007b. *Working in China: Ethnographies of Labor and Workplace Transformation*. London: Routledge.

Le Méner, Erwan. 2011. Evaluer des demandes, ou la justesse comme travail invisible: Le cas du 115 de Paris. Online at www.ethnographiques.org/2011/LeMener, accessed October 2012.

Lin, Li-Wen. 2009. Legal Transplants Through Private Contracting: Codes of Vendor Conduct in Global Supply Chains as an Example. *American Journal of Comparative Law* 57, pp. 711–744.

Liu, Mingwei. 2010. Union Organizing in China: Still a Monolithic Labor Movement? *Industrial and Labor Relations Review* 64(1), pp. 30–52.

Locke, Richard and Romis, Monica. 2007. Improving Work Conditions in a Global Supply Chain. *MIT Sloan Management Review* 48(2), pp. 54–62.

Lora-Wainwright, Anna, Yiyun Zhang, Yumei Wu and Rooij, Benjamin van. 2012. Learning to Live With Pollution: The Making of Environmental Subjects in a Chinese Industrial Village. *The China Journal* 68, pp. 106–124.

Mercure, Daniel. 2013. Le nouveau modèle de pouvoir et de domination au travail dans le mode de production postfordiste. *SociologieS*. Online at http://sociologies.revues.org/4227, accessed January 2014.

Nader, Laura. 1991. *Harmony Ideology. Justice and Control in a Zapotec Mountain Village*. Stanford, CA: Stanford University Press.

Newendorp, Nicole. 2006. Teaching "Responsibility:" Social Workers' Efforts to Turn Chinese Immigrants Into Ideal Hong Kong Citizens. In: Vanessa L. Fong and Rachel Murphy, eds. *Chinese Citizenship: Views From the Margins*. London and New York: Routledge, pp. 123–150.

Off Our Backs. 1993. China: Women Start Hotline. *Off Our Backs* 23(6), p. 4.

Ong, Aihwa. 1996. Cultural Citizenship as Subject-Making: Immigrants Negotiate Racial and Cultural Boundaries in the United States. *Current Anthropology* 37(5), pp. 737–762.

Ong, Aihwa and Collier, Stephen J., eds. 2008. *Global Assemblages: Technology, Politics and Ethics as Anthropological Problems*. Oxford: Blackwell Publishing.

Ong, Aihwa and Zhang, Li. 2008. Introduction: Privatizing China. Powers of the Self, Socialism From Afar. In: Li Zhang and Aihwa Ong, eds. *Privatizing China: Socialism From Afar*. Ithaca, NY: Cornell University Press, pp. 1–19.

Pun, Ngai. 2005a. Global Production Company Codes of Conduct, and Labor Conditions in China: A Case Study of Two Factories. *The China Journal* 54, pp. 101–113.

Pun, Ngai. 2005b. Quanqiuhua gongchang tizhi yu "daode linian chonggou" (The Global Factory System and "Ethical Reconstruction"). *Kaifang Shidai* (*Open Times*) 2, pp. 108–125. Online at www.opentimes.cn/bencandy.php?fid=100&aid=1312.

Pun, Ngai. 2008. "Reorganized Moralism:" The Politics of Transnational Labor Codes. In: Aihwa Ong and Li Zhang, eds. *Privatizing China: Socialism From Afar*. Ithaca, NY: Cornell University Press, pp. 87–102.

Pun, Ngai, Chan, Jenny and Selden, Mark. 2016. *Dying for an iPhone: The Life of Chinese Migrant Workers*. Lanham, MD: Roman and Littlefield.

Rodriguez-Garavito, César. 2005. Nike's Law: The Anti-Sweatshop Movement, Transnational Corporations, and the Struggle Over International Labor Rights in the Americas. In: Boaventura de Sousa Santos and César Rodriguez-Garavito, eds. *Law and Globalization From Below: Towards a Cosmopolitan Legality*. Cambridge: Cambridge University Press, pp. 64–91.

SACOM, 2009. *Towards a New Worker-Based CSR Model: A Pilot Labor Rights Training Program in China*. Online at www.sacom.hk/?p=585, accessed August 2014.

Sahlins, Marshall. 1985. *Islands of History*. Chicago: Chicago University Press.

Seeley, Mary Frances. 1998. Hotlines and Mental Health Services. *The Journal of Crisis Intervention and Suicide Prevention* 19(1), pp. 4–5.

Spires, Anthony J. 2011. Contingent Symbiosis and Civil Society in an Authoritarian State: Understanding the Survival of China's Grassroots NGOs. *American Journal of Sociology* 117(1), pp. 1–45.

Stern, Rachel E. and O'Brien, Kevin J. 2012. Politics at the Boundary: Mixed Signals and the Chinese State. *Modern China* 38(2), pp. 174–198.

Thireau, Isabelle and Linshan, Hua. 2001. Le sens du juste en Chine. En quête d'un nouveau droit du travail. *Annales. Histoire, Sciences Sociales* 6, pp. 1238–1312.

Wedel, Janine R., Cris Shore, Gregory Feldman and Stacy, Lathrop. 2005. Toward an Anthropology of Public Policy. *Annals of the American Academy of Political and Social Science* 600, pp. 30–51.

Weikert, Jochen. 2011. Chinese Companies" Response to Corporate Social Responsibility. In: Christoph Scherrer, ed. *China's Labor Question*. Mering: Rainer Hampp Verlag, pp. 182–198.

World Bank. 2003. *Strengthening Implementation of Corporate Social Responsibility in Global Supply Chains*. Washington, DC: World Bank Group.

Yan, Yunxiang. 2011. The Changing Moral Landscape. In: Arthur Kleinman, Yunxiang Yan, Jun Jing, Lee Sing and Everett Zhang, ed. *Deep China: The Moral Life of the Person*. Playfield: University of California Press, pp. 36–77.

Yin, Juelin and Zhang, Yuli. 2012. Institutional Dynamics and Corporate Social Responsibility (CSR) in an Emerging Country Context: Evidence From China. *Journal of Business Ethnics* 111(2), pp. 301–316.

Zajak, Sabrina. 2013. Transnational Private Regulation and the Transformation of Labour Rights Urbanizations in Emerging Markets: New Markets for Labour Support Work in China. *Journal of Asian Public Policy* 6(2), pp. 178–195.

Zhang, Li. 2006. Contesting Spatial Modernity in Late-Socialist China. *Current Anthropology* 47(3), pp. 461–484.

4 Judging publics and contested exclusion

The moral economy of citizenship in China

Alan Smart and Josephine Smart

Introduction

People always make judgements, whether on institutions or other people. What makes people into a public, to a substantial degree, is their ability to make such judgements publicly. If they cannot publicly judge their rulers, or if the rulers carefully circumscribe what kind of judgements are accepted without punishment, we could conclude that a public does not exist. As this volume demonstrates, judging publics have clearly begun to emerge in China. But the restraints and limits on expression of such judgements publicly are still considerable.

In a conventional usage, judging involves the rules against which an action or performance is evaluated. But what rules are used by judging Chinese publics? – the explicit constitution and laws of the People's Republic of China? the informal rules that officials and institutions use and insist on conformity to, which De Herdt and De Sardan (2015) call "practical norms", even when they are in conflict with the formal rules? or the grounds for judgement of ordinary people, which may be consonant with either formal or informal official rules, or dissonant with both? For both ordinary citizens and civil servants, there are distinctions between legitimate acts, regardless of whether the law might consider them bribes or corruption, for example, and socially illicit acts that are in no way illegal.

Multiple rule systems are ubiquitous in all societies (Moore 1978). The nature of the relationship between these rule systems varies greatly. Colonies were often characterized by legal pluralism: ethnic or citizenship status determined which rules applied to particular people or situations, custom for native populations, extraterritorial provisions for judgement by home country rules for colonizers or expatriates in Chinese treaty ports (Merry 1992). In a less formal way, legal pluralism is found everywhere, with churches and voluntary associations applying their own rules to those who want to be members, such as gated communities, for example. In liberal democracies, such particular rule systems are expected to be subordinate to the national legal system: enforceable only to the extent that they are not incompatible with formal law or charters of human rights. From another perspective, however, some communities, particularly religious communities, may feel that their sacred rules transcend those of worldly governments (Erie 2016), and resist a variety of laws such as conscription, vaccination, monogamy, and so on. More broadly, many citizens feel that certain formal rules, particularly as implemented by their rulers or leaders, are less ethically acceptable than the mores that the citizens attempt to live by (Heyman and Smart 1999).

Rather than discussing judging in general, we concentrate on a particular set of discourses and dynamics that we label the "moral economy of citizenship". We have argued that because of the household registration system, China has a distinctive regime of "local citizenship" where the rights, entitlements and responsibilities of citizenship are primarily set by the locality in which a household is permanently registered (Smart and Smart 2001). Those who move to other localities and do not or cannot transfer their permanent household registration (*hukou*) have temporary registration, if any, which confers a much lesser set of privileges. While this has often been discussed in a dualistic fashion of urban *hukou* as privileged and rural *hukou* as disadvantaged (Beitz 1983; Solinger 1999), the situation is more complicated: some holders of rural *hukou* in some prosperous villages resist becoming urban to avoid losing valued privileges. Similarly, some urban people oppose the liberalization of the household registration system because they think it results in rural people getting the 'best of both worlds', the safety net of land back home and the same rights (which have often been eroded quite drastically) as local-born people in the cities. We explore this complex mesh of moral evaluations surrounding citizenship in order to consider the ways in which judgements are made by Chinese publics about what is just and unjust about the changing situations of contemporary China.

In the next section, we outline our theoretical perspective on judging publics and private judgements, with an emphasis on moral economy and exclusionary citizenship. The following two sections consider how Chinese judging has changed over the course of thirty-four years of reform, contrasting the first decade of reform with the period after 1992. In the former period, informal criticism such as gossip was most important, whereas open criticism of the state and government officials became more feasible in the later period (O'Brien and Stern 2009). Along with this, we suggest that changes in the political economy have resulted in the lesser effectiveness of informal judging and criticism, which may be encouraging the growth of more contentious and open resistance and dissent. In the conclusion we offer some comments on what the Chinese experience might say about the intersections among moral economy, law and political economy. The different forms of judging and evaluation operating within each discursive domain interact to influence the dynamics of transformation of reforming socialist societies.

Theoretical perspectives

Citizenship is inherently exclusionary: different rights and entitlements apply to those inside the circle than to those outside. John Rawls's theory of social justice relied on a thought experiment, the original position, where people could choose the political and economic systems into which they would be born without knowing the personal characteristics they would have at birth, such as family, wealth or ethnicity. Any system which people would not choose without knowing their fate was seen by him as unjust. From this perspective, national citizenship can be seen as inherently unjust. If you didn't know if you would be born British or Somali, you would be unlikely to opt for the present system of citizenship, so it is an unjust system that arbitrarily favors the status quo (Beitz 1983: 596). Building on Rawls's principles, Carens (1987: 252) states: "Citizenship in Western liberal democracies is the modern equivalent of feudal privilege – an inherited status that greatly enhances one's life chances. Like feudal birthright privilege, restrictive citizenship is hard to justify when one thinks about it closely" (see also Kipnis 2004). It must be noted that Rawls himself explicitly restricted "membership in the original position to compatriots until after the principles of distributive justice have been chosen" (Beitz 1983: 594). However, the basic procedural principle seems to logically lead to its extension to the global level. Whether open borders would be *feasible* or even desirable from non-ethical grounds is another matter, of course. Non-liberal ethical theories, such as the communitarian position of Michael Walzer (1994), have stronger grounds for supporting exclusionary citizenships in order to preserve desired ways of life (Carens 1987; Smart 2010b).

Despite such defenses of national citizenship, exclusionary forms of citizenship *within* a nation, for example South African apartheid, are harder to justify as socially just arrangements. And this is precisely the situation within contemporary China resulting from the *hukou* system, which initially prevented unauthorized rural-urban migration and since 1979 has allowed movement only at the cost of exclusion from rights and welfare provisions accorded to local citizens (Chan 1994). Resistance to inclusive policies may be slowing *hukou* reform despite higher-level support for reform. The phenomenon of local citizenship (Smart and Lin 2007; Smart and Smart 2001) means that increases in citizen participation in local politics and government have serious potential for encouraging greater exclusionism against outsiders. There is considerable evidence that this has indeed occurred in certain areas in China (Cho 2013). There might be parallels to contemporary populist and nativist politics around migration in the EU and USA.

The existing literature on *hukou* in China concentrates on the exclusion of rural migrants from urban citizenship, following dualistic assumptions that "urban citizenship" is always the more advantaged status in comparison to "rural citizenship". This provides a less useful account of contemporary inequality than a more nuanced concept of "local citizenship". Solinger's (1999) concept of "urban citizenship" is only part of the story. She neglects comparable exclusivist tendencies in rural China, often framed as "local corporatism" (Oi 1992), in which the benefits of development, facilitated by migrant labor, are monopolized by the locally born. While overall it is clear that discrimination against rural migrants to the cities is of the utmost importance, analytically we need to recognize that "rural citizenship" can also bear advantages and that when there are desirable local resources and opportunities, rural areas also act on the basis of xenophobia and exclusion. Furthermore, rather than "urban citizenship" operating as a generic category, it is citizenship in particular cities that determines the kinds of entitlements that are provided. For these reasons, we see urban citizenship as just one component of a broader category of local citizenships which include both rural and urban localities, and which focus on the specific jurisdiction rather than more general categories of urban and rural.

People who live in urban areas without an urban *hukou* totaled 245 million in 2013, about 18% of the total population, a proportion that has continually risen since 1980 (Chan 2014). The *hukou* as a system of exclusion persists through:

> social and official groups that supported it, namely most urbanites, along with the powerful bureaucracies of public security and labor, and the wealthier, magnet regions of the country. Because of this weighty, if latent, coalition disposed to conserve this one institution, the influences of market incentives had by no means changed the model of official urban citizenship as the century drew to a close.
>
> (Solinger 1999: 8)

The same can still be said now, despite local experiments and gestures toward reform from the top leadership. It has become clear that the barriers to entry through *hukou* conversion are closely correlated with the wealth of a locality: the greater the interest of outsiders to move to a place, the higher the barriers.

The advantages, entitlements and obligations of citizenship in a particular locality vary greatly between cities and between rural municipalities, sometimes as much or more than between urban and rural locations. The dualism of Solinger's conception of citizenship in China is limiting and requires some revision to cope with the complex and changing situation. Urban-registered people "who cross an administrative boundary to work or live (whether to an urban or a rural area) can become just as much excluded outsiders as rural migrants" (Woodman 2011: 22).

Economic decline in various cities simultaneously have been eroding the rights of many urban citizens, particularly in the rustbelt of the Northeast (Cho 2013). The result is that the advantages of holding a *hukou* in a particular place are increasingly differentiated, not binary between urban and rural.

Public judging of legal practices as socially illegitimate has a long genealogy, usefully framed by the British historian E. P. Thompson as "moral economy" (see Introduction, this volume). The way we use the term presents a problem, however. As used by E. P. Thompson (1991 [1971]: 188), the moral economy of the poor involves a "consistent traditional view of social norms and obligations, of the proper economic functions of several parties within the community". Marc Edelman (2005: 331) notes that Thompson's discussion of moral economy has spawned a diversity of approaches, many of which Thompson (1991 [1971]: 341) sees as losing in focus what they may gain in breadth. There are advantages in maintaining conceptual clarity by keeping the concept close to its most prominent expositions. We extend the idea beyond the original inspiration because it is so 'good to think with'.

All economies involve moral judgements and restrictions. Moral economies influence systems of production, exchange and consumption. A moral economic examination pays close attention to the ways in which moral practices and discourses structure economies, and vice versa. We go beyond Thompson's particular usage of moral economy operating, which we call moral economy 1, and develop the idea more generally to allow us to dissect the particular forms of moral claims, limits and practices that operate in *all* historical and contemporary economies. The latter we refer to as moral economy 2 (Smart and Smart 2016). For the remainder of this chapter, we refer to moral economy in the second sense.

The pioneering reform period

The concept of local citizenship, as we first coined the term in 2001, includes the bifurcation of citizenship in the People's Republic of China into agricultural and non-agricultural (urban) *hukou*, which created a legal and formal system of inclusion/exclusion in matters of spatial mobility, access to public resources and services, employment opportunities and housing conditions. Before the 1978 economic reform, an urban *hukou* was considered superior and more desirable than a rural *hukou* by all measures of quality of life.

Our fieldwork in a rural township in the Pearl River Delta from 1987 to 2002, however, pointed to the complexity of local citizenship beyond the simple dual model of rural vs. urban. The rapid influx of migrant workers from all parts of China, of both rural and urban *hukou*, rapidly expanded the local population from 12,000 to 150,000 by 1991, and then, after becoming part of an expanded Shenzhen, to over 2 million by 2009. These outsiders are in the community on temporary permits of residence, even though many of them may stay for many years for employment and business purposes. Their migration to this rural township in the Pearl River Delta did nothing to change their status as 'outsiders', and their original *hukou* designation rooted in a specific locality remained unchanged. This distinction of local citizenship vis-à-vis all outsiders has tremendous implications. Thanks to the economic reform, this rural township flourished under foreign direct investments (mostly from Hong Kong) and rapidly urbanized and industrialized. The new income streams from rental properties and land leases created new wealth for the original residents who have local *hukou*, a local citizenship status that is now fiercely guarded with pride because local resource redistribution is strictly reserved for people with local *hukou* claims.

In this township, as in other rural parts of Guangdong's Pearl River Delta, the opportunities and risk accompanying the early reforms resulted in the widespread sense that other villagers needed to be at least partially incorporated into the new wealth-generating machine. This was because of the potential for instability through envy and political suspicion of the new wealth of local elites (Smart 2010a). There was still at that time widespread ideological discomfort with wealth disparities, markets, competition, and other capitalist practices which caused a great deal of local resentment against the new wealthy class. Government officials could squeeze resources out of these new classes (Osburg 2013). Local opinion at that time put constraints on opportunistic behavior by officials, encouraging them to apply their rent-seeking efforts partially to the common good of the locality (Smart 1999). The welfare provision of local citizenship results in part from constraints on the freedom of action of local officials. Lily Lee Tsai (2002) found that wealth alone cannot explain how public services are provided. Villages with active temple associations and strong lineage organizations were found to be more likely to avoid imposing unpopular policies due to the efficacy of social disapproval. She also found that temple associations were often used in these cases to collect contributions for community projects. The most predatory practices were found in villages with neither active village-wide social institutions nor elected village representative assemblies. Social networks that incorporate both village officials and citizens "restrict predatory behaviour and facilitate public projects that might not otherwise become a reality" (Tsai 2002: 26).

Spreading the wealth to all locals in one way or another reduced the likelihood of insiders judging officials' behaviour as unacceptable and reporting dubious practices to outsiders. Personal benefit that also benefited the locality as a whole was seen as more legitimate, whatever the technical legal status of actions. And dubious practices were the order of the day given the fuzziness of the new rules of the game during the first reform decade (Smart and Smart 2012). Smart and Hsu (2007) found that the operation of tact in *guanxi* relations reveals countervailing forces against unrestrained corruption. Officials and others felt pressure to present their actions as 'reasonable' *guanxi* rather than exploitative corruption, to show that they were acting on behalf of the collective good rather than just selfish gain. After all, outsiders had the power to discursively transform the actions they observed by judging them to be corruption – and in the context of the anti-corruption campaigns of the 1990s, accusations of corruption could have serious consequences. People still had incentives not only to appear to be acting for the collective good, but also to actually do it in order to avoid grievances that might circulate as gossip.

During the time of our research, a portion of this new wealth was redistributed in the form of a yearly dividend (in cash) to members in the nine rural village administrative units in the township. The amount of the dividend varied widely from village to village, reflecting uneven economic development. In one well-to-do village, the dividend was about 8,000 yuan per person, equivalent to more than a year's income for a factory worker in the region at that time. Since this dividend was given to all members of the village with a local agricultural *hukou* (those with positions in town enterprises had received urban *hukou*, earlier a privilege, but now having certain disadvantages) regardless of age and sex, it was considered a good thing to give birth just before the end of the year so that the newborn would receive this cash bonus. Because of the high value of the dividend, there emerged in this well-to-do village disagreements about the ineligibility of married daughters (whose parents hold a local village *hukou*, and who choose to remain in their natal village after marriage) to receive this year-end cash bonus, despite the laws that stated that males and females should be treated the same for inheritance purposes.

Traditionally, a married daughter moved to live with her husband in his village. Household members include all unmarried children (of both sexes) and all descendants traced through the patrilineal line. Since the economic reform, and under the incentive of the cash dividend, more people marry someone from the same village (contrary to the traditional preference for exogamy, marrying someone from a different locality), and more married daughters remain in their natal village with a husband who may be from another locality. In some villages, married daughters and their husbands who live in the wife's natal village were counted as local residents with full entitlement to collective resources, including the yearly dividend. In other villages, married daughters were not eligible to receive this dividend even though they remain in their natal village after marriage. This situation of each village administrative unit having the authority to define who is a local citizen with the associated entitlement is evidence that the definition of local status is a distinctive legal and social practice differing from the more general inequality based on gender, age, wealth, the strength of relationship or connections and other attributes that are common in all social groups. For this reason, we are reluctant to accept Woodman's (2016: 349) suggestion to expand the idea of local citizenship to include cultural processes of local belonging. Only when such cultural processes of exclusion impact the political and judicial definition of who is eligible for rights, benefits and duties of citizens is such an extension useful. Otherwise, it is better seen as part of broader processes of status and social exclusion.

One result of this kind of development was the exclusion and exploitation of outsiders in wealthier rural areas, much less well known than discrimination against rural migrants in cities. Wealth was often generated by limiting local entitlements, particularly 'dividends' from development, to those born there but who have not attained urban *hukou*. In extreme cases, such as the township where we did several periods of fieldwork from 1987 to 1993, less than a tenth of people residing there were citizens in this sense, rates of exclusion comparable to those of the United Arab Emirates. Rapidly developing townships generate substantial revenues, making it possible to offer benefits unthought of in poorer regions (Guo and Zhou 1997: 260). Andrew Kipnis (2011) describes the consequences of such entitlement in the educational arena, with schools in Zouping, Shandong possessing facilities comparable to those at the most elite of Western private schools. In such circumstances of enhanced entitlements to local citizens combined with lesser or almost no services for migrants, tensions naturally result between insiders and outsiders.

In the township we studied, many new income-generating opportunities were created in the wake of the 1978 economic reform. Within the hierarchy of the new economic structure, the best or most desirable options were reserved for people with local *hukou*. One of these plum jobs was the position of a factory manager. When Hong Kong investors came to the local region to set up a factory, it was required that they hire a 'local' person to be a factory manager on the assumption that s/he had the local connections to deal with all government offices and all the necessary paperwork. At the shoe factory where we did a multi-year study, the local authority with whom the investment contract was signed identified Ms. Yeung as the person to be the manager at this shoe factory. Ms. Yeung was not locally born and raised. Her father was born in this community but was sent to Guangxi in his youth during the Cultural Revolution. He stayed and married and had a family. His younger brother remained in the local community where they were born. When the economic conditions in this community improved after 1978, Ms. Yeung moved back with her husband and their young son. Through her paternal uncle's connections, and on the strength of her patrilineal membership to the local community traced through her father, she was able to establish her local citizenship status and secured highly desirable employment as a factory manager, although some felt that she did not deserve her treatment. Her move from Guangxi to the Pearl River Delta was a calculated relocation driven by the promise of better economic and other gains. By that time, both Ms Yeung and her husband had government-assigned employment in Guangxi. Her personal decision to relocate required her to pay a penalty to her work unit (state employer) in cash equivalent to her monthly income for an agreed upon period. However, she did not receive a share of the yearly dividend.

In the 1980s, systems of rural social security were generated from the bottom up and with little financial support or effective political regulation from central authorities. It is tempting to admire the use of revenues for collective rather than simply individual benefit in these townships. However, boundaries of local citizenship reinforce rather than ameliorate inequality. In most cases, those with rural *hukou* who need welfare only qualify for it by returning to their place of birth (Woodman 2016). Migrants to rapidly industrializing rural municipalities were frequently privately critical of their poor treatment, but until recently generally opted for exit (to other factories in the same area, or to other places, or returning home) rather than voicing their criticisms publicly or joining a collective action.

The phenomenon of wealthy villagers appears inconsistent with many accounts of rapid growth in conflict over land between villagers and officials resulting from land being taken with minimal compensation by predatory governments and their allies (Lin 2009; O'Brien and Li 2006). How can we reconcile predatory land grabbing with ideas that, at least in some areas, rural citizens are becoming affluent through various distributions, entitlements and rent-seeking opportunities with widespread perceptions that villagers are being dispossessed without fair compensation? A key element in reconciling these phenomena is that there are great differences over time and place in the terms of local citizenship for rural residents. In the early reform era, we suggest, uncertainty created a situation where it was politically useful for officials to include ordinary villagers in the redistribution of wealth created by the reforms, to prevent gossip about exploitation and taking the capitalist road. Entitlements grew out of a situation of profound ambiguity about the nature and limits of the reforms. While such concerns are still held by many ordinary people, the routinization of market Leninism or capitalism with Chinese practices, particularly since 1992 and China's inclusion in the WTO since 2001, means that such resentments are less likely to result in proactive consideration of their sentiments by power-holders. The result seems to be that tacit bargains are being replaced by more open predation, and in some places more open political contestation by those whose land is expropriated and resources despoiled. We turn to this post-1992 situation in the next section.

Local citizenship in the era of routinized reform

Local citizenship has changed greatly, even while retaining its centrality to the social organization and political economy of contemporary China. We emphasize only three of the many relevant issues here: land grabbing by local governments, preferences to retain rural *hukous* in some areas, and the recent *hukou* reform initiatives launched by the central government.

The conversion of agricultural land to other uses is one of the most important processes of wealth creation in reform China. Changes in how this wealth is created has fundamentally challenged the operation of local citizenship in rural areas, since it has been the economic basis for the dividends and other benefits distributed to locals that we discussed in the previous section. Most observers of the situation agree with the conclusion that farm households "rarely receive adequate compensation" and have "been unable to exercise their rights as owners of collective land"; with "no institutional safeguards to guarantee equal voice for individual farmers, a handful of local officials gain at the expense of individuals" (Zhou 2009: 125). We suggest that outright predatoriness was less blatant and extreme in the first reform decade than after 1992 because of the constraints that had earlier been created by uncertain property rights and rules for economic enterprise.

Yan Sun concluded that prior to 1992, bribery and associated activities "did not result in overwhelming harms that strangled reform" (Sun 2004: 80). Rampant bribery did produce unfairness in access to resources and contributed to income inequality, but also contributed to the flow of goods and information, and played an overall constructive role in a system (Sun 2004). After 1992, however, bribery could no longer be seen as circumventing "barriers to equal access. Rather, it undermines a dominant market and thus the reform program itself, making unequal . . . competition the rule of the game" (Sun 2004: 86). Illegal and corrupt practices had often been seen differently if done for the collective advantage of a locality rather than solely for an official's benefit (Smart 1993).

More radical reforms after 1992 were accompanied by a reversal of the previous trend of decentralization. The central state's share of total budgetary revenue had dropped from 40 percent in 1983 to just over 20 percent in 1993. As a result of a new tax assignment system, the centre's take soared to almost 60 percent in 1994; although a substantial portion of this was reallocated to the provinces, the new system still gave Beijing much more effective power (Yang 2004: 74).

Fiscal decentralization in the 1980s may have facilitated corruption, but Kang Chen (2004) has argued that recentralization in the 1990s did not end it. Instead, it channelled it into a more destructive form. The previous tax system provided incentives for local officials to promote local development, since they would share in the proceeds. This produced what Chen (2004: 1002) describes as "helping hand" corruption, such as "collective bribery" done in the interests of the locality. Recentralization undermined these incentives, encouraging "short time-horizon, grabbing-hand behaviour that was uncoordinated and more opportunistic, and which inhibited private sector development and economic growth, and so contracted the local tax base for both budgetary and off-budget taxes" (Chen

2004: 1002). Zhou (2009: 123) points to new tax-sharing arrangements and value-added taxes in 1994 as also encouraging much more predatory approaches by local governments to land seizures.

There is a widespread belief that the last two decades have seen growth in predatory, rather than developmental, forms of local government (O'Brien and Li 2006). A key dimension of this shift has been the growth of exploitative forms of land seizure and increases in active resistance against the governments that engage in such predatory seizure. Changes in administrative scale have been a major cause of this shift. Control over land conversion has been transferred from local collectives and townships to higher levels more distant from local voice and influence. The land administration system is characterized by hierarchical relations between municipal governments and rural collectives. When rural land is subject to state expropriation and rural-urban conversion, collectives and their members are in a poor position to negotiate with the municipal or county governments. This is why the "expropriation and conversion of rural land have been so controversial and contentious" (Lin 2009: 11). Recentralization since the late 1980s and its re-empowerment of the centre have moved key decisions over land and local livelihoods farther away from local citizens so that their informal voices have been muted. In the silences created by this rescaling, predatory government has increased, and more forceful actions to resist the injustice of land expropriation have emerged in a variety of localities. Strong feelings of moral economy operate in the creation of such reactions, but often in ironic ways. O'Brien and Li (2006) document how exploited villagers frequently adopt a pattern they call "rightful resistance": attempting to mobilize support from the centre against local officials to protect rights that they have on paper but rarely in practice. The local causes of their suffering and exploitation are much more apparent than the structural circumstances that prompt the predation to arise in the first place.

Yet, this situation is not universal in rural China. While quantitative analysis would be necessary to fully support this, it seems plausible to us that in those areas where capitalist development occurred before 1992, the enhanced local citizenship that developed helped to insulate them from the more predatory forms of local governance emerging under routinized reform. If nothing else, much of the agricultural land base had already been redeveloped, and the dividends and other benefits received. The emergence of an exploitable labour force of non-local workers meant that local citizens had resources that they could build on to continue to enhance their growing prosperity, often by becoming rentiers and landlords. It is harder to remove privileges than to avoid bestowing them in the first place, so that villagers in areas that industrialized during the first reform decade have done better than those in the later period. One phenomenon that supports this analysis is the emergence of resistance by some villagers to being converted to urban status. An explanation of this situation has to be situated within the ongoing processes of *hukou* reform.

From the beginning of *hukou* reform in 2000, the central government has "empowered" local governments by devolving financial burdens associated with reform to them (Li and Smart 2012). In doing so, administrative authority over *hukou* reform was also decentralized. One outcome of *hukou* decentralization is that it allows different localities to set different barriers to entry (*men kan*). The *hukou* reform is implemented differentially along a spatial and scalar axis – the lower-level cities and towns are the first to undertake intensive *hukou* reform, whereas the higher-level cities and towns are the slowest and the last to adopt reform. Since implementation of the "Opinions on Promoting Reform of the Management System for Household Registration in Small Cities and Towns" in 2001, small cities and towns have become open to rural-to-urban resident status conversions. However, an anticipated rush by rural residents to convert to urban status did not happen. Many rural residents are not attracted to urban household status. First, many prefecture-level cities and provincial capitals have created barriers to entry designed to favor 'high-quality' migrants with skills and financial or educational advantages at the exclusion of ordinary migrant workers. Bigger cities impose even higher admission requirements on migrants, making urban status near impossible for people. Gains in services and benefits that traditionally came with a change from rural to urban *hukou* status for migrants in cities are now greatly diminished due to other policy reforms that improve employment security, health care insurance and housing. In other words, migrant workers in smaller cities and townships are enjoying almost all the urban services and benefits without having to change their *hukou* status (Li and Smart 2012).

Given the almost universal scholarly dualistic accounts of urban *hukou* as privileged and rural *hukou* as disadvantaged, it is almost always assumed that *hukou* reform will be welcomed by rural residents. That such is not the case seems a surprise. In some cases, there was active resistance by some rural residents against *hukou* reform. As urban boundaries are redrawn to include previously rural/agricultural units since 1978, many rural *hukou* are upgraded to become urban *hukou*. Before 1978, such an upgrade would have been welcomed with delight. But now having a rural *hukou* in at least some areas is considered advantageous. As a result, there is a new phenomenon of contestation among rural *hukou* holders to keep their original status despite their new administratively defined status as a resident within an urban locality. Ethnographic data collected in a township in Zhongshan county in southern China showed the successful resistance to becoming urban by residents of a village that did very well after the reforms, so much so that welfare benefits for village members include loans for housing upgrade, pension supplements and yearly banquets and gifts for the aged (Li and Smart 2012). By safeguarding their rural *hukou* status, the village remains an autonomous administrative unit with the authority to collect and redistribute collective income and resources. If the village accepted the *hukou* "upgrade", the collective income and resources would automatically be controlled by the municipality, and entitlements tied to local citizenship as defined by the village would be lost. In this instance, local citizenship is a process of exclusion of others in an effort to safeguard the entitlement of selected individuals.

Most active resistance to *hukou* conversion takes place in highly developed coastal areas, urban villages, and suburban areas of big and medium cities. These rural sites tend to be economically developed with public infrastructure and services comparable to those available in cities. A crucial issue central to the emergence of active resistance to *hukou* reform in some rural communities in highly developed areas has to do with land use and its direct benefits to its users or owners. Many local governments initiate *hukou* reform to acquire land for urban and industrial/commercial development. The Economic Information Center of Sichuan Province notes that the idea of *hukou* reform is to "exchange land for social security and turn farmers into city residents" (*yi tu di huan she bao, bian nong min wei shi min*). Urban residents have social security but not land; farmers have land but not social security. Critics of these policies say that farmers should turn in their land to become city residents; otherwise they will become super-citizens who have both land and social security, which is unfair to city residents (Sichuansheng jingji xinxi zhongxin ketizu [The Economic Information Study Group of Sichuan Province] 2007: 28).

According to Li and Smart (2012), there are many reasons why rural residents resist attempts to convert them to urban status. In contested cases, village collective land has long been capitalized for industrial and rent-seeking uses. Villagers are given "shares" which pay a dividend at the end of each year according to the revenues collected. The local villages have become corporate groups in this process. With urbanization, land prices have risen greatly, and the amount of land dividends received by villagers also go up accordingly. Each rural household is also entitled to receive a building site for housing construction. After conversion, rural residents stand to lose not only the legitimacy of profiting from collective land, but also entitlement to a housing site. With so many vested interests involved, it is less surprising that rural residents resist becoming urban residents. Family planning policy is another important factor that hinders *hukou* reform, since the former one-child policy was less stringently applied in rural areas. Rural residents were already allowed under the policy to have two children (Cooney and Li 1994; Hsu 1985). The criterion of differential fertility as stipulated in the national family planning policy was governed by the parents' *hukou* status. If both husband and wife were of rural *hukou* status and their first child was a girl, they were entitled to bear a second child, a practice known as "one and half" (*yi tai ban*). If one member of a couple had urban *hukou* status, the one-child policy for urban residents applied. Since *hukou* status is directly linked to reproductive opportunities, people who want more than one child paid attention to *hukou* status in their mate choice, so that rural *hukou* status is preferred (Li and Smart 2012). These circumstances combine in some situations to make conversion to urban status undesirable, in contrast to common expectations.

The household registration system is again under scrutiny since a national urbanization plan issued by China's national planning authority was approved by the Chinese Communist Party at its third Plenum in November 2013. The Plenum "admitted that China's dual rural-urban social structure . . . remains a major obstacle to development" and "vowed to accelerate *hukou* reform" (Chan 2014: 4). The plan set a target of 100 million new urban *hukous* in the next six years, which will require increasing registration conversions at a rate of about 50 percent compared with recent years. However, the plan intends to continue the "current practice of easing *hukou* restrictions in towns and small cities, while also extending controls on migration to the big cities" (Chan 2014: 6). While providing more people with urban registration, the plan will also extend the trend explored above towards ever more diverse forms of local citizenship rather than a simple urban/rural dichotomy. Debates going on in various venues raise too many issues relevant to moral economy to be discussed here, from ideas of whether this should only be done in conjunction with the marketization of rural land, to popular ideas of who deserves *hukou* status in the big coastal cities, to the desirability of much more radical moves to erase the divisions and separations in contemporary China (Cho 2013; Mobrand 2015). How these discussions and conflicts work out in practice will only be seen in the years and decades to come.

Concluding comments

Moral economic discourse frequently centers on questions of economic justice (Brandtstädter this volume). Although disagreements and debates about what constitutes economic justice permeate all sectors of policy debates, few issues have greater economic weight than the question of how to deal with the exclusionary characteristics of *hukou*-based local citizenship. To take only one of the main concerns about urbanizing migrant workers, the associated fiscal burden on local governments, estimates of the costs are immense. In Guangdong, "it is estimated that on average it takes 80–120 thousand Chinese yuan to 'citizenize' a migrant worker, and it will cost about 149 billion Chinese yuan to localize 1.5 million migrant workers in Guangzhou City alone" (Zhu 2016: 12). Using these estimates, providing urban *hukous* to 160 million migrant workers would cost 1.8 trillion yuan (Zhu 2016). On top of this, there are suggestions that the rebalancing of the Chinese economy towards domestic consumption rather than exports cannot be achieved without increased income for migrant workers. Similarly, a reduction of the high savings rate and increased consumption is less likely if migrant workers cannot trust in a future safety net of pensions and government-supported health care. Thus, contestation over the economic justice of continuing or reforming the *hukou* system has immense implications for the political economy.

Reforms of the household registration system are difficult because moral economic ideas held by different kinds of actors describe the situations and choices using disparate narratives, predictions and prescriptions. Zhu (2016: 26) found that "when respondents are stimulated to think about economic consequences of migrant inflows, considerations of migrants' impact on the local labor market and public finance" shape urbanites' attitudes toward internal migration. The provision of prompts influenced how they answered, but differences persisted between different kinds of people. Highly skilled urbanites "are more likely than low-skilled urbanites to favor inflows of migrant workers; rich urban natives have stronger anti-migrant sentiments than the poor". His survey questions found that "nonmaterial factors, such as national pride and sympathy for worker strikes and legal rights, have a strong effect on pro-migrant sentiments" (Zhu 2016: 26).

All descriptions and ideas about "what is to be done" are permeated by moral judgements, usually contested ones. As the judgements become public, their character and consequences change. *Hukou* systems constrain and channel people's choices and lives, forming a meshwork (Ingold 2011) of administrative relations that subtly influence every aspect of life, from marital choices to migration, not just whether but most importantly *how*. Ethnographic accounts are particularly useful when they illuminate how people get things done despite the formal rules.

The household registration system divides the Chinese "public" in profound ways, making it impossible to identify a public in any singular sense. Mun Young Cho (2013: 120) describes the paradoxical situation of the partial but unequal integration of migrants into cities as "inclusive exclusion". Even the provision of services to rural migrants can rebound on them negatively, through "dividing the poor", which has the effect that China's "urban poor are not merely excluded from the wider society; they are prompted to voice their grievances not against the state but against other poor people" (Cho 2013: 146–147). Impoverished urbanites and rural migrants

> aggravate their misery by insisting, on one side, that rural migrants 'work like hell and take all the jobs in the city' and, on the other, that urban workers are still 'raised and fed by the state'.
>
> (Cho 2013: 147)

Judging and voicing grievances about the other group of poor people, rather than the government, serves to prevent a public coalition of the poor, and empowers the state.

More generally, just as undocumented international migration creates a population of denizens without rights of citizenship, being resident in a place where you do not have local *hukou* makes you removable, and potentially more controllable. This greatly increases the difficulty and risks of publicly airing one's negative judgements of the state. This situation supports Rawls's "original position" principle: if you didn't know what kind of *hukou* you would be born with, you probably wouldn't vote for such an exclusionary system.

The silencing of people without local *hukou* can be extreme. Jaesok Kim's (2013) ethnography of a Korean run factory in rural Shandong revealed how the managers relied on the village leaders to intimidate the factory's workers, who were mostly migrants from other rural areas. One of the ways in which they did this was through cooperation with gangleaders, widely referred to in China as the "merger of the black and white . . . whereby criminal organizations are allied with local government officials . . . to promote their common illegal interests" (Kim 2013: 178). Kim documents the fear that this created, and how it encouraged exit over voice, facilitating despotic forms of worker control in the factory. What we have tried to demonstrate, however, is that exclusions and divisions generated by the *hukou* system are more complicated than a simple urban/rural dichotomy. Similar logics can divide the (relatively) privileged and the disenfranchised in rural places as well. Reform efforts can produce even more diverse forms of exclusion and division, as the pathways to local citizenship become increasingly varied from one locality to another. Perhaps we will also see a parallel proliferation of how local publics judge and criticize local administration of *hukou*. We can only hope that such local moral economies will interact in progressive rather than exclusionary ways with ongoing national discussions of the overall frameworks that should be in place to produce better forms of urbanization for China's future development.

References

Beitz, Charles R. 1983. Cosmopolitan Ideals and National Sentiment. *The Journal of Philosophy* 80(10), pp. 591–600.

Carens, Joseph H. 1987. Aliens and Citizens: The Case for Open Borders. *The Review of Politics* 49(2), pp. 251–273.

Chan, Kam Wing. 1994. *Cities With Invisible Walls*. Hong Kong: Oxford University Press.

Chan, Kam Wing. 2014. China's Urbanization 2020: A New Blueprint and Direction. *Eurasian Geography and Economics* 1(55.1), pp. 1–9.

Chen, Kang. 2004. Fiscal Centralization and the Form of Corruption in China. *European Journal of Political Economy* 20, pp. 1001–1009.

Cho, Mun Young. 2013. *The Specter of "the People": Urban Poverty in Northeast China*. Ithaca, NY: Cornell University Press.

Cooney, Rosemary Santana and Jiali, Li. 1994. Household Registration Type and Compliance With the "One Child" Policy in China, 1979–1988. *Demography* 31(1), pp. 21–32.

De Herdt, Tom and Olivier de Sardan, Jean-Pierre, eds. 2015. *Real Governance and Practical Norms in Sub-Saharan Africa: The Game of the Rules*. London: Routledge.

Edelman, Marc. 2005. Bringing the Moral Economy Back In . . . to the Study of 21st-Century Transnational Peasant Movements. *American Anthropologist* 107(3), pp. 331–345.

Erie, Matthew. 2016. Sharia, Charity, and Minjian Autonomy in Muslim China: Gift Giving in a Plural World. *American Ethnologist* 43(2), pp. 311–324.

Guo, Zhenglin and Zhou, Daming. 1997. Rural Development and Social Security. In: Gregory E. Guldin, ed. *Farewell to Peasant China: Rural Urbanization and Social Change in the Late Twentieth Century*. Armonk, NY: M.E. Sharpe, pp. 248–261.

Heyman, Josiah M. and Smart, Alan. 1999. States and Illegal Practices: An Overview. In: Josiah M. Heyman, ed. *States and Illegal Practices*. Oxford: Berg, pp. 1–24.

Hsu, Mei-Ling. 1985. Growth and Control of Population in China: The Urban-Rural Contrast. *Annals of the Association of American Geographers* 75(2), 241–257.

Ingold, Tim. 2011. *Being Alive: Essays on Movement, Knowledge and Description*. New York: Routledge.

Kim, Jaesok. 2013. *Chinese Labor in a Korean Factory*. Stanford: Stanford University Press.

Kipnis, Andrew. 2004. Anthropology and the Theorisation of Citizenship. *The Asia Pacific Journal of Anthropology* 5(3), pp. 257–278.

Kipnis, Andrew. 2011. *Governing Educational Desire: Culture, Politics, and Schooling in China*. Chicago: University of Chicago Press.

Li, Cuiling and Smart, Josephine. 2012. Resistance to Becoming Urban: Hukou Politics in a Pearl River Delta Community, China. In: Zai Liang, Steven F. Messner, Cheng Chen and Youqin Huang, eds. *The Emergence of a New Urban China: Insiders' Perspectives*. Lanham, MD: Lexington Books, pp. 61–85.

Lin, George C. S. 2009. *Developing China: Land, Politics and Social Conditions*. London: Routledge.

Merry, Sally Engle. 1992. Anthropology, Law and Transnational Processes. *Annual Reviews in Anthropology* 21, pp. 357–379.

Mobrand, Erik. 2015. Legitimising and Contesting Exclusion: Discussions About Shiminhua in Urban China. *China: An International Journal* 13(2), pp. 108–122.

Moore, Sally Falk. 1978. *Law as Process: An Anthropological Approach*. London: Routledge and Kegan Paul.

O'Brien, Kevin J. and Li, Lianjiang. 2006. *Rightful Resistance in Rural China*. Cambridge: Cambridge University Press.

O'Brien, Kevin J. and Stern, Rachel E. 2009. Introduction: Studying Contention in Contemporary China. In: Kevin O'Brien, ed. *Popular Protest in China*. Cambridge, MA: Harvard University Press, pp. 11–25.

Oi, Jean. 1992. Fiscal Reform and the Economic Foundations of Local State Corporatism in China. *World Politics* 45(1), pp. 99–126.

Osburg, John. 2013. *Anxious Wealth: Money and Morality Among China's New Rich*. Stanford, CA: Stanford University Press.

Sichuansheng jingji xinxi zhongxin ketizu [The Economic Information Study Group of Sichuan Province]. 2007. yi tudi huan shebao, bian nongmin wei shimin [Making the Land Change for Social Security, Transforming the Peasants to Urban Residents]. *Sichuan gaige [Sichuan Reform]* 10, pp. 27–32.

Smart, Alan. 1993. Gifts, Bribes and *guanxi*: A Reconsideration of Bourdieu's Social Capital. *Cultural Anthropology* 8(3), pp. 388–408.

Smart, Alan. 1999. Predatory Rule and Illegal Economic Activities. In: Josiah M. Heyman, ed. *States and Illegal Practices*. Oxford: Berg, pp. 99–128.

Smart, Alan. 2010a. The Strength of Property Rights, Prospects for the Disadvantaged, and Constraints on the Actions of the Politically Powerful in Hong Kong and China. In: Fulong Wu and Chris Webster, eds. *Marginalization in Urban China: Comparative Perspectives*. London: Palgrave Macmillan, pp. 90–111.

Smart, Alan. 2010b. Tactful Criticism in Hong Kong: The Colonial Past and Engaging With the Present. *Current Anthropology* 51(Supplement 2), pp. S321–330.

Smart, Alan and Hsu, Carolyn. 2007. Corruption or Social Capital? Tact and the Performance of *guanxi* in Market Socialist China. In: Monique Nuitjen and Gerhard Anders, eds. *Corruption and the Secret of Law: A Legal Anthropological Perspective*. Aldershot, UK: Ashgate, pp. 167–190.

Smart, Alan and Lin, George C. S. 2007. Local Capitalisms, Local Citizenship and Translocality: Rescaling From Below in the Pearl River Delta Region, China. *International Journal of Urban and Regional Research* 31(2), pp. 280–302.

Smart, Alan and Smart, Josephine. 2001. Local Citizenship: Welfare Reform, Urban/Rural Status, and Exclusion in China. *Environment and Planning A* 33, pp. 1853–1869.

Smart, Alan and Smart, Josephine. 2012. Hong Kong Petty Capitalists Investing in China: Risk Tolerance, Uncertain Investment Environments, Success and Failure In: Gordon Mathews, Gustavo Lins Ribeiro and Carlos Alba Vega, eds. *Globalization From Below: The World's Other Economy*. New York: Routledge, pp. 103–119.

Smart, Alan and Smart, Josephine. 2016. Tangled Up in Food: The Moral Economy of Food Politics in the Transpacific Region. In: Eveline Dürr and Philipp Schorch, eds.

Transpacific Americas: Encounters and Engagements: Between the Americas and the South Pacific. New York: Routledge, pp. 150–166.

Solinger, Dorothy J. 1999. *Contesting Citizenship in Urban China: Peasant Migrants, the State, and the Logic of the Market*. Berkeley: University of California Press.

Sun, Yan. 2004. *Corruption and Market in Contemporary China*. Ithaca, NY: Cornell University Press.

Thompson, Edward Palmer. 1991 [1971]. *Customs in Common: Studies in Traditional Popular Culture*. New York: New Press.

Tsai, Lily Lee. 2002. Cadres, Temple and Lineage Institutions, and Governance in Rural China. *The China Journal* 48, pp. 1–27.

Walzer, Michael. 1994. *Thick and Thin: Moral Argument at Home and Abroad*. Notre Dame, IN: University of Notre Dame Press.

Woodman, K. Sophia. 2011. *Local Citizenship and Socialized Governance: Linking Citizens and the State in Rural and Urban Tianjin, China*. Phd, diss. University of British Columbia, Vancouver, BC.

Woodman, K. Sophia. 2016. Local Politics, Local Citizenship? Socialized Governance in Contemporary China. *The China Quarterly* 226, pp. 342–362.

Yang, Dali. 2004. *Remaking the Chinese Leviathan: Market Transition and the Politics of Governance in China*. Stanford: Stanford University Press.

Zhou, Feizhou. 2009. Creating Wealth: Land Seizure, Local Government, and Farmers. In: Deborah Davis and Feng Wang, eds. *Creating Wealth and Poverty in Postsocialist China*. Stanford: Stanford University Press, pp. 112–125.

Zhu, Boliang. 2016. Public Attitudes Toward Migrant Workers in China (July 16, 2016). *Social Science Research Network*. Online at http://ssrn.com/abstract=2819056, accessed August 22, 2016.

5 Policy documents

Imaginations of the state and the struggle for justice in a Chinese land-losing village

Chi-Pui Cheung

This chapter seeks to spell out the complexity of local articulations of central documentary practices in rural Chinese 'rights defense' (*weiquan*) activities. It describes how in Meicun, a land-losing village in Jiangxi Province in the midst of urban change, 'central policy documents' (*zhongyang zhengce wenjian*) became the basis for social imaginaries of a just state, and relatedly, for critically engaging with local authorities, who seized rural lands for urban and industrial development. During my fieldwork, Meicun villagers often complained to me that the local authorities "failed to comply with central policy rules" (*weifan zhongyang zhengce*), and even "fell foul of law" (*weifa*) when developing rural land. Villagers' evidence for local administrative malpractices were policy documents, promulgated by the central government and circulating in the countryside, which in turn became a basis for judging the situation at hand as both illegal and unjust. Meicun villagers' particular 'documentary practices' raise the question of the relation between the nature of evidence on the one hand, and standards of judgement on the other. As Matthew Engelke has pointed out, anthropological evidence and thus anthropological judgement is shaped by the fact that "the roots of anthropology are grounded in social experience, *not documents*" (2008: S3, emphasis added). Engaging recent work that renders documents a new object of ethnographic study (Riles 2006), contrariwise, this chapter seeks to show that circulating 'policy documents' (*zhengce wenjian*) do not just conjure up evidence for villagers' judgements of what is right or wrong, and just or unjust, but also produce a shared social experience of injustice. Such documentary practices in rural China thereby bring forth rural publics, or carve out a rural public sphere where villagers can both imagine and judge the state.

In contemporary China, new forms of citizenship have emerged from the rise of civic activism (see Perry and Selden 2010, Brandtstädter 2011). Although the nature of this civic activism is open to debate (Perry 2009), the frequent invocation of 'rights defense' (*weiquan*) has become a central theme in the literature on socio-legal activism. *Rightful Resistance in Rural China* (O'Brien and Li 2006) is a major study of rights claims and resistance in the Chinese countryside. It offers an account of Chinese farmers who resist local government politics by invoking government slogans about the 'rule of law' (*fazhi*), by citing concrete laws and policies, and generally by adopting the burgeoning rights-defense discourse in

China in order to point out political wrongdoings and question local officials' political commitments. For this particular strategy of resistance, which strives to remain within state-approved boundaries of contention, O'Brien and Li have coined the term 'rightful resistance', or 'policy-based resistance' (Li and O'Brien 1996). As Chinese resisters pursue strategies that exploit the fragmented, divided structure of the Chinese state at various administrative levels, the authors point to the need for "unpacking the state" (O'Brien and Li 2006: 51) in order to understand contentious politics, and argue for an 'anthropology of the state' that takes heed of theories of the conflict-laden state (e.g., Migdal 2001). 'Rightful resistance', as they show, capitalizes on the contradiction between an ideal image of the state on the one hand and actual practices of governments at different administrative levels on the other.

I here suggest that, moreover, an 'anthropology of the *affective* state' is needed to illustrate the wider struggle for righteousness and justice in rural China that includes, yet also goes beyond 'rightful resistance'. How should this be understood? The affective turn in the social sciences draws attention to the general role of emotions in social life (see Clough and Halley 2007). Warner (2002) in his work on emergent publics, for example, has emphasized the role that emotional responses to public address – beyond rational deliberation – play in the formation of publics. In this chapter, I confine myself to an analysis of how publics come into life, first, as a result of the circulation of policy documents and, second, as part of the political rationalities of the state expressed in affective terms (Stoler 2004), i.e. grounded on the social experience (including affects, shared imaginations of the state and visions of a just society) conjured by policy documents. Documentary practices are "affectively loaded phenomena" (Navaro-Yashin 2007) that help to forge a specific sphere of publicity in which policy documents project an image of the central Chinese state as a 'policy benefactor', planning pro-rural policies. The 'complex causality' of affect (Hart 2007: ix)[1] here means that sentiments (e.g., hope for justice, righteous indignation and a mood of despondency), from which the Chinese state exudes, come to inhabit resisters' struggle for justice or a better society. Emphasizing affect, in other words, implies that Chinese rural resistance is not just driven by a spasm of grievances, or by strategic use of policies for the purpose of rightful resistance. Rather, it is also driven by moral indignations and hopes for a just society; not just by 'reified policy' but by an 'imaginary policy' represented by and in policy documents.

In the following, I use the term 'social imaginary' to refer to publics as stranger-relationalities formed around public addresses in Warner's sense (Warner 2002; also see introduction, this volume), and in addition to refer to a collectively imagined moral order of a society that makes political norms realizable (Taylor 2004: 10). Overarching state policies and their materializations as policy documents set the scene for developing a social imaginary in which the central state appears as a 'benefactor' which not only makes good policies but also renders them *implementable*. Such a social imaginary in some measure constitutes that part of a public which is inseparable from the discourse which addresses it (Warner 2002: 54). In other words, a focus on policy shows that publics are created in a conjunction between state and society; yet while policies create publics attached to the political legitimacy of the state, policy documents also become a basis from where publics come to judge the state.

This chapter, in sum, looks at a specific sphere of public life in the Chinese countryside where circulating policy documents congeal with existing visions of a just society to imagine the state as an ideal policy benefactor that not just promulgates policy plans and regulations but also stands for their translation into practice. It starts by grounding the analysis of Meicun's contentious politics within the context of policy documents that for many rural people exemplify the gap between the ideal and the real state, or between the 'ought' and 'is' of rural politics. In the subsequent sections, I draw on my ethnographic material to explore emotional responses to 'imaginary policies' that result in hopes for justice (and subsequent disillusions) at the center of which stands the central government or central state. Finally, I close this chapter with a brief discussion of the role problems of local policy implementation play in Meicun's land disputes.

Policy documents, land disputes and the politics of 'truth'

Documents, particularly policy documents at issue, serve as a channel by which the state assumes control over citizens and by which it manages citizens' subjectivity. Yet they do not merely generate forms of sociality as instruments of control, but also as vehicles of social imagination (Hull 2012: 260). Rights consciousness has not emerged in a cultural, historical vacuum; nor must it be understood in purely legal terms. Rather it exists in relation to cultural and historical contexts in which civic engagements unfold, shape particular forms of citizenship and nurture particular 'senses of justice' in rural law activists (see Brandtstädter 2011, 2016).[2] Here I would like to bring to the fore a particular context, namely that of the 'paper medium' of policy documents. Policy documents can open up a particular space for civic engagements.

In China's rural contentious politics, it is worth noting that many rural people are engaged in 'paperwork' in their quest for justice. Chinese rural studies (e.g., O'Brien and Li 2006; Yu 2011) have also produced ethnographic material on documentary practices that have a part in forming rural publics. As China steers itself toward rapid urbanization, land is the fulcrum of social disputes in the country (Yu 2005). However, what lies behind collective protests in the countryside is not only the land question itself, but also contested interpretations of policy documents promulgated by the central government. Protesters are often roused to political action by a large difference between an ideal of political practice emerging from national policy documents and the actual practices by local authorities. Contested interpretations of official policy documents between protesters and local authorities become a focal point of heated debates over the legality and legitimacy of local development. The following is a statement by a rural protest leader, taken from Yu's work, himself a leading figure in Chinese rural studies:

> I obtained it [a policy document about reducing rural taxes] during the day but I didn't read it until at night. My wife read it first and then told me that the county government regulations were different from those laid down in the provincial government documents (*wenjian*). . . . After reading it, I have found that there exists such an enormous gap between the Party Center's policies (*dang zhongyang de zhengce*) and what basic-level cadres do.
>
> (quoted in Yu 2011: 68–69, translation mine)

In this particular case, the person who obtained the policy document was a middle-aged man discharged from the army. Being part of the rural elite, he played a leading role in organizing his fellow villagers to collectively protest onerous impositions of taxes and fees by his local government. Central to this role was the circulation of 'central documents' (*xuandu zhongyang wenjian*) (Yu 2011: 69) in the village, 'texts' with which he addressed his fellow villagers as a relevant public and that induced in them a strong sense of injustice (also see O'Brien and Li 2006: 38). Another extract from Yu's work supports this important role that documents play in producing a sense of injustice, and subsequently in raising people to public action:

> When [government officials] came to my house to collect the 'pork tax' (*shengzhu shui*), I was not at home. . . . My mother was in a rush to borrow money. . . . I said that if leaders wanted to collect the 'pork tax', [they] could not do so on a per person basis, and they should produce the respective documents (*wenjian*). I could not pay it without documents. . . . That is how one is being duped. I was furious when I thought that cadres were so corrupt that they tried to deceive peasants! I went on to lodge administrative appeals (*shangfang*) because of this.
>
> (quoted in Yu 2011: 71, translation mine)

In both cases, the concrete matter of dispute were fiscal exactions. Yet, what rural people de facto argued is that local authorities should comply with policy document regulations and produce appropriate documents when collecting taxes. This recourse to policy documents can be read as a rights defense strategy. But, at the same time, such documents in themselves constitute a focal point of rural public life as people come to debate, and pass public judgement on, rural politics in light of these policy documents. In contemporary Chinese political imagination, 'central policy' (*zhongyang zhengce*) physically manifests itself in what is generally called 'documents' (*wenjian*), a term that embraces all authoritative pronouncements (O'Brien and Li 2006: 5). Policy documents are thus materializations of state power and suffused with state authority. On the one hand, these items of state power are used to legitimize rural people's (policy-based or rightful) resistance. On the other hand, scholars working on rightful resistance have often overlooked how documents – similar to other images of power – may be part and parcel of the "construction and expression of the social imaginaries of modernity" (Kapferer 2012: 8). Policy documents, albeit representative of state power, thus can be 'bent' in popular politics to buttress a particular social imaginary of a well-governed, prospering (or 'developed') rural society, where the obligations of good citizens and the duties of responsible government match each other. To realize such a 'just' society is the ultimate aim of many acts of resistance in China – a reason to "fight to the end", in the words of this Chinese farmer called Hong:

> I [Hong] participated in lodging appeals (*shangfang*), because I saw something bad happening in rural areas. . . . Policies laid down in central and provincial policy documents (*wenjian*) are being ill-implemented locally. . . . Why did I persist in lodging appeals? Primarily because I am a determined person upholding justice. As long as there are central, provincial and municipal government documents (*wenjian*) calling for easing the peasant burden (*nongmin fudan*), I fight them [the local government representatives] to the end.
>
> (quoted in Yu 2011: 76, translation mine)

In modern societies, bureaucratic documents are elements of everyday knowledge formation (cf. Miyazaki 2004). Chinese policy documents do not only represent the authority of the central state, but they are also a materialization of its political 'will'. If we consider how policy documents have come to dominate rural people's social experience in China, it can be argued that they have come to constitute an overarching (political) 'truth'. As a result, their circulation prompts many rural people not just to test local realities against them, but also helps them to obtain the 'truth' about right and wrong in public action. Hong, in the above quote, called himself a "determined person upholding justice" (*zhuchi zhengyi de ren*), struggling to uphold the truth and the political values represented in policy documents. He would "fight to the end" (*douzheng daodi*), as he said, as long as there were such policy documents *existing*. Policy documents appear here as a repository of knowledge about the truth from which to judge the actions of local authorities. One may ask: how is this knowledge verified and turned into evidence? An answer to this question can be found in the rural politics of policy documents.

Disputes over the authenticity of documents, and thus over what constitutes the 'truth' are part and parcel of rural politics and an arena for producing and contesting evidence for administrative malpractice. The Chinese have long captured enduring problems with local policy implementation in an aphorism: "When there are policies from above, there are countermeasures from below" (*shangyou zhengce, xiayou duice*). The second half of the idiom characterizes a rural China where local governments, partaking in the complexity of institutional arrangements, implement central policies only partly or in their own way (Wu 2007; Zhong 2003). 'Local policies' (*tu zhengce*) may thus bend and, at worst, break central policy regulations. To mobilize opposition to such local policies, rural resisters thus typically distribute policy documents (O'Brien and Li 2006: 69) and thereby attempt to produce evidence about government malpractice. Yet the local governments can refute any allegations of malpractice, arguing that the copies of policy documents that rural people have obtained are 'black documents' (*hei wenjian*) or 'fabricated documents' (O'Brien and Li 2006: 85; Yu 2011: 205) and thus contain no political truth. The authenticity of documents may be buried away in bureaucratic discretion and thus become something difficult or impossible for rural resisters to establish. Authentic policy documents are nevertheless something they *yearn for*.

In reality, local governments as 'street-level bureaucracy' (Lipsky 2010) work in a complex institutional environment in a way that allows them to use their own initiative and discretion in navigating through complex local situations and issues. Moreover, policies are implemented in such a way that allow such local policy experiments to produce national policy models which can later be adopted in other provinces (Heilmann 2008). Viewed in this light, the policy process involves messiness and ambiguity in some measure. This, together with the complexities of the institutional framework, adds complications to the working setting of local governments that in some measure need to 'bend the rules' (*biantong*) to fulfill their duties with respect to local development and fiscal growth. In such a situation, a general public excluded from political participation has difficulties identifying the original policy author (cf. Shore and Wright 2011: 10).

Policy documents and the 'murkiness' of local policy processes in China have produced the widespread social imaginary of a 'bifurcated state' (Guo 2001), in which a well-governed, 'white' central state is opposed to a corrupted, 'black' local state. Anthropologists have argued that ordinary ethics in contemporary China involve subtle nuances of moral judgement (Stafford 2013). Yet, when Meicun villagers used central documents to morally judge political action, their judgements reproduced these stark moral oppositions. The state's policy message that reverberates in these judgements is one that links beneficial policies promulgated by the central state with local development, 'justice' (*gongzheng*), and the 'rule of law' (*fazhi*). This is incorporated into Meicun villagers' everyday moral narratives that evaluate whether the state at different levels lives up to popular expectations (Cheung 2015). Such everyday moral narratives about the state involve the speaker in reshaping public opinion, and thus may be seen as having a public-making capacity. This public-making capacity also includes their 'rights defense' (*weiquan*) activities or forms of public action directed both at local authorities and as appeals to the central state. As I will show below, when Meicun villagers suffered injustices at the hands of local authorities and tried hard to resolve land disputes, they resorted to rights defense not only to defend their rightful interests, but also to rouse local publics and act righteously in the light of the state's policy messages.

Fact and fiction: contested interpretations of policy documents and senses of injustice

In Meicun, land conflicts between villagers and local authorities that involved divergent interpretations of policy documents often crossed the line between fact and fiction when referring to rural development. A reason for this might also be found in the illegibility of spatial development projects for many rural and urban dwellers. Urbanization studies have argued that the ideal image of a city must be 'legible' enough for city dwellers to identify the spatial meanings of the city (Lynch 1988). The urban image projected in Meicun, in contrast, was for its residents suffused with 'blackness' or 'illegality'. Based on their experience of local land requisition, which in turn was shaped by their interpretation of policy messages and documents, Meicun villagers came to perceive of local authorities as a 'black society' (*hei shehui*) using illegitimate or even illegal practices to develop rural land. In contrast, local authorities claimed to act in the name of local development and public interest – to them the 'real message' of policy documents. Contestations between villagers and local authorities over rural policies arose typically in grey areas where 'informal practices' by local authorities could indeed lubricate economic development, but at the immediate expense of local households. Also the fine line remaining between a bending of rules and the breaking of the law effectively contributed to the 'black' image of the local state.

The fact that local governments adopt 'informal strategies' in the process of rural development might induce us to perceive them as predatory actors. Yet they are better understood as agents of a 'developmental state' who act in the context of the 'developmental politics' (*kaifa zhengzhixue*) (Wu 2007: 62). Relatedly, the intensification of land conflicts in China since the 2000s could induce us to see them as a new phenomenon. It is de facto the persistence of the financial crisis of the local state in the 1990s that is fuelling them; in other words, when considering their underlying causes, the disputes should be viewed as "old wine in a new bottle". However, arguments brought forth in land conflicts hardly reflect the very real institutional constraints of rural development policies in China. Rather, they supplement 'policy facts' with 'policy fiction' to produce evidence for the moral judgement of political practice (and the need to engage in 'rightful resistance'). As social imaginaries are fuelled by the existence of 'authentic documents', the possibility to locate such documents further intensifies hopes of identifying that which is rightful and truthful through documents (cf. Miyazaki 2004: 47) as well as hopes that struggles of ordinary people against injustices will in the end succeed. The story of Meicun's urban development and resulting land conflicts well exemplifies these processes that have come to shape land conflicts in many areas of contemporary China.

Meicun falls under the administration of Fengmei, an urban district government, which tried in the late 1990s to restore momentum to the local economy by the requisition of local lands. The 1990s constituted a watershed in China's urban development program. Following Deng Xiaoping's southern tour in 1992 that again cranked the country's reforms, a series of institutional changes – such as the use of more market-oriented economic models for local development, the restructuring of state-owned enterprises, the 1994 fiscal reforms that placed responsibility for fiscal growth on local authorities, and so on – were realized. These institutional reforms meant that local governments came to rely heavily on land to attract investors in the face of stiff peer competition (see Tao 2011).

For the same reasons, Fengmei started to use rural lands for urban and industrial development. The district government set up a new urban development zone in and around Meicun, with the effect that much of Meicun's and the surrounding villages' rural land disappeared under concrete. Regardless of whether this particular local development project was properly executed or not, in the new institutional environment the requisition of rural lands for new developmental zones meant to do the 'right thing' for Chinese street-level bureaucrats. In jumping on the property development bandwagon like many local governments in China, Fengmei followed the officially sanctioned 'land enclosure movement' (*quandi yundong*), which has allowed the local state to administratively seize, and not just to economically privatize, rural lands in the name of public interest. Yet, in this process, local governments often came to view peasant households as a drag on urban development, particularly when they were asking for more compensation (Cao 2005: 83). Urban development can in principle further the public good. Constituting a form of 'land-based finance' (*tudi caizheng*) of local development, land development alleviates a financial situation shaped by local governments' chronic shortage of tax revenues and raises the necessary finances for urban construction. Nonetheless, the situation becomes at least 'complex' when street-level bureaucrats use discretion in the execution of their administrative work.

What if local governments would not push new developmental plans? This is the question Wu Yi (2007: 44) asked in his seminal work on Chinese rural politics. Fiscal growth provides a crucial measure for the success of Chinese street-level bureaucratic work. Like local governments across the country, Fengmei's local authorities felt impelled to develop land to avert a fiscal crisis, thus setting up the developmental zone that breathed new life into an ailing local economy. In 2000, the majority of Fengmei's fiscal revenues (up to 80%) came from coal-mining and relevant industries (Zhang 2006: 77). In the late 1990s, the central government had executed a crackdown on unlicensed coal mines that badly hit Fengmei's fiscal income. Even so, Fengmei managed to bump up fiscal revenues and thus avert the fiscal crisis by promoting urban development, particularly property development (Liu and Zhang 2000). In recent times, land has acted as a magnet for local states consolidating their territorial power in the face of fiscal and administrative decentralization (Hsing 2006: 576). Despite the fact that the central government has placed stricter limits on land development, local states are so keen that they still develop land *and* sometimes use informal practices to do so.

'Illegitimate', or in some sense 'extralegal', ways were used in the process of Fengmei's local authorities that carried out land clearances involving land expropriation and the demolition of houses to establish the developmental zone. As these ways of developing rural land did not correspond with the ideal 'white' image of the Chinese state (as righteous, just, responsible and so on), they reproduced the notion of the 'bifurcated' Chinese state on the local level (Guo 2001). As we will see in the last section, the 'white' ideal of the state that came to manifest itself in policy documents and narratives both shaped rural people's struggle for justice, and kept their hopes to ultimately achieve justice alive throughout this process.

As I pointed out above, Meicun villagers such as Xu Jie perceived the local state to be like a 'black society' (*he shehui*) or 'triad'. In her forties, Xu Jie had been relocated to a resettlement community that accommodated Meicun villagers and others from adjacent villages who had been affected by urban development. Like other villagers, she had developed a deep sense of injustice when her house was demolished. Xu Jie was especially enraged that local authorities were trying to reduce compensation costs by calculating compensation rates based on an outdated policy document – as Xu Jie said, on the "1991 version of a government policy document". Xu Jie explained to me that the compensation rate for housing demolition in the old version of the policy document was lower than that stated in the more recent, updated version. Xu Jie and other villagers had eventually unearthed the latest version of the same policy document, and based their resistance to Fengmei cadres' policy interpretation on this version. However, as the key agents of producing bureaucratic knowledge, local cadres hold powers of privilege when determining the 'authenticity' or applicability of policy documents. Accordingly, Fengmei's local government officials denied the villagers' claim that only the most recent policy document was 'authentic' and therefore applicable.

This case resembles another I encountered in 2014, when my colleague and I conducted pilot field research on 'policy remaking' at the local levels in northwestern China's Ningxia Province. During the fieldtrip, we visited a household in a *Hui* or Chinese Muslim resettlement community. The community was designed to accommodate displaced *Hui* and other residents whose original villages had given way to an industrial park established in the early 2000s. Lan, a female head of household in this community, harboured a grievance against the local authorities for having expropriated her land in what she regarded to be an improper or unjust way. More than ten years later, her grievances had not faded away. These derived from the fact that before establishing the industrial park, the local authorities had introduced a new policy that encouraged local residents to reclaim wasteland for agricultural production. Later, however, under new local leadership, reclaimed land was expropriated for the industrial park. At this time, Lan's rights to her reclaimed lands had not yet been officially established, with the result that she could not receive any compensation when local authorities seized the land for industrial development. That was such a great injustice to her, as she had not "illegally reclaimed land" and the land had been under the plough for years. To her, she thus should have been awarded government compensation in accordance with relevant policy documents. Effectively, one government official had told Lan that disputes went unresolved, as incoming new governments with their own new policies on local development were unwilling to solve problems arising from the previous leadership's policymaking. The dispute between Lan and the township government thus stayed unresolved due to fast-changing policies on local development, following short terms or the rotation of leaderships.

'Interpretive policy analysis' (Yanow 1996) has furthered our understanding of how policymaking is expressive of meanings, including values, beliefs and feelings; policies are representations (and thus interventions) interlaced with the constitution of social life. Yet it cannot ignore that policy is interpreted in such a political way that the lapse of time between policies introduced under different leaderships breaks the continuity of previous policies, and so disguises the authenticity of policy documents. The examples provided above have demonstrated that policy involves interpretations that can itself be contested over time. Despite the fact that the local authorities do interpret policy in their own terms, rural people regard state policies as authoritative pronouncements that the local authorities are politically and morally supposed to obey.

In Meicun there was a so-called 'nail household' (*dingzi hu*) – a popular term for households who refuse to give up their homes and thus to make way for urban development. Mr. Xu and Mrs. Xu, the elderly couple representing the nail household, told me that the local authorities had enlisted thugs to break anything breakable in their house, and to threaten hurting their grandson. The area around their house had already been levelled for pending construction work. Yet the Xus insisted on remaining in their home. As they told me, they were not prepared to vacate their house before being granted a higher amount of monetary compensation. Monetary compensations are today a key issue in nationwide land disputes. However, the main point in this dispute was the Xus' belief that local authorities had failed to comply with a relevant policy document concerning the on-site replacement of demolished housing. As the Xus saw it, it behooved the local authorities to uphold policy regulations laid down in policy documents, and in their case particularly the one stipulating on-site replacement. Yet the whereabouts or the relevance of this document remained mysterious. "We had our own way to procure it", Mrs. Xu answered when I asked her, but also failed to produce it. No other villagers affected by urban development mentioned this policy document during fieldwork. It later became clear that this particular policy was implemented elsewhere in Fengmei, and not by Meicun authorities. At the beginning of their negotiation with the township government, they vociferously demanded on-site replacement as stipulated in this document. Later on, however, they had to soften their stance vis-à-vis local authorities and face the fact that on-site replacement would never materialize. This did not mean that the Xus dropped their fundamental belief in the 'truth' of documents. Instead, Mrs. Xu remained convinced that local authorities were duty-bound to follow 'documents', i.e. policy rules.

The above three cases of rural document practices and land disputes point to a number of ways that senses of injustice are formed in the context of policy and policy documents. In contemporary China, relations between local people and local authorities are typically shaped by mistrust (see Li 2004). In the first case, villagers harboured doubts about the version of the policy document the local government had used for calculating compensation fees. Their sense of injustice was aroused not merely by the factual 'authenticity' of the policy document, but also by the way the local authorities had bent the 'truth' of central policies and hid a more updated version of the document. In the case of land disputes in Ningxia, what in contrast aroused a sense of injustice in Lan was that the 'whole truth' about the policy on reclaimed wasteland was disapproved by local authorities. Here, it appeared as if the shift in leadership had rendered a former policy 'non-existent'. Yet this – then – 'non-existent policy' only intensified her strife to defend her rights. This again was similar to the case of the 'nail household', where the Xus' anger over the failure of local government officials to provide on-site housing replacement actually related to a non-existent policy, at least when it came to Meicun. To give their claim more political weight, the Xus appropriated the political narrative of the central government pushing 'the rule of law' (*fazhi*) in China, and blamed the local government for not carrying out central policies. Their yearning for a county governed according to written laws and central policy regulations was certainly reinforced by the threats the family had faced from local thugs. As Mr. Xu said to me on many occasions, "local governments must follow policies in their work" and "the country will be finished if laws are not put into effect".

Hope and disillusion: "going to Beijing" (*qu Beijing*)

In Chinese policymaking, there is one model for setting policy agendas in which ordinary citizens participate, namely the 'popular-pressure model' (Wang 2008), where public opinion has a part in shaping the policy process. I have documented above how central policies and their materializations in the form of documents constitute a rallying point for villagers to judge, talk about and even reject local authorities. Yet public opinions and moral judgements place pressure not only on the policy process, but also on local authorities to closely follow and act upon policy documents and agendas coming from the central government. The circulation of policy documents in rural China thus helps to bring about new publics – it helps to shape moral sentiments and shared senses of injustice in a given locale, and it informs public judgements that rural people pass on local governments, their representatives and policies. It is also evocative of the affective Chinese state as one that upholds justice and rolls out 'good policies'. This imagery of the state, represented in policies that project good governance, comes to shape social imaginaries that guide Meicun villagers both in their *local pursuit* of justice and their *translocal hope* for justice. I will now turn to the latter to show how villagers turned to the central government for support in their struggle against local authorities, and how this experience was a source of both hope and disillusion.

As pointed out above, local authorities in Meicun were perceived to be 'bad' or 'black' because they did not comply with central policy regulations. In the same vein, some villagers felt compelled to take legal action against Meicun's 'black' authorities. However, for ordinary Chinese citizens, suing the local government is an arduous task. The Confucian idea of 'harmony' (*hexie*) encourages Chinese people to seek mediation in disputes rather than file lawsuits against each other (Wall and Blum 1991: 4). Yet contrary to this age-old convention, contemporary Chinese citizens have been empowered by the Administrative Litigation Law (ALL) to seek justice by filing lawsuits against local authorities in cases of administrative malpractice (see O'Brien 2004). Nevertheless, Chinese local courts are often ineffective in settling administrative disputes primarily because judges remain subject to the administrative ranks (Zhang 2006: 149); in other words, there is no judicial independence. Also Chinese lawyers have little inclination to take on cases of administrative litigation (Cai and Yang 2006).

At the time of my fieldwork in Meicun, I was told that several villagers had tried to file lawsuits against the local authorities – cases that had been summarily dismissed by the local court. This then led them to lodge 'capital appeals' (*jingkong*) similar to Chinese petitioners in the Qing Dynasty (Ocko 1988), that is to say to collectively travel to Beijing to 'lodge petitions' (*shangfang*). Before lodging 'capital appeals', Meicun villagers had held a demonstration in protest against land expropriation. They also had complained to different levels of government, from district (*qu*), municipal (*shi*) to provincial (*sheng*), about 'illegal' land expropriation and under-compensation. Yet each level of government had refused to hear their complaints. Having exhausted all other possibilities (i.e. filing lawsuits, collective protests, and local petitions), villagers sought help from the central state as their *last hope* to find justice. As Old Li, together with Old Yan and Old Xu, one of the most active protest leaders in Meicun, told me:

> We went to Beijing to seek a solution to the problem [of land disputes]. We had gone to the town and district governments. The lower-level governments (*xiamian*) brushed aside our appeals, and did not come up with a solution to the problem.

Yet also their trip to Beijing remained unsuccessful. After their return to Meicun, Old Yan told me his thoughts about their capital petition:

> After we came back from Beijing, I ruminated over our capital petition again and again. Our petition was of 'no use at all' (*mei yong*). We met with the people from the 'State Bureau for Letters and Calls' (*Xinfang Ju*) who made a phone call back to the municipal government officials, and asked them to handle our case and to treat us well. Municipal officials promised that they would solve our case. The people from the 'State Bureau for Letters and Calls' then said "you see, your leaders are going to handle your case, so you should go back to your home town."

Also in the case of the Xu 'nail household', the elderly couple systematically linked their local pursuit of justice with translocal hopes for justice. Remaining local typically produced little or no result. As they told me helplessly, they had no choice but to "go to Beijing" (*qu Beijing*). "Going to Beijing" seemed to be the last hope they held out for redressing the injustice they had experienced:

> When the local government does not solve our problem, I [Mrs. Xu] must go to Beijing. When I was in Beijing, I did not cause any trouble. We just turned to the central party committee (*dang zhongyang*) for help.

As shown above, Meicun villagers pinned their hopes on "going to Beijing", i.e. on the central state and the country's age-old petitioning system. And while some villagers like Old Yan became disillusioned in the process, for others like

Mrs. Xu the central government continued to be a beacon of hope. Although she had lodged capital appeals several times, she still hoped against hope that justice would be done as long as she kept going to Beijing. When I was doing fieldwork in Meicun in October 2007, Mrs. Xu left Meicun and made another capital appeal again. She had not told me she would make another attempt to find justice in Beijing. Mr. Xu only said to me: "She will continue going to Beijing until the local authorities solve the problem." For villagers like Mrs. Xu, the state was and remained a 'hope-generating machine' (Nuijten 2003). For villagers like Old Yan it had also become what I call a 'disillusion-generating machine'.

Concluding remarks

Unlike the 1990s, when the Chinese state experienced a decline in state capacity, in the 2000s its institutional structures were better adapted to changing economic conditions (Yang 2004). Ahlers and Schubert (2014: 23) thus paint a bright picture of Chinese local governance in which stricter central regulations, coupled with increasing popular pressure, can prod the local state(s) into engaging in better policy implementation, yielding a greater "procedural and output effectiveness". Nevertheless, as this article has shown, there is still a large gap between these developments and the public perception or judgement of local authorities as 'black', 'bad' or 'corrupt'.

Contrary to the negative image of local authorities, the central state retains a lot of political support on the ground in contemporary China. Overarching state policy and policy documents have produced an image of the central state as a defender of justice and a source of beneficial or 'good' policies, creating bonds of affection. These shaped not only villagers' experiences of injustice when facing the actions of local authorities, but also a sense of righteousness and hope that propelled them forth in their struggles for justice. There is 'procedural effectiveness' of policy implementation in Chinese local governance, yet it was different interpretations of policy documents and their implementation that furthered land disputes in Meicun. To understand these, it has been necessary to look beyond 'reified policy' – a 'thing' utilized by rural people for rightful resistance, as described in the literature on contemporary peasant protests – to include 'imaginary policy', a social imaginary based on a well-governed, just public sphere that has come to be represented by policy documents. Policy is more than rational governance *per se*; it is a vehicle for state imagination and representation and, thus, for intervention from above and below, as we have seen. Policies are what people plan, but planning in itself is more than the exercise of human rationality (Robertson 1984: 1). In effect, policies are "intention, the product of creative human imagination" (Goodin, Rein and Moran 2006: 19). In this chapter I have shown that Meicun villagers did not merely utilize policies to draw on the central state's political leverage for their resistance, but more importantly also the social imaginary or 'imagined policy' reframing the way they reimagined the Chinese state as one that makes policies *implementable*. Viewed in this light, when the Chinese government launches policy campaigns to uphold 'core socialist values' (*shehui zhuyi hexin jiazhi*) – particularly including 'justice' (*gongzheng*) and the 'rule of law' (*fazhi*) – these campaigns are likely to shape the general public's political imagination and their perception of what an ideal society should look like, thereby also shaping emergent publics. The 'complex causality' of affect (Hart 2007: ix), in a word, contributes to a process where the more conscious of citizenship rights the general public becomes, the more seriously the Chinese government will take her policy promises.

Acknowledgements

Early versions of this chapter were presented at the conference 'Material Asia: Objects, Technologies and Rethinking Success', Jeonju, Korea, 1–5 August 2011, organized by SEAA, AAA, and The Korean Society for Cultural Anthropology, and at the workshop 'Justice, Popular Politics and the Chinese State', Oslo, Norway, 27–28 June 2012, organized by the Department of Social Anthropology at the University of Oslo. I am grateful for all the comments the participants made on these occasions. Special thanks also go to Susanne Brandtstädter, who invited me to join the workshop. The research for this paper was partly supported by the Humanities and Social Sciences Research Grant Programs of the Ministry of Education of China for Early Career Scholars (the research project '*guanyu Zhongguo binzang zhengce de renleixue yanjiu*', No. 15YJC850025).

Notes

1 The affective turn calls for an epistemological shift when talking about causality – first, for a new synthesis between body and mind, and passions and reasons, and second, for a more complex view of causality itself: "[A]ffects belong simultaneously to both sides of the causal relationship. They illuminate, in other words, both our power to affect the world around us and our power to be effected by it, along with the relationship between both these powers" (Hart 2007: ix).

2 Brandtstädter (2011, 2016) locates rural legal activism within a broad context of social change from socialist China to a neosocialist one. In such a radical social transformation, there is a growing segment of the population that is discontent with the situation or with 'society' (*buman shehui renshi*), which includes, but goes far beyond, rural law activists. How this segment organizes itself and which public action it pursues are closely associated with the Maoist inheritance and political movements in that period (see Brandtstädter 2016). Yet equally pertinent here is the historical 'laxness' of policy implementation or the amount of discretion used by local authorities (e.g., in the 1980s crackdown on rampant crime [*yanda*] that involved many unjustified arrests).

References

Ahlers, Anna L. and Schubert, Gunter. 2014. Effective Policy Implementation in China's Local State. *Modern China* 41(4), pp. 372–405.

Brandtstädter, Susanne. 2011. The Law Cuts Both Ways: Rural Legal Activism and Citizenship Struggles in Neosocialist China. *Economy and Society* 40(2), pp. 266–288.

Brandtstädter, Susanne. 2016. The Rebel as Trickster and the Ironies of Resisting in Rural China. In: Hans Steinmüller and Susanne Brandtstädter, eds. *Irony, Cynicism and the Chinese State*. London: Routledge, pp. 122–137.

Cai, Yongshun and Yang, Songcai. 2006. State Power and Unbalanced Legal Development in China. In: Zhao Suisheng, ed. *Debating Political Reform in China: Rule of Law vs. Democratization*. Armonk, NY: M. E. Sharpe, pp. 164–179.

Cao, Yu. 2005. Quanmian Tuijin Pingxian Xiandaihua Xinjincheng (Making Pingxiang's New Modernization Progress). In: Chen Anzhong, and Kuang Xiaoping, eds. *Pingxiang Shi Jinzhongqi Jingji Shehui Fazhan Zhanlue Yanjiu (A Study of the City of Pingxiang's Economic and Social Developmental Strategies in the Mid- and Short-Term)*. Pingxiang: Pingxiang Shiwei, pp. 79–84.

Cheung, Chi Pui. 2015. Moral Narratives of State Policy: Urban Development in Meicun, China. *Critique of Anthropology* 35(4), pp. 351–372.

Clough, Patricia Ticineto and Halley, Jean, eds. 2007. *The Affective Turn: Theorizing the Social*. Durham, NC: Duke University Press.

Engelke, Matthew. 2008. The Objects of Evidence. *Journal of the Royal Anthropological Institute* 14 (issue supplement S1), pp. S1–S21.

Goodin, Robert E., Rein, Martin and Moran, Michael. 2006. The Public and Its Policies. In: Michael Moran, Martin Rein and Robert E. Goodin, eds. *The Oxford Handbook of Public Policy*. Oxford: Oxford University Press, pp. 3–35.

Guo, Xiaolin. 2001. Land Expropriation and Rural Conflicts in China. *The China Quarterly* 166, pp. 422–439.

Hart, Michael. 2007. Foreword: What Affects Are Good For. In: Patricia Ticineto Clough and Jean Halley, eds. *The Affective Turn: Theorizing the Social*. Durham, NC: Duke University Press, pp. ix–xiii.

Heilmann, Sebastian. 2008. From Local Experiments to National Policy: The Origins of China's Distinctive Policy Process. *The China Journal* 59, pp. 1–30.

Hsing, You-tien. 2006. Land and Territorial Politics in Urban China. *The China Quarterly* 187, pp. 575–591.

Hull, Matthew S. 2012. Documents and Bureaucracy. *Annual Review of Anthropology* 41, pp. 251–267.

Kapferer, Judith. 2012. Introduction: Images of Power and the Power of Images. In: Judith Kapferer, ed. *Images of Power and the Power of Images: Control, Ownership, and Public Space*. New York and London: Berghahn Books, pp. 1–8.

Li, Lianjiang. 2004. Political Trust in Rural China. *Modern China* 30(2), pp. 228–258.

Li, Lianjiang and O'Brien, Kevin J. 1996. Villagers and Popular Resistance in Contemporary China. *Modern China* 22(1), pp. 28–61.

Lipsky, Michael. 2010. *Street Level Bureaucracy: Dilemmas of the Individual in Public Service* (2nd revised edition). New York: Russell Sage Foundation.

Liu, Changwei and Zhang, Zengyou. 2000. Anyuanqu fahui youshi tuixing dichanxingqu (Anyuan District Takes Advantage of Property Development). *Pingxiang Daily*, July 25, p. 1.

Lynch, Kevin. 1988. *The Image of the City*. Cambridge, MA: MIT Press.

Migdal, Joel S. 2001. *State in Society: Studying How States and Societies Transform and Constitute One Another*. Cambridge: Cambridge University Press.

Miyazaki, Hirokazu. 2004. *The Method of Hope: Anthropology, Philosophy, and Fijian Knowledge*. Stanford, CA: Stanford University Press.

Navaro-Yashin, Yael. 2007. Make-Believe Papers, Legal Forms and the Counterfeit: Affective Interactions Between Documents and People in Britain and Cyprus. *Anthropological Theory* 7, pp. 79–98.

Nuijten, Monique. 2003. *Power, Community and the State: The Political Anthropology of Organization in Mexico*. London: Pluto Press.

O'Brien, Kevin J. 2004. Suing the Local State: Administrative Litigation in Rural China. *The China Journal* 51, pp. 75–96.

O'Brien, Kevin J. and Li, Lianjiang. 2006. *Rightful Resistance in Rural China*. Cambridge: Cambridge University Press.

Ocko, Jonathan K. 1988. I'll Take It All the Way to Beijing: Capital Appeals in the Qing. *The Journal of Asian Studies* 47(2), pp. 291–315.

Perry, Elizabeth J. 2009. A New Rights Consciousness? *Journal of Democracy* 20(3), pp. 17–20.

Perry, Elizabeth J. and Selden, Mark, ed. 2010. *Chinese Society: Change, Conflict and Resistance* (3rd revised edition). London: Routledge.

Riles, Annelise, ed. 2006. *Documents: Artifacts of Modern Knowledge*. Ann Arbor: University of Michigan Press.

Robertson, Alexander Foster. 1984. *People and the State: An Anthropology of Planned Development*. Cambridge: Cambridge University Press.

Shore, Cris and Wright, Susan. 2011. Conceptualising Policy: Technologies of Governance and the Politics of Visibility. In: Cris Shore, Susan Wright and Davide Però, eds. *Policy Worlds: Anthropology and Analysis of Contemporary Power*. New York: Berghahn Books, pp. 1–25.

Stafford, Charles, ed. 2013. *Ordinary Ethnics in China*. London: Bloomsbury.

Stoler, Ann Laura. 2004. Affective States. In: David Nugent and Joan Vincent, eds. *A Companion to the Anthropology of Politics*. Malden, MA: Blackwell Publishing, pp. 4–20.

Tao, Ran. 2011. *Zhongguo Dangqian Zengzhang Fangshixia de Chengshihua Moshi yu Tudi Zhidu Gaige – Dianxingshishi, Zhuyaotiaozhan yu Zhengcetupo (Urbanization and Land Reform under China's Current Growth Model: Facts, Challenges and Directions for Future Reform)*. Brookings-Tsinghua Center for Public Policy Working Paper Series, Washington, DC and Beijing, China.

Taylor, Charles. 2004. *Modern Social Imaginaries*. Durham, NC: Duke University Press.

Wall, James A. and Blum, Michael. 1991. Community Mediation in the People's Republic of China. *Journal of Conflict Resolution* 35(1), pp. 3–20.

Wang, Shaoguang. 2008. Changing Models of China's Policy Agenda Setting. *Modern China* 43(1), pp. 56–87.

Warner, Michael. 2002. Publics and Counterpublics. *Public Culture* 14(1), pp. 49–90.

Wu, Yi. 2007. *Xiaozhen Xuanxiao: Yige Xiangzhen Zhengzhi Yunzuo de Yanyi yu Chanshi (The Tumult of Little Town: An Account and Interpretation of a Township's Politics)*. Beijing: Shenghuo Dushu Xinzhi Sanlian Shudian.

Yang, Dali L. 2004. *Remaking the Chinese Leviathan: Market Transition and the Politics of Governance in China*. Stanford, CA: Stanford University Press.

Yanow, Dvora. 1996. *How Does Policy Mean? Interpreting Policy and Organizational Actions*. Washington, DC: Georgetown University Press.

Yu, Jianrong. 2005. Tudi Wenti Yichengwei Nongmin Weiquan Kangzheng de Jiaodian: Guanyu Dangqian Woguo Nongcun Shehui Xingshi de Yixiang Zhuanti Diaoyan (Land Problems as the Focus of Farmers' Struggles for Rights Defense: A Study of Rural Conditions in Contemporary Chinese Society). *Diaoyan Shijie* 3, pp. 22–23.

Yu, Jianrong. 2011. *Kangzhengxing Zhengzhi: Zhongguo Zhengzhi Shehuixue Jiben Wenti (Contentious Politics: Fundamental Issues in Chinese Political Sociology)*. Beijing: Renmin Chubanshe.

Zhang, Qianfan. 2006. The People's Court in Transition: The Prospects for Chinese Judicial Reform. In: Zhao Suisheng, ed. *Debating Political Reform in China: Rule of Law vs. Democratization*. Armonk, NY: M.E. Sharpe, pp. 138–163.

Zhang, Youchang. 2006. Pingxiang Shi Anyuan Qu: Jingji Zhuanxing Fazhan Gei Zhongbu Diqu de Qishi (Pingxiang's Anyuan District: The Inspiration of Anyuan's Economic Transformation for Central Regions). *Zhongguo Keji Touzi* 7, pp. 77–78.

Zhong, Yang. 2003. *Local Government and Politics in China: Challenges From Below*. Armonk, NY: M.E. Sharpe.

6 Fighting for one's life

The making and unmaking of public goods in the Yunnanese countryside

Andrea E. Pia

As discussed in different other chapters in this volume, in today's China, state-sanctioned discourses of justice, fairness and desert (legal rights included) are often appropriated and recombined by political activists as well as ordinary citizens in more or less organised forms of struggle to express disgruntlement and dissent towards power. With this chapter, I make the further effort of analysing instances of failed appropriation of such discourses or of their positive disavowal. Basing my discussion on long-term fieldwork conducted in Yancong, a rural, destitute township of north-east Yunnan,[1] I will explore one of the ways in which Chinese citizens are commonly made aware of the limited and uncertain efficacy of appealing to state-sanctioned discourses, and in particular to legal rights, to gain access to local resources. The chapter will argue that the course of actions taken in response to that awareness enables alternative regimes of public goods, premised on the notion of popular participation in their production, and give way to progressive demands of support from the state. In doing so, Yunnanese villagers give shape to an alternative form of social contract, one rooted in past ideas of consensual management and dependency from authority but which has now been effectively marginalised by the state's strategic recourse to the discourse of rights to regulate and also limit the growing demands of its most neglected subjects.

To support this argument, the chapter draws from Susanne Brandtstädter's introduction and elaborates on the idea of "world-making publics", i.e. a regime of organised or semi-organised politically informed actions that attempts to rewrite codified relations between "self, society and the state". However, my objective here is to ground this notion on the concretely material demands advanced by my research participants. At stake here is not simply the possibility of constituting themselves as a public endowed with a "voice", the capacity to express one's mind in relation to power, but more prosaically the capacity to have a "say" (Pils 2016: 144), that is, the power to determine how locally essential goods ought to be produced and distributed. Thus, this chapter extends and entangles the idea of the public with that of *public goods*. According to my Yunnanese informants, the Chinese legal framework currently in place is de facto making its collective effort of governing and accessing essential resources more strenuous. Moreover, it is inhibiting local residents' capacity to take part in the government and the making of local public goods.

In what follows, I explore both analytically and ethnographically the growing tension between local villagers and state officials in relation to the use and development of local resources, such as land and water. In particular, I focus on the discursive dimension of and pragmatic responses to this tension, showing the diverse political logics underpinning state-imposed development projects and the aspirations, concepts of justice and strategies of legitimation of rural communities in relation to the government of local affairs. In conjuring this tension, an important role is played by the Chinese state codification of access to public goods in terms of 'rights'. The state enjoys "ownership rights" over land and water supply, while the villagers only have "use rights" (Ho 2005; Hu 2006: 78; Pils 2014).[2] In Yancong the government is now inclined to recur to legal arguments and "rights" talk, to justify its own political economic choices regarding essential resources to its citizens. When village land is requisitioned or water services are privatised, local state agents provide legal explanations for such occurrences. If pushed, they will concede that privatisation and requisitioning are indeed pursued in the nation's greater interest (*guojia de liyi*) and are therefore legitimate (*an falü*).

Against this, villagers usually articulate and take on an alternative register to talk about and gain access to land and water. This register hinges upon an understanding of essential resources such as public goods that ought to be consensually (*xieyi*) and responsibly (*fuze*) used and managed (*guanli*), that is, upon prior discussion and agreement with all the parties involved. This latter configuration of public access opposes the argument of rightful management advanced by the state – which formats access as legal title – that of mutual obligation (*yiwu*), a moral force. As the ethnography will show, these mutual obligations extend and include state actors in the everyday making of public goods. The force of obligations is here supposed to compel state agents to first fulfil their roles, that is, taking care of common citizens, and to give them something back if they take decisions that might negatively impact the local community. In bringing to the fore the local strategies of legitimation that north-eastern Yunnanese villagers employ to envision and perform alternative regimes of public goods, this chapter hopes to contribute to recent discussion in anthropology, political science, legal and Chinese studies (Wang, Lee and Fischer 1994; Elyachar 2012; Woodman 2015; Pils 2016) as to how public goods are enclosed, disclosed and more importantly remade under conditions of differential distribution of power, voice, status and wealth.

The first section will set out the theoretical backdrop against which the ethnography in the following part should be cast. Here I will introduce the historical and philosophical backdrop of the repertoire of practices, values and forms of judgement that informs widely supported ways of holding goods in common in present day Yancong and trace their configuration in relation to contemporary theories of public goods. I will then move to clarify this chapter's argument in relation to recent scholarly works on the advent of the "rights age" in China. The second section will move to the ethnography. My stay in Yancong involved long afternoons spent in what I will call the Dong Village Committee's Archive, hand-copying the minutes of numerous disputes. From some of the "requests for hearing" (*shenqing*) found there I will first show the contentiousness of resource management in my field site. Second, I will use substantial excerpts from my field notes to recount the story of how the management of water and land by local officials creates a site for negotiation and establishes expectations of role fulfilment. It is here that the reference to obligations seems to disclose a renewed space for public participation and stands out as effective in securing villagers' interests.

In the final section, I will look at how these expectations break down by telling the story of how legal provisions help delimit the province of villagers' political involvement in the public life of their own community. I will show this through a brief description of the arguments made against land requisitions and the upending of water provisions at the hands of the local state. These will be used to highlight the resentment many felt toward 'rights talk', and common people's support for an engagement with counter-practices of public goods making that is rooted in obligations and responsibility.

Values

Chinese public-making: theories and practices

Chinese culture is enriched by a long-standing tradition of thought regarding the handling and production of public goods. This has at its roots an understanding of individual access to public goods – what we could call a 'right' – as underpinned by the idea of human interdependence. Many scholars have already suggested that the concept of 'rights' in China has developed along its own trajectory, conceptually divergent from that of the West (Angle 2002: 206–207). In relation to access to land, Philip Huang has stressed that the possession of land has always been firmly coupled in China with the obligations one has towards one's household or lineage (Huang 2010: 165). As a consequence, no abstract principle of absolute ownership has ever been consolidated in this moral landscape (Huang 2010: 148). Peerenboom noted that, in the Western tradition, "the essence of a right is that it protects an individual against the interests of others, including, most importantly, the majority" and that, on the contrary, Chinese legal culture understands rights "as contingent interests rather than as moral principles that stand apart from, and cannot be weighed or balanced against" (Peerenboom 1995: 354, 366).

In Confucian thought, these "contingent interests" are premised upon the notion that property relations are social relations entertained by differently positioned individuals who maintain mutual obligations with one another and whose roles come to be actually defined by these very obligations (Ames 2011: 167–168). Thus, under the Confucian ethos, which has profoundly informed Chinese politics and social thought, access to essential resources happens through agreements occurring between interdependent social roles. This means two things: firstly, that before one can claim access, one should first fulfil the obligations one has towards one's social circle, that is, to fulfil one's role. Second, a decision over local public goods cannot be taken unilaterally, as a person's rights over such goods always entail social obligations.

This philosophical point is supported by a great deal of historical evidence. Rowe argues that up to the Qing period the responsibilities for keeping access to land and water available at the local level rested strictly upon local public figures or institutions such as lineages or religious associations (1990: 322). These institutions were organised around the principle of collective participation of household heads in what was a local and de-centralised regime of public governance (Duara 2015: 84). Key here is to notice that when lineages referred to their own pool of common land they called it *gong*, a term later used to translate the Western notion of "public" (Wang, Lee and Fischer 1994: 600; Hua 2009: 36). Tellingly, however, during the early modern period, this regime started to be seen as existing in formal contrast with the central state's intrusive power (*guan*) over local communities and their resources, as well as with self-interested claims to tradable market assets and private accumulation (*si*).

It is with the advent of communist China, though that for the first time *gong* undergoes a process of dislodgement from its spatially bounded, kinship-encircled discursive frame. Chinese socialist thought subsumed *gong* into the Party's all-encompassing space of reference, thus justifying the new government increased level of intrusion in the country's rural society (Day 2013: 938). This was achieved by stigmatising private and lineage-based modes of production as selfish and feudal (Wang, Lee and Fischer 1994: 601), while at the same instigating the adoption of simultaneously deliberative and disciplining mechanisms of self-government in the countryside, like the "mass line" and "speaking bitterness" sessions (*suku*) (Lin 2006: 143–144). In this respect, the most profound legacy of Maoism is its ambivalent representation of public interest: something in which all socialist citizens were expected to partake but the attainment of which was ultimately considered only within the Party's reach.

In concluding this section, I wish to tie my historical detour to this volume's introduction in with broader discussions in anthropology and cognate disciplines as to the modality by which publics and public goods are symbolically and materially constituted and given purpose. While building on the notion of publics as "virtual entities" constituted by their "members' attention" and the "reflexive circulation of discourses" this attention gives rise to (Warner 2002: 419–420), the Chinese ethnography presented here compels us to shift the focus away from publics' dependency on intersubjective reasoning (Habermas 1981) or their potential for facilitating mutual recognition of intent, affects and identity among their members (Elyachar 2012: 120–121). Rather, here I focus on the political techniques through which a specific way of life acquires self-consciousness by going public and establishes the conditions for its own survival (see Hirschkind 2001: 5).

In today's rural Yunnan, these public-making techniques ensue from past collective experiences of self-rule and are oriented towards the installation of utopian forms of social contracts (Bear and Mathur 2015: 18–20) through the pragmatic project of maintaining distributed input into the management of local livelihood. "Goods" stand here as a way of translating what my informants called *minsheng* (lit. the people's livelihoods) or borrowing from Mao's terminology *shengmingxian* (lifeline), a shorthand to describe regimes of access to essential resources based on the individual and collective responsibility of their reproduction. However, and crucially to the ethnography that follows, when such regimes fail for whatever reason, it is still down to the Party, the state and its agents – those whom the philosophy and practices of Chinese public goods making long identified as the ultimate arbiters of the country's welfare – to fulfil their obligations of support towards their subjects.

Right-bearing vs. life-bearing subjects

In Yancong, Chinese citizens are actively resisting legally coated dispossession by articulating an alternative figuration of public goods. As such, this argument problematises recent attempts in political sciences and anthropology at gauging the extent to which the Western concept of the "rights-bearing subject" is entering Chinese society and winning its citizens' hearts and minds (Gallagher 2006; O'Brien and Li 2006; Perry 2008, 2009; Li 2009; Cai 2010; Woo and Gallagher 2011). Here I will briefly summarise two aspects of this debate that are germane to this chapter. First, in O'Brien and Li's account of collective resistance in rural China, the authors propose that the many cases of outright resistance towards local governments happening throughout rural China signal the willingness of Chinese citizens to fight for their "rights". This is usually taken by much of the scholarship following O'Brien and Li (Chan and Pun 2009; Cai 2010; Chen 2013) to mean that Chinese citizens are starting to take rights seriously, meaning that they are beginning to conceptualise themselves as subjects whose rights should not be infringed by an external authority.

However, my findings show a more complicated picture. In this chapter, I show that in Yancong, local villagers maintain an active distrust of legal rights. In particular, villagers are suspicious of the official discourse of "use rights" and the state's right to lawful requisition in favour of top-down development. For one thing, it is the state that is actively exploiting the "rights" rhetoric to pursue a unilateral agenda of rural development, one that is not immediately beneficial to or discussed with the local communities, and to shirk responsibilities when the fallouts of development have to be allocated. Rather, Yancong villagers try to oppose and circumvent the right-based dispossession practised by the state by appealing to an alternative, specific way of referring to and performing public goods. The management of land and water – the "people's livelihood" – establishes obligations among people. One cannot simply decide by oneself what should be done with essential resources; one ought to discuss with others what to do with them. Local state actors have to be part of this discussion and should be accountable for their unilateral choices.

Second, the mainstream narrative about the introduction of a 'rights' discourse into Chinese society holds that this can provide an effective tool – a 'language' as it were – for bottom-up reclamations of greater individual and political latitude. According to this view, the "innovative use of laws, policies, and other officially promoted values to defy disloyal political and economic elites" (O'Brien and Li

2006: 2) is a strategy now largely adopted in China to reclaim citizens' freedom in the face of an authoritarian government. While not disproving this position, in this chapter I show that opposition towards the government could also be staged in a discursive register different from that of 'rights'. This form of opposition belongs to "the official discourse of deference" (Scott 1990: 101) towards authority and it is largely supportive of an idea of society based on differentially positioned and privileged roles, e.g. not ideologically against the idea of ultimate ownership vested in the state (see Perry 2008: 24–25). In this way, my Yunnanese interlocutors can be seen not to be simply fighting for their "rights", but rather for their "life" – a particular and morally valued way of producing and allocating essential resources.

Practice

The un-making of public goods in Yancong

One day in December 2011, I was crossing some paddy fields positioned alongside Yancong Township's main thoroughfare in north-east Yunnan Province. These fields were covered with a suspiciously iridescent slick, resembling petrol. The sprouting rice plants were rotting beneath it. Suddenly a man, who was walking confidently over a narrow ridge separating two different plots of land, started pointing at me in apparent anger. Getting closer, he bombarded me with questions, his tongue a fast-cadenced rifle. So overwhelmingly agitated was he, it took a while for him to finally realise I was not a local. He then cautioned me about what was going on in Yancong, how petty developers and the local government had forced the former owners of the now swampy plots to undersell the land to a construction company. "Who did this land belong to?" I asked. "To the *laobaixing*. The land is the people's livelihood (*minsheng*). Farmers work the land and *they* sell it before the rice is even ripe. This is why the fields have been flooded, to make it clear to everyone that land is no longer of value in China, that what farmers do is of interest to no one (*tajia dou wusuowei*)."

That day Mr Liu, the angry farmer, made what to me sounded like a sweeping remark. Yet, to my surprise, the feeling that farmers in Yancong Township were being disenfranchised was widespread. There were many reasons for feeling this way. Land was constantly under attack: drought and monsoon downpours were depriving farmers of precious terraced plots. At the same time, few alternatives to farming were viable for local villagers. While agricultural productivity was reported to be on the rise, gains from the non-agricultural sector were still meagre, representing only 0.9 percent of Dong villagers' annual income, and around 17 percent of the net value of the Township's economy. Large numbers of young people migrating towards Kunming – Yunnan's capital city – meant that the ratio of able workers to land was diminishing. Many farmers reported having plots of land they were no longer able to farm, or that it was no longer convenient to do so, mainly because of their distance or size. And then there was the issue of prolonged droughts.[3] To turn requisitioned land to the construction of emergency water reservoirs was common practice in many surrounding highland communities. The local government estimated a pace of requisition of almost 50 ha per year, if the soaring water demand was to be met. Farmers thus faced losing additional portions of land. Thereby, when not directly displaced and relocated by water security projects, as the literature has documented extensively for China and for its southwest in particular (e.g. Ying and Jun 2000; Jun 2007), farmers around Yancong had their actually workable land allotments reduced to almost nothing.

Besides the struggle of the local agricultural economy and the endangered livelihood of its inhabitants, there was also the issue of land development. An example may illustrate this. Further north of Yancong lies another township called Shuitan. This township is richer than Yancong and the local government, in its commitment to infrastructural development, was trying its very best during the time of fieldwork to complete the ambitious north-eastern passage, a highway linking Yunnan's capital city to Guizhou Province and ultimately the whole province with the hyper-modern coastal regions of eastern China. For such a project to be possible, conversion of agricultural land to other uses was the first, most basic requirement.

However, the restitution of farmland to the village authorities for precisely this type of project is becoming the subject of heated controversies in China (e.g. Yu 2007: 419–517; Pils 2016), because it is often carried out regardless of the former leaser's consent. As said, Chinese farmers do not actually "own" the land they work. Since 1982, the redistribution of land in Yancong has been carried out according to the number of household members. Such a procedure meant that farmers were requested to stipulate a thirty-year lease with their appointed authority (i.e. the various village committees), which remains the "ultimate" owner of local agricultural land (Ho 2001: 396–397). For poorer households, such an agreement could be beneficial, as redistribution is undertaken similarly from one peasant family to the next with land allocation varying according to actual needs. However, the fact that farmers do not actually ever own the requisitioned land does not necessarily lead to easier and less contested land reallocation (see Guo 1999, 2001).

In Shuitan, a woman had allegedly taken her contempt towards the highway project – which caused forced demolitions throughout the community – to the extreme, blowing herself up inside a government office. The event, while not officially acknowledged by the local government, did to a large extent impact the imagination of Yancong's neighbouring farmers. In a private conversation with a group of farmers working at a construction site in Bei Village, I was asked whether I thought such an attempt could coax the government back to reconsider the highway project, perhaps to rethink its original route, this time leaving farmers' precious land alone. Later in the chapter I will return to the public display of contempt towards the government. For now, let me just make the simple point that land and water, according to my research participants, were increasingly becoming resources in dire straits. Scarce, poorly managed and of poor quality, land and water were the cause of some trouble and quarrelling not just when the state was seen encroaching upon them, but also when villagers' competing interests clashed.

What rights cannot do

Quarrels on public goods were objects of many "requests for hearing" filed to the Dong Village Dispute Committee, an administrative village under Yancong's jurisdiction. The data I collected in the dispute archive exposes the amount of contentiousness that access to land and water use foments in the community. Of the forty-eight disputes resolutions documents I collected, spanning a period of six years (2006–2012), eleven (22 percent) involved issues of land, and fifteen (31 percent) were related to water. Of the former, three involved the state encroaching on someone's property; the other eight, boundary and land use disputes between villagers. With this material, I am trying to show two things: that a concern for unmet expectations of role-fulfilment, e.g. unmet obligations on the part of officials, informs ordinary grievances and that villagers complain about being excluded from participating in the public life of their own community.

In one "request of hearing" signed by "all villagers" (*quanti cunmin*) of Wang Family Village and filed to the Committee on 12 January 2007, the applicant demanded the suspension or redirection of a segment of the north-eastern passage highway. After lamenting that the construction works began without any consultations with the locals, the author moves on to a critique of the local party cadres.

> All these works were not agreed upon by us (*dabucheng xieyi*) [. . .] the case was mediated collectively by the local VC [Village Committee], the Township Government and the organ that supervises the reallocation of leased land plots. Compensation has been given out per square metre. All the parties to whom compensation was due have been already paid. Among these, however, there were some who did not get compensation. To those, one of the local VC cadres, whose name I do not dare to reveal here, said that he could not give me the money, that I wanted to go against the public interest (*yao nale chonggong*). The VC subsequently mediated the case with the abovementioned individual. Even if now my personal request has been answered, I wish that the VC comrades now come to our village, redressing all other villagers' cases, asking this unmentionable individual to step forward. I want him to say in front of everyone (*dangren dangzhong*), in the light of day (*zhengda guangming*), how things really went. He has to say that we deserved what we got and that we did not get anything more than that. I call this "when a noble man loves wealth he/she has a noble way of obtaining it, when a small man loves it, he/she resorts to tyranny" (*junzi aicai quzhi youdao; xiaoren aicai hengxing badao*).

In one case mediated by the VC in April 2012, a 42-year-old man complains about the damage to his property caused by one of his neighbours:

> The offender intentionally encroached (*guzhan*) upon the applicant's drainage ditch, discharging waste and pig excrement onto it. This has caused several damages to the applicant's domicile. His behaviour infringed on the

> applicant's ability to produce a secure environment to sustain a safe living (*bu liyi shengqinren de rensheng anquan shengchan*). All these years the applicant has already lamented the offender's behaviour, filing several applications to the competent authority. He has never been considered by the administration. This is because the VC and the offender entertain a "complicated" social relationship with one another (*cunzaizhe fuza de shehui guanxi*).

In these first two cases, we see citizens asking for cadres' intervention in relation to third party misconduct. While it should be noted that resorting to mediation by cadres was unusual for Dong villagers,[4] these cases show two things. First, applicants appear to care about the obligations (towards a person or the community) the authorities are expected to meet. In the two disputes, for instance, officials are accused of not living up to the standards of conduct imposed on them by their role. Second, these cases show that villagers ask for extended involvement in public affairs. Both cases seem to treasure villagers' participation in public life. Villagers lament when state–society relations are "complicated", thus hampering public, genuine engagement with their own community. They complain when infrastructural projects are carried out without their consent or supervision. They feel ashamed when their public persona is slandered to the point that further contribution to village life will be irremediably compromised. To the authorities, villagers demand more involvement in public life.

The above cases have been primarily about confrontation between villagers and officials. In the archive, though, the VC seems to be dealing far more often with cases involving villagers. In a long 'request', a 23-year-old man asks the Committee to uphold his usufruct rights over his father's estate. In fact, having suffered mental problems, his father was no longer in possession of the legal requirements for meeting usufruct.[5] In his statement, the young man reports how his patrilineal kin reacted to his request:

> In 2002 I turned 18 and I felt that it was time for me to shoulder my family's responsibilities. For that reason, I called my paternal uncle (*erdaye*) and his wife. I told them my intention, that I wanted back my father's properties (*yaohui wo fuqin de tudi caichan*), so that I could better take care of him (*rang wo lai zhaoguan wo fu*). My aunt replied: "Your mother does not know who she dealing with". My uncle added: "You call me to talk how to take care of your father and then you end talking about the land? The land stays where it is, no one needs you". I did not reply to that, but I knew that I could have relied on the "People's Republic of China Inheritance Law" (*Zhonghua Renmin Gongheguo Jichengfa*). It is my right to inherit my father's land.

While Chinese contract law would have accorded to the claimant the management of his father's land as his legally certified guardian, local authorities exploited the plaintiff's invalid appeal to Chinese inheritance law to negotiate compensation with the applicant's patrilineal kin, who also maintained an interest in keeping access to this land. In the cadres' response, it is specified that the claimant has to show "care" and "responsibilities" for his kin, regardless of the validity of his claim to his father's land. This last case complements my previous reading with two more points. On the one hand, 'rights talk' can be selectively de-activated by local authorities to protect their own (undisclosed) agenda and possibly vested interests in everyday village politics (Pia 2016b). On the other, it reveals that requests for reclaiming individual rights may still be re-couched in the language of "responsibility" and "care" (*fuze, zhaoguan*) – a language that directly relates to the obligations applicants have towards their families or lineages, but which, as I show below, may potentially spill over into relations with state agents.

Office vs. rights

In May 2012, Dong Village was seeing its water infrastructures turned upside down, as the government was intending to radically transform the pattern of land use in the locale, by converting most of the flat plots to tobacco. That day a man from the Township Government visited the Village Committee. He was accompanied by a well-dressed, bulky man holding a checked black and gold bag. The bag looked overstuffed and heavy. It contained numerous wads of red bills. After some preliminary exchanges of remarks and cigarettes, two older women dressed in farm clothes came along. They started talking in a high-pitched and angry tone to the Township official: "You and your friends talked about several hundred *yuan* to be given out, not merely two hundred! To build up the small dam requires much more money than expected. We need to buy more material, and the task is more difficult than we initially imagined. We talked to the group leader (*xiaozuzhang*) and he said, 'Don't ask me to get into this (*wo bu chengdan*)'. His supervisor also said 'I'm not getting into this, I have no right to do so (*mei you quanli*)'. How could they say that! Aren't they supposed to assume responsibility over precisely these types of issues?"

The official, clearly annoyed by the request for more money, denied that he had any leverage to pull off a more profitable contract with the working unit, and he challenged the two women to provide evidence that what they were saying was true: "Do you think that I can give money to anyone's asking? You should prove to me (*shuoming*) that you need the money for the dam, bring the master mason (*shigong*) here and let's see what he thinks about it. Besides, when we agreed on the budget, two hundred seemed fair enough (*gongping de*)." One of the women, outraged by the official's refusal, retorted, "Fair what? (*zenme gongping*!) Do you even know what being a *laobaixing* means? Living costs are so huge I can't save a penny! Telly costs me 60 *yuan* per month! Again, this year we've had no water: I will have to throw the rice away! We want four hundred. We are asking you to cover our living expenses (*shenghuofei*), really." Finally, a middle-aged man, hair whitened by a thick layer of concrete dust, entered the room, causing some relief to the two women. In a laconic manner, the man confirmed the women's story. The money-bag man responded by handing out four wads of bills to the newly formed trio.

As is clear from the vignette, to meet an official could be a good thing. Negotiation could lead to material benefit in a context where legal guarantees are absent.

Let me give a further example. One day at Dong Village Committee, Party Secretary L was discussing with an engineer the impact on the community of a water-related project. A number of group leaders were also present, representing the interests of their own constituencies. One of the group leaders refused to give his approval to the project, and thereby refused to provide the essential labour for the construction of a new irrigation channel, unless with the irrigation infrastructure a communal drinking water tap (*longtou*) was also installed in his own community. The negotiation progressed, and afterwards the water tap appeared at the entrance of Wang Family Village.

In contrast with how rights operate in the community – entailing overt confrontation and the risk of jeopardising one's position within one's own social network, as in the case of the young boy requesting his father's land – approaching an official in Yancong allows for a variety of strategic manipulations of one's claim, and thereby for greater chances of success. Despite their attempts at shirking responsibility – I have no right to do so! – officials could be used as proxies for wealth, and when face-to-face negotiations do not succeed, legal trickery does. One last case clarifies this point. In Pear Field Village, a young man had built a house at the turning point of a hairpin turn. Village cadres contested that in that position the house could, and did, clog up traffic. They then proceeded to demolish the unauthorised building.

Soon after that, the man sued the two cadres in court, demanding huge compensation. The young man claimed in court that the cadre used the "obstacle to transportation" clause as a pretext (*jiekou*), and that they wanted to hurt him for some other undisclosed reasons. The court agreed with the plaintiff, demanding 15,560 yuan from the two cadres. When I met the two officials to discuss this case, they looked terrified. They told me that in a previous extra-judicial settlement they had already bargained for 3,000 yuan and that they now did not know how to afford the compensation. One of them was sure that the young man was colluding with the court and erected the house in that position only because he knew that it was illegal to do so. This would prompt the officials to call for demolition, which the conniving judge would rule against, going all-in for the loot. That was a well-played scam they unfortunately had fallen into.

To hold an office in Yancong means to be in the position of presiding over the flow of funding the state can generate by virtue of ad hoc administrative decisions. As all my informants would easily recognise and lament about, this is the breeding ground of corruption and injustice. Yet, in a context of weak legal guarantees and the selective activation of 'rights talk', Yancong villagers go to great lengths to press officials to maintain their obligations to secure livelihood or "living expenses" for their local communities. In a twist that further complicates Chinese observers' enthusiasm for Chinese citizen's recourse to 'rights talks', the ethnography above has not only shown that rights may appear way too ineffective a 'weapon' for their purposes, but also that 'rights' may be strategically adopted by unscrupulous villagers towards illicit ends. In Yancong, in a context where basic livelihood is a matter of public concerns and debate, the register of rights intersects with that of obligations and both are recruited or rebutted by villagers as well as officials to advance private and collective strategies of legitimation against one another. This is the bread and butter of fighting for one's 'life'. The following and last section will show when such intersecting leads to political breakdown and to competing projects of public goods making.

Judgement

"What's a use right for?"

Let me now turn to some conversations I had with a group of informants who, during fieldwork, took part in a mass protest against one construction project involving the requisitioning of farmland (Pia 2016a). Most of them stressed that without land the requisitioned families will now be more insecure (*mei tudi mei anquan*), regardless of the amount of compensation given. All of them openly complained about the little involvement of locals in the decision-making process. One of my interlocutors commented: "You have to understand that the requisition was lawful (*an falü*). It is because of the temporary use of land. What could that possibly mean? The law in China is another way for the government to make a profit." In the eyes of the protestors, "use rights" limited, rather than expanded, the kind of demands villagers could express. Cases of lawful land requisition cannot be properly contested on the grounds that farmers' rights have been infringed, because "use rights" are temporary and are devised for expropriation to be possible.

Moreover, "use rights" entails devolving responsibilities onto common citizens. In the second protest I witnessed during fieldwork, the waters flooding out of a shoddy irrigation canal damaged several acres of cropland. To the angered farmers, local officials simply said that the upkeep of the canal was their duty and that they would be legally entitled to only limited compensation. As a consequence of this, "use rights" limit the intelligibility of dissent, as they recompose opposition exclusively in terms of neglected or unsatisfactory compensation. In reference to the metaphorical migration of Chinese contentious politics to the terrain of law, Sophia Woodman has pointed out the rights discourse: "validates some ways of speaking and invalidate others" (2011: 191). Her point is widely supported by my Yunnanese material. After the first protest, the Dong Village Party Secretary told me that the compensation given out to the affected farmers was massive, equalling forty years of farming the plot. Because of that, he claimed that he couldn't possibly empathise with the greedy rationale (*zisi zili de*) driving the protest. "Use right" works to deny villagers the opportunity to negotiate their claims with officials, as protesting against assumedly fair legal provisions makes the former look like a greedy, unintelligible mob in the eyes of the latter.

Another legal instrument of collective disenfranchisement put to work in Yancong is the locally infamous "water use permit" (*yongshuizheng*) and its related "right to water" (*yongshuiquan*). In the early 2000s, prior to the beginning of a slow political process of reform of the provision of drinking water in the locale (Pia 2017), Yancong dwellers had their water delivered to their houses in two ways. Through an open air channel collectively constructed during the Great Leap

Forward and secondly via a series of privately built but publicly accessible water wells disseminated throughout the countryside. By the early 90s, the above mentioned channel had been diverted by the local government to bring water to a newly built hydropower station. Further, the drilling of water wells was made illegal by a new environmental legislation concerned with the increasingly declining water table of Chinese underground water sources (Wang et al. 2007: 52). Central state control tightened on the management of water, drinking water included. Water meters started to be installed in every household, providing water for a fee.

Thereby, what was the public good of drinking water slowly became the exclusive province of the local water bureaucracy, with villagers being effectively expelled from the everyday management of the service. The terms regulating water services were clearly spelled out in a small booklet, called "water use permit", which every household was required to keep updated with the monthly amount of water use and fees paid. It was the household's right to receive 15 m^3 of free water daily, its responsibility to bear the maintenance costs of the water meter (*weixiu baoyang yiwu*). While my research participants working in the local water bureaucracy understood this system as a step forward towards a more efficient and safe system of resource consumption and delivery, local villagers talked of it as a "shady" service (*huise de fuwu*), muddled by an "unintelligible" right (*nan lijie de quanli*) and falsehood (*jiahua*). Because it was entirely devised by the local government – i.e. without the input of the locals – and more significantly based upon the appropriation of a pre-existent and participatory delivery system, villagers were actively resisting state water provisions. In fact, wilful disruptions to the water system, such as broken meters or severed pipes, had become quite common occurrences around Yancong.

How then did Yancong villagers get their daily share of drinking water if they almost refused to have access to what they called, only slightly joking, state water (*guojia de shui*)? They simply put greater effort and resources into building more publicly accessible water wells. Official documents recorded 970 wells in the Crooked Cart's Township for a population of slightly more than 96,000, although farmers claimed that in the area one could find one well for every ten households.[6] Unlike the state-sponsored drinking water network, which suffered continuous disruptions to its service, gaining access to wells was unrestrained and on a purely individual basis. The practice of supplying water through wells was totally and utterly a second-tier distribution network. During interviews with water wells' owners, respondents stressed that well water was used in common, with no right to exclude others from its use. In practical terms, the owner's consent to withdrawal was largely understood as the owner's obligation to give (*zeren*).

Conclusions

In Yancong the local state is recurring to a particularly dismissive and dispossessing form of 'rights talk' in the effort to subtly reframe the terms of villagers' participation in the making of local public goods. This reframing has to do with the fact that legal titles to land and water redesign and more relevantly shrink the boundaries of citizen's collective political agency. In fact, by virtue of the "use right to land" and of the "water use permit", local residents find their access to these public goods made precarious or even illegal. For this reason, rather than looking at the alleged emerging of a 'rights consciousness' in the Chinese countryside as an exclusively positive development for Chinese citizens living in the poorest parts of the country – as many commentators of China seem to do – attention should be paid on the one hand to how such discourses about rights are appropriated by the State and on the other, to what Chinese citizens really do, what political register they employ and what consequences this may have for future configurations of Chinese public goods and for the very possibility of their figuration.

This chapter provides a theory of public goods making in China that purports a reconsideration of recent analysis, quoted at the beginning, of the rise of a 'rights' discourse in China. The discussion, I contend, cannot be grounded in the reductive dichotomy of rules/rights. This is a dichotomy that characterises Chinese people's reclamations as stemming either from the idea that national rules and proper procedures are not being followed (Perry 2008) or from people's subjective feelings of violated entitlements (Li 2009). Rather, when disputing access over land and water, people in Yancong show greater concern for the social obligations maintained by the party who consents or gives way to someone's enjoyment of said goods. Villagers' anguish towards land requisitions or water distribution, driven by what they perceive as inscrutable or deceitful rationales, appears to be linked to feelings of violated obligations; obligations which join "the people" (*laobaixing*) and the state together and whose fulfilment falls on the latter.

Thus, my discussion here should rebalance the view of those scholars who argue that Chinese citizens are homogeneously starting to think of themselves as being endowed with individual or collective rights *against* the state. While an "obligation to give" and a "right to use" could be taken to mean the same thing – that people think of land and water as something that they deserve and hence as something from which they cannot be separated, i.e. as something inalienable – there is indeed a difference between reclaiming one's right and demanding official redress, one which generates a specific type of contention and bellicosity between local villagers and the state. This bellicosity is not cast in terms of the opposition between private interests (*si*) and the state (*guan*), but of a particular notion of justice that sees locals as entitled to have a say in matters of public concerns (*gong*). 'Rights' thus come to be seen by local villagers as a scapegoat, a strategy employed by officials when the imperatives of development urge them to sever obligations and to take unilateral choices in favour of a self-serving economic agenda.

Yancong villagers maintain a strategic relationship with the local state officials. Discussing with officials one's own involvement in the management of land or water means being able to set the conversation on the moral obligations that the former have towards the common people. Local officials thus intercede to secure the villagers' interests, uphold locally crafted rules, redress their grievances and impose compensation. However, as seen with the young man's request to gain control over his father's land, the register of obligation may also turn against villagers' interests to reinstate patriarchal values and the accompanying authoritarian practices of government. As the literature has widely shown (e.g. Ku 2003), this at times instrumental relationship with local officials is often able to secure small individual benefits for local villagers (that is, able to secure their *si*). And yet, the reliance on these relationships may prove to be too little too late for the participatory, popular government of rural Yunnanese villages. In fact, the same strategy is arguably falling short of winning villagers back their *gong* – i.e. their rights to collectively participate in the governance of a local public good.

Notes

1 Due to confidentiality agreements, I will make use of pseudonyms throughout the chapter. A deep thanks to the Chiang Ching-Kuo Foundation, the Chinese Scholarship Council, the Universities' China Committee in London, the John Wright Memorial Trust and the LSE Financial Support Office for support of this project.

2 The legal literature on land requisition in China highlights three main issues with the current legal framework governing land use in China. First, the actual users of the land have no say in terms of whether their land could be purchased by third parties. Second, the law does not include any provision for assessing "just compensation". Third, the law defines the "public interest" as the Party State's (i.e. forced urbanisation and economic growth are the default definitions of public interest). See Chan 2003 and Pils 2009.

3 During the time of fieldwork, Yancong was going through its fourth year of "drought". I have no space here to further problematise this statement, but the reader should note that fluctuating rainfall patterns linked to monsoonic weather were not the root cause of the diminishing availability of water in the locale.

4 The data relevant to access to justice from a thirty-household survey run by me and two assistants reports that, of those who declared having experienced "problems" (*maodun*) with fellow villagers in the last five years (i.e. 43.3 percent of the respondents), only 15.3 percent asked the VC for intervention. The majority (46.1 percent) dealt with these "problems" "privately" (*ziji guan*), while the second best option was either to ask the Water Engineer Office (23 percent) or to "lump" the grievance altogether (23 percent). See for similar yet much more generalisable results Michelson 2007 and 2008.

5 This is an abridged version. Attached to this, the claimant also submitted legal evidence certifying his status of "guardian" of his father (*fading baohuren*). According to Chinese Contract Law, persons with no capacity for civil conduct (as the mentally ill) are appointed guardians as administrator of their property (see 1986 Chinese Civil Code, Art. 17). The claimant, however, mistakenly derives from the Inheritance Law his rights to manage his father's land.

6 Yancong's governmental data also show that between September 2011 and April 2012, farmers' households contributed privately (*minying*) to the Township water sector's investment for an amount of 3 million and a half *renminbi* (567,000 US dollars), which equals 2.4 percent of the total investment in water infrastructure for that period. The sum invested by farmers is not part of the irrigation water fees farmers pay according to the amount of irrigated land they work, but it is an independent, unwarranted investment in the water service on the farmers' part.

References

Ames, Roger T. 2011. *Confucian Role Ethics: A Vocabulary*. Honolulu: University of Hawaii Press.

Angle, Stephen C. 2002. *Human Rights in Chinese Thought: A Cross-Cultural Inquiry*. Cambridge: Cambridge University Press.

Bear, Laura and Mathur, Nayanika. 2015. Remaking the Public Good: A New Anthropology of Bureaucracy. *The Cambridge Journal of Anthropology* 33, pp. 18–34.
Cai, Yongshun. 2010. *Collective Resistance in China Why Popular Protests Succeed or Fail*. Stanford: Stanford University Press.
Chan, Chris K. and Pun, Ngai. 2009. The Making of a New Working Class? A Study of Collective Actions of Migrant Workers in South China. *The China Quarterly* 198, pp. 287–303.
Chan, Nelson. 2003. Land Acquisition and Compensation in China. Problems and Answers. *International Real Estate Review* 6(1), pp. 136–152.
Chen, Jie. 2013. *A Middle Class Without Democracy: Economic Growth and the Prospects for Democratization in China*. Oxford: Oxford University Press.
Day, Alexander. 2013. A Century of Rural Self-Governance Reforms: Reimagining Rural Chinese Society in the Post-Taxation Era. *Journal of Peasant Studies* 40(6), pp. 929–954.
Duara, Prasenjit. 2015. *The Crisis of Global Modernity: Asian Traditions and a Sustainable Future*. Cambridge: Cambridge University Press.
Elyachar, Julia. 2012. Next Practices: Knowledge, Infrastructure, and Public Goods at the Bottom of the Pyramid. *Public Culture* 24(1), pp. 109–129.
Gallagher, Mary E. 2006. Mobilizing the Law in China: "Informed Disenchantment" and the Development of Legal Consciousness. *Law & Society Review* 40(4), pp. 783–816.
Guo, Xiaolin. 1999. The Role of Local Government in Creating Property Rights: A Comparison of Two Township in Northeast Yunnan. In: Jean Oi and Andrew G. Walder, eds. *Property Rights and Economic Reform in China*. Stanford: Stanford University Press, pp. 71–94.
Guo, Xiaolin. 2001. Land Expropriation and Rural Conflicts in China. *The China Quarterly* 166, pp. 422–439.
Habermas, Jürgen. 1981. *The Theory of Communicative Action*. Cambridge: Polity.
Hirschkind, Charles. 2001. Civic Virtue and Religious Reason: An Islamic Counterpublic. *Cultural Anthropology* 16(1), pp. 3–34.
Ho, Peter. 2001. Who Owns China's Land? Policies, Property Rights and Deliberate Institutional Ambiguity. *The China Quarterly* 166, pp. 394–421.
Ho, Peter. 2005. *Institutions in Transition: Land Ownership, Property Rights and Social Conflict in China*. Oxford: Oxford University Press.
Hu, Desheng. 2006. *Water Rights: An International Comparative Study*. London and Seattle: IWA.
Hua, Shiping. 2009. *Chinese Utopianism. A Comparative Study of Reformist Thought With Japan and Russia, 1898–1997*. Stanford: Stanford University Press.
Huang, Philip C. C. 2010. *Chinese Civil Justice, Past and Present*. Plymouth: Rowman & Littlefield.
Jun, Jing. 2007. State Comrades and an Elderly Woman's Suicide. *Critique of Anthropology* 27(2), pp. 147–163.
Ku, Hok Bun. 2003. *Moral Politics in a South Chinese Village: Responsibility, Reciprocity, and Resistance*. Lanham, MD: Rowman & Littlefield.
Li, Lianjiang. 2009. *Rights Consciousness and Rules Consciousness in Contemporary China*. Prepared for delivery at the 2009 Annual Meeting of the American Political Science Association, Toronto, Ontario, Canada, September 2–6.
Lin, Chun. 2006. *The Transformation of Chinese Socialism*. Durham and London: Duke University Press.
Michelson, Ethan. 2007. Climbing the Dispute Pagoda: Grievances and Appeals to the Official Justice System in Rural China. *American Sociological Review* 72, pp. 459–485.
Michelson, Ethan. 2008. Justice From Above or Below? Popular Strategies for Resolving Grievances in Rural China. *The China Quarterly* 193, pp. 43–64.

O'Brien, Kevin and Li, Lianjiang. 2006. *Rightful Resistance: Contentious Politics in Rural China*. New York: Cambridge University Press.

Peerenboom, Randall. 1995. Rights, Interests, and the Interest in Rights in China. *Stanford Journal of International Law* 31, pp. 359–386.

Perry, Elizabeth J. 2008. Chinese Conceptions of "Rights": From Mencius to Mao – and Now. *Perspectives on Politics* 6(1), pp. 37–50.

Perry, Elizabeth J. 2009. A New Rights Consciousness? *Journal of Democracy* 20(3), pp. 17–20.

Pia, Andrea E. 2016a. "We Follow Reason Not the Law:" Disavowing the Law in Rural China. *PoLar, Journal of Political and Legal Anthropology Review* 39(2), pp. 276–293.

Pia, Andrea E. 2016b. *On Chinese Pedagogical Legalism (and Its Anthropological Ghost)*. ALLEGRA Laboratory. Online at http://allegralaboratory.net/on-chinese-pedagogical-legalism-and-its-anthropological-ghost-fictions/

Pia, Andrea E. 2017. Back on the water margin: the ethical fixes of sustainable water provisions in rural China. *The Journal of the Royal Anthropological Institute* 23, pp. 120–136.

Pils, Eva. 2009. *Waste No Land: Property, Dignity and Growth in Urbanizing China*. Cornell Law Faculty Working Papers. Paper 59.

Pils, Eva. 2014. Contending Conceptions of Ownership and Property in Urbanizing China. In: Hualing Fu and John Gillespie, eds. *Resolving Land Disputes in East Asia: Exploring the Limits of Law*. Cambridge: Cambridge University Press, pp. 115–172.

Pils, Eva. 2016. Voice, Reflexivity and Say: Governing Access to Land in China. In: Olivier de Schutter and Katharina Pistor, eds. *Governing Access to Essential Resources*. New York: Columbia University Press, pp. 127–155.

Rowe, William T. 1990. The Public Sphere in Modern China. *Modern China* 16(3), pp. 309–329.

Scott, James C. 1990. *Domination and the Arts of Resistance: Hidden Transcripts*. New Haven, CT: Yale University Press.

Wang, Jinxia, Huang, Jikun, Blanke, Amelia, Huang, Qiuqiong and Rozelle, Scott. 2007. The Development, Challenges and Management of Groundwater in Rural China. In: Mark Giordano and Karen G. Villholth, eds. *The Agricultural Groundwater Revolution: Opportunities and Threats to Development*. Colombo, Sri Lanka: IWMI, pp. 37–62.

Wang, Hui, Lee, Leo O. and Fischer, Michael J. 1994. Etymologies: Is the Public Sphere Unspeakable in Chinese? Can Public Spaces (*gonggong kongjian*) Lead to Public Sphere? *Public Cultures* 6, pp. 597–605.

Warner, Michael. 2002. Public and Counter-Publics. *Public Culture* 14(1), pp. 49–90.

Woo, Margaret K. and Gallagher, Mary E. 2011. Introduction. In: Margaret K. Woo and Mary E. Gallagher, eds. *Chinese Justice: Civil Dispute Resolution in Contemporary China*. Cambridge and New York: Cambridge University Press, pp. 1–24.

Woodman, Sophia. 2011. Law, Translation and Voice: Transformation of a Struggle for Social Justice in a Chinese Village. *Critical Asian Studies* 43(2), pp. 185–210.

Woodman, Sophia. 2015. Segmented Publics and the Regulation of Critical Speech in China. *Asian Studies Review* 39(1), pp. 100–118.

Ying, Xing and Jun, Jing. 2000. Jiti Shangfang Zhong De Wentihua Guocheng: Xinan Yige Shuidianzhan De Yimin De Gushi (The Process of Problemization in Collective Visits: A Story of Migration Caused by a Hydroelectric Plant in Southwest China). *Qinghua Shehuixue Pinglun* 1, pp. 80–109.

Yu, Jianrong. 2007. *Dangdai Zhongguo nongmin de weiquan kangzheng: Hunan Hengyang Kaocha* (Organized Peasant Resistance in Contemporary China: An Investigation of Hengyang County of Hunan Province). Beijing: Zhongguo Wenhua Chubanshe.

7 Public Buddhist philosophy

Civic engagement and discursive space among a religious group in Shanghai

Weishan Huang

Since the 1980s we have witnessed immense historical changes in China, also in the increasing number of religious associations and religious populations. Beyond the existing statist categories of five traditional religions, there are also many new religious groups emerging domestically, or being brought into the country, with new agendas. At the same time, we have witnessed the emergence of urban voluntarism organized by religious groups in China. In Prasenjit Duara's book, he asks if Buddhist environmentalism could be an alternative social force for sustainable development in the crisis of global modernity, including the situation in China (Duara 2014). The roles of religion in fostering civic engagement in contemporary Chinese society is a thought-provoking question. While much literature on religion and the state in contemporary China focuses on tensions (Ying 2016; Kindopp and Hamrin 2004; Chan 2016), I will look at one conformist group and how it seeks to enact social reforms through urban volunteerism. In this chapter, I will look at a lay and long-standing religious movement, the Buddhist Tzu Chi Foundation (hereafter Tzu Chi), in urban Shanghai as an example of how social niches are created that focus on community voluntarism and grassroots education for moral reform. I argue that reflexive Buddhist environmentalism may develop a more creative and discursive space in a women-led civic sphere. Furthermore, I will examine how religious teachings and practices are translated into secular language and actions by adherents in order to adapt to the statist discourse in China.

Religious populations have increased steadily in China since the religious recovery in the early 1980s. Buddhists are reportedly the largest religious group in China, but the country will also soon become a global center of evangelical Christianity in terms of population[1] (Kindopp and Hamrin 2004; Ying 2016). Many religious groups have expanded rapidly or have had conflicts with the Chinese state in the last two years, generating public attention and political significance. However, these are not the movements generally considered as contributing to civil engagement, in Jose Casanova's (1994) sense, which I shall elaborate on in the next section.

The Tzu Chi Foundation in China was planted by Taiwanese immigrants in the early 1990s but has indigenized its membership in the last decade since its successful registration as a civic association. Unlike other civil activists seeking to transform the state, this religious movement seeks to accommodate state regulations in inventive ways to create long-lasting moral reform. Due to governmental restrictions in province-level municipalities, religious practices are less visible in public spaces, but they show considerable vitality in private and semi-open spaces in Shanghai. Although most religious groups have a limited scope in influencing the state, their actions create greater autonomy within Chinese society. For religious groups, the price of expressing political discontent is typically too high. Instead, they focus on changing the 'public culture' or engaging in 'moral reform' in religious terms. Tzu Chi is not a 'pressure group', since the pressure is still only coming from the direction of the state. The Tzu Chi movement diverts such discontent toward personal transformation and redirects the tension away from state control. Instead, their collective actions are seeking to transform the morality of society as a whole.

The organization of this chapter is as follows. First, I will raise the question concerning the concept of 'public' in China, followed by a brief introduction on statist discourses on religion and its social role. Third, in using the case of the Tzu Chi movement in a highly controlled municipal city, I will shortly introduce its organizational structures and religious discourse. The main section will focus on Tzu Chi's civic engagement and how this religious movement helps us reconsider the conceptual boundary between 'private' religious practices and the public societal imaginary.

Defining 'the public' and 'public religion'

How is the border between the private and public defined in the highly controlled society of China? Due to state regulations, many religious groups have involuntarily held their gatherings in households or in private manufacturing companies (Kindopp and Hamrin 2004: 133–140; Hattaway and Yun 2005; Potter 2003; Huang 2012), and might be classified as private religions since they are hidden and personal, or what Thomas Luckmann once called 'invisible' (Luckmann 1967). Private religious phenomena do not explicitly challenge either the dominant structure or the dominant paradigms of a society. Yet, I am interested in examining how the appearance of such religious groups and their discourses are linked to the concerns of the wider public.

In the broader comparative literature, the term 'civil society' has implied a number of political possibilities. According to White, who in the 1990s discussed the potential for the rise of a civil society in China,

> the use of civil society [first] reflects an attempt to define a type of relationship between state and society, regarding them as separate spheres. Second, it implies a certain power relationship between state and society, such that there are limitations on the state's capacity to pervade and control society, and a certain power on the part of members of a society to insulate themselves from the state. Third, in this realm of autonomous social power and space, 'civil society' denotes an associational realm in which autonomous organizations

are formed through voluntary association to represent the interests and aspirations of members of society.

(White 1993: 65)

As White argued, with the societal changes wrought by economic reforms in China, a social space had begun to open up between the state and social agents. His observations also referred to a parallel shift that occurred in the balance of power between the state and the new non-state players (White 1993:86). In his book *Alternate Civilities: Democracy and Culture in Taiwan*, Robert Weller instead proposed the term ‘civil association’ to avoid the theoretical assumptions and historical connections connected with the term ‘civil society’, for example those organizations must be formally organized or against the state. Yet, also civil associations as ‘alternate civilities’ are critical factors in state–society relations (Weller 2001).

Erving Goffman (1959, 1963) uses a more critical distinguishing reference point between the private ‘backstage’ sphere of self and the field of ‘public life’. Public life is where face-to-face interaction takes place and where one can distinguish between private individual religiosity and all of the public forms of associational religion. This differentiation between private and public appears as the distinction of individual and group religiosity at the interaction level of analysis. Applying the face-to-face definition of Goffman to the current political circumstances in China, I would classify Tzu Chi practices as belonging to the category of group religiosity, a public form of associational religion, at the interactional level of analysis. However, it is the distinction between religion and the ‘world’ at the societal level of analysis that makes the Tzu Chi practice in general a public religion, a point I will elaborate on later in this chapter.

In line with José Casanova’s critique of theories that reduce the political to the governmental and with feminist critiques of female spaces as domestic, apolitical and moral realms, I analyze how the merging of religious and domestic spaces can render the latter more public and political. Tzu Chi practitioners are part of the political community because they articulate a concern for the public good. Following José Casanova, I am interested in how “religious institutions and organization refuse to restrict themselves to the pastoral care of individual souls and continue to raise questions about the interconnection of private and public morality and to challenge the claims of subsystems” (Casanova 1994:35).

Municipal regulation and statist discourse

The post-Mao government has permitted limited freedom of religious belief and behavior, which is subject to legal and regulatory restrictions. Since 1979, a number of Protestant and Catholic churches, Buddhist and Daoist temples, and Islamic mosques have opened or reopened for religious services (Potter 2003). In 1982, religious toleration was formally reinstated. The basic policy on religious affairs during the socialist period granted legal status to Buddhism, Daoism, Islam, Protestantism, and Catholicism under the government-sanctioned “patriotic” associations, but not to groups outside of the five religious associations or to other religions (Laliberté and Lanteigne 2008). Yet it should be noted that other forms of religious practices had survived through the Cultural Revolution and were restored, such as in the Putian area of Fujian Province (Dean and Zheng 2010). While religion is still a sensitive issue in China, many scholars have contributed to the study of its revival and development, such as that of Buddhism and Christianity in both rural and urban areas.[2] Yet little of the literature touches on the issue of the development of religion in China through transnational networks.

What makes the political control of Shanghai different from other places, such as rural areas in China? In my fieldwork, I found out that one important but unspoken regulation among house churches in Shanghai is the separation of 'foreign' and 'non-foreign' congregations or fellowships. For example, the "Regulations on the Religious Affairs in Shanghai" (*Shanghai shi zongjiao shiwu tiaoli*) states that these regulations are formulated in accordance with the Constitution and relevant laws for the purposes of ensuring citizens' freedom of religious belief, maintaining harmony among and between religions, preserving social concord, and regulating the administration of religious affairs. Yet such freedom of religious belief is limited. In the name of 'harmony', many restrictions have been established on faith practices. Since it is 'illegal' for citizens to practice religious rituals without religious clergy even at permitted religious sites, almost all religious rituals conducted outside of state-sponsored sites are 'underground'. And these rules also apply to foreigners. Religious activities of aliens within Chinese territory includes the religious ceremonies that aliens conduct or participate in in accordance with their own religious beliefs and customs, their contacts with Chinese religious bodies, their sites for religious activities, and religious personnel.[3] It reflects the government's fear of foreign influence on domestic congregations (Ying 2006). The Chinese government still treats Christianity as a foreign religion, and these regulations are not imposed on Buddhists in Shanghai. Despite all of these constraints, local and foreign residents are still 'doing religion' in Shanghai, though in a climate of political uncertainty.

The second unspoken regulation I discovered is not only that 'nationality' matters in Shanghai, but that the size of a group is also critical. The Shanghai city government will be tolerant if each private religious group (such as a house church) has an attendance of lower than fifty people at a single event. Therefore, faith-based groups have to stay small in order to survive. The state does not take their small and submissive presence as a threat. This has to do with crowd control to prevent the outbreak of disorder and possible mobilization. This number is imposed by the municipal government to quarantine religious groups by isolating them into small groups.

In turning to the statist discourse on social roles of religions (especially the roles of Buddhism) in China, the Chinese government had recognized the influence of charitable works within the religious communities after the Sichuan earthquake in 2008. Yet the state discourse never advanced reasons connected to the development of humanitarianism, but rather it associated benevolence work with its benefits for the collective society and state. Since 2008, the increasing institutionalization of benevolence work has been under a process which allows the government to manage the flow of charitable funding.

The basic forms of charitable activities were also included in the document of the State Administration for Religious Affairs, 2008, number 6. The religious organizations were encouraged to make monetary donations to the public welfare and to set up internal charitable projects. The establishment of charitable projects and related activities, however, need to be reported to the government and relevant authorities, such as the Religious Bureau. The religious organizations were strongly encouraged to set up foundations to manage their special funds. During my fieldwork, I noticed that most Buddhist temples in Shanghai have set up such charitable foundations based on the encouragement of local government and have donated money to the district or city Red Cross offices.

In terms of management, it is stated in this document that tax exemption, discounts on utilities, and state reimbursements could be applied to legally register religious charitable entities. However, it was also stated that the state would determine which roles religious charitable organizations should play. They included issues of disaster relief, disabilities, childcare, elderly care, poverty, medicine service, and environmental protection. In some ways, the mission of the Tzu Chi Foundation fit well within the parameters of the statist discourse. Although the Tzu Chi Foundation was registered as a non-governmental organization (NGO), not as a religious entity, in China, it is stated that the Tzu Chi Foundation is still under the supervision of the Religious Bureau. The reassertion of state regulations in charitable work for religious groups provided a structural opportunity for the rapid development of the Tzu Chi Foundation after its official registration in 2008.

The Tzu Chi Foundation: the renewal of a historical movement

The Buddhist Tzu Chi Foundation is an international Buddhist relief organization founded in 1966 in Hualien, Taiwan, which has today millions of members in Taiwan and overseas. There are more than 300 Tzu Chi offices in forty countries, and four major missions. As of 2012, there were 1081 commissioners and 276 members of Tzu Cheng Faith Corp in Mainland China, which makes the Chinese overseas group the third largest, behind those of the United States and Malaysia. The Tzu Chi denomination (*ciji zongmen*) was officially established in Taiwan in 2006 by Master Chengyen.

The main mission emphasis of Tzu Chi is on social service, which is different from conventional Buddhism. The eight core missions of Tzu Chi include charity, medicine, education, culture, international relief, bone marrow donation, environmental protection, and community volunteering. Due to political restrictions, out of these core missions only five have been better implemented in China. They are: charity, culture, international relief, environmental protection, and community volunteering. Year-end poverty relief in Jiangsu province, for example, is one of the most significant charitable events for Tzuchians (*cijiren*), since it touches on the historical memory of organizational establishment in Taiwan and involves large-scale relief in the countryside in China. The Tzu Chi Foundation teams up with rural governments in Jiangsu province to organize the relief distribution, though the event has gradually brought concerns to the local county government because of the mass mobilization it involves. The first Tzu Chi hospital in China was established in 2012 in Suzhou after a year-long negotiation with the city government. Tzu Chi hospitals have also become social spaces for members to serve as volunteers. The establishment of private religious schools in China is unlikely to receive approval. However, the Tzu Chi Foundation has had enormous success on its missions of environmental protection and the mobilization of community volunteers in urban areas in China. These missions require less institutional formation and tend to be easier implemented.

The settlement of ethnic Chinese immigrants in many major cities worldwide is a significant factor behind the emergence of Tzu Chi's global network. The pioneer of Tzu Chi in China was a Taiwanese merchant known as Sister Chiou. As is the case with most Taiwanese merchants, Chiou's decision to transplant her manufacturing company to China was not an easy one. She felt forced to relocate her IT company's investments from Taiwan to China because of the rising cost of labor in Taiwan. With the hope that China was a new promised land for business expansion, she was also determined to bring her faith with her without assistance from the headquarters. After relocating her company to China, and with it Tzu Chi to Shanghai in 1992, Sister Chiou has faced harassment, interrogation, and short periods of detention from the government. After an early house gathering had attracted local police and officials' scrutiny, Tzu Chians in Shanghai, many of whom were bosses of private firms, decided to convene in companies and factories. Between 1998 and 2008 they worshipped in the *Jinshi* Halls located inside their factories and companies. My fieldwork on this transnational religious movement showed how immigrant entrepreneurs used their economic power to shadow religious practice before Tzu Chi gained legal status in 2008. People were practicing religion at the risk of losing their businesses.

The major Tzu Chi publications are *Tzu Chi Monthly* and its digital copies on the Tzu Chi website. However, Tzu Chi China is not permitted to publish religious content in both its magazine and website. The official website of Tzu Chi China, therefore, concentrates on reporting stories and news related social services and volunteerism, as in poverty relief, medical relief, and environmentalism. Only a few Buddhist education materials are distributed in the form of PowerPoint presentations or videos for study groups in the district centers or entrepreneurs' companies.

Organizational structure in Shanghai

The general organizational structure of Tzu Chi Shanghai basically follows that of Taiwan; but there are some differences. In leadership, Tzu Chi China is the only overseas branch where Master Chengyen is serving as the executive director. This is given important symbolic meaning. According to the staff in Suzhou, this is the second country where the Master will be able to preach in Chinese, suggesting the cultural intimacy and historical connections between Taiwan and Mainland

China. It also demonstrates the desire for further development in China among Tzu Chi's leadership.

Once Tzu Chi 'successfully' registered as an NGO in 2008, the organization could recruit local Chinese members, which was a significant breakthrough for the expansion of organization membership. Ninety percent of the new commissioners (and converts) in 2015 were Chinese. Yet even after gaining 'legal' status, as a religious group Tzuchians still have to practice their belief in a subtle way, within small groups. Tzu Chi activities remain also under the supervision of the Bureau of Religious Affairs.

Another significant change in the internal culture of the organization has been to integrate the mission into members' residential communities. In 2006, there was a structural reform known as 'Four in One'[4] within the Tzu Chi Foundation in Taiwan. The reform was gradually implemented in overseas branches, including China in 2014. The fundamental nature of the reform is to integrate social service within the territorial based residential communities. This is also a way to integrate the junior members in local missions so that they do not feel left out in a big organization. It is not simply a concern about efficient mobilization; it is also about diversifying the leadership in ethnic terms. "Integrating with the community" represented a shift of organizational development in 2014, but it was also an indigenization of leadership intended for the long term.

Community-based education and volunteerism

Sister Mei, who like Sister Chiou is a Taiwanese entrepreneur who migrated to Shanghai in the early 1990s, has converted the storefront space of her construction company into a gathering space where Tzu Chi activities in her district are organized. When I visited her, the office was completely converted into a Tzu Chi local center with clear Tzu Chi interior design elements. Tzu Chi posters were part of her storefront decoration. Most of the posters featured detailed information on environmentalism. Every Tuesday, there was a study group gathering members of all ages from the nearby residential community. Members, mostly females, watched video clips and listened to senior commissioners' lectures about environmentalism and Buddhist teachings. Putting Buddhist ideas into action was something new to them. Some of them were former 'mainstream' Buddhists and enthusiastic about grassroots environmental education in their neighborhood and poverty relief in rural areas. While senior members teach new members how to plan and implement organizational activities, new converts bring new ideas about how to localize this transnational Buddhist teaching in housing communities. In 2011, there were about twelve to fifteen people attending the Tuesday study group. In 2013, the size had grown to fifty to sixty people. In community-based gatherings, the number of members must nevertheless remain small.

Campaigns for environmental promotion in residential communities (*xiaoqu*) have always been important grassroots events for Tzu Chi Shanghai. In 2011, on the weekends, residents could also hear music and witness up to seventy-five people singing and dancing to Tzu Chi music outside of Mei's company. These people, who wore the grey uniforms of trainees, were dispersed into four residential communities for environmental protection campaigns, mainly promoting recycling. A team of sixteen to twenty members would set up a booth in the plaza or another open space to maximize the visual impact. Campaigns promote the concept of recycling and environmentalism. During the several very high profile outdoor campaigns I observed, only one complaint was received by the Residential Community Committee (*juweihui*; hereafter RCC), which also includes a Communist party representative. This complaint was quickly resolved after Sister Mei made a few phone calls. This is typical for Tzuchians who seek to bring the concept of sustainable development to their communities. Ceaseless efforts at communication and the skillful cultivation of personal relationships with RCC and party leaders are the keys for Tzu Chi development in residential neighborhoods. At the end of 2013, the environmental promotion and community education campaign had broken into even more groups to keep the size of attendees on the site appropriate. Larger groups can attract unwanted attention from community residents.

Similar stories have been unfolding in different districts in Shanghai. When I interviewed the commissioners in a Tzu Chi center in Pudong in 2010, they still mentioned the challenges they faced in staging events outdoors. In Ji District in 2013, however, a Tzu Chi recycling site had finally been set up with the assistance of the local RCC. RCC party members even encouraged community volunteers to join Tzu Chi environmental protection events. Since then, members have gathered every two weeks to organize their recycling collection. Ms. Feng, for example, a local task force leader, had been trained about recycling at the Tzu Chi Changfeng Center. Feng would negotiate with community residents to leave their recycling materials in a hidden area of their buildings and collect them after work on a daily basis. To her, Tzu Chi Buddhist environmentalism can be implemented in daily life. In the summer of 2016, she also planned to teach community residents how to make bio-enzyme from kitchen waste. At that time, Tzu Chi's Pudong branch was gradually able to promote its missions in the public spaces of its residential communities.

It requires two years of training before members can be promoted to become Tzu Chi commissioners. During these two years, trainees must attend all of the classes as well as Tzu Chi public events. Attendance for each trainee is documented in print. Those classes and events are a way of socialization into the 'Tzu Chi spirit' and the proper behavior of a Tzuchian. Besides participating in the community events, trainees are also required to attend volunteer training camps and public lectures held in the Shanghai center in Chengning district. Once trainees attend a certain number of district and city activities, they will be recommended to attend the regional training camps in Tzu Chi's Suzhou headquarters.

Creating urban voluntarism through discursive spaces

The religious discourse of Tzu Chi is one example of an internal secularization of a modern religious organization. What makes Tzu Chi's teachings different from other forms of traditional Mahayana Buddhism? What makes them more societal and, in the end, political? 'Relieve suffering, embrace all beings' is a core teaching of Master Chengyen. The focus on 'this world' and on 'others' is central to the doctrine of Tzu Chi Buddhism, and 'good deeds' are seen as more potent in creating good karma than sutra chanting or meditation. Internal secularization in the Tzu Chi Foundation happens in four ways: by creating discursive spaces for individual education, by rendering action more important than chanting, by working on self-cultivation, and by emphasizing collective karma.

Creating discursive space

According to Weedon, discourse in Foucault's work means "ways of constituting knowledge, together with the social practices, forms of subjectivity and power relations which inhere in such knowledge and relations between them. Discourses are more than ways of thinking and producing meaning. They constitute the 'nature' of the body, unconscious and conscious mind and emotional life of the subjects they seek to govern" (Weedon 1987: 108). During Tzu Chi events, members not only passively receive the information about the ecological crisis and environmental protection, lectures also emphasize environmental action by members globally and locally. Members' religious identities as Tzuchians are exemplified through religious activism for environmental protection.

In public testimonies on converting to vegetarianism, for example, members typically no longer mention the Buddhist commandment not to kill but the need to be compassionate to all living beings and have love for the earth. The religious rationale for promoting environmentalism is to promote the value of a life of wisdom (*huiming*). Environmentalism provides the only possible earthly field for self-cultivation. Thus, in many public speeches, Master Chengyen calls Tzuchians "Environmental Buddhas," "Purified Buddhas," or "Buddhas of Embracing Earth." Chengyen often emphasizes the relationship between reviving decency, decorum, ethics and virtue and environmental protection. Chengyen uses modern slogans in her speeches, such as "Love the Earth." As a Buddhist, this has a double meaning, which includes treasuring the cultivation of *huiming* (the life of wisdom) in our lives. Buddha taught that human beings cannot become Buddha in heaven, or in hell. In the world of the ten directions (*shifang* or the whole universe), the only place where people can cultivate themselves and become Buddhas is the earth. This has created a double impetus, both secular and religious, for the environmental protection mission. The rationale has been internalized, connecting the individual to larger society and, therefore, leading members to engage with social action.

Acting for the common good is more important than chanting

One important organizational motto is the active practice of sutras (*xing jing; xingru ciji dazangjing*). One can often hear the saying, "Just do it" (*zuo jiu dui le*) in the group. Action is regarded as more important than chanting sutras, as

Tzuchians view ethical action as separating believers from non-believers. The Buddhist Tzu Chi Compassion Relief Association was established as a secular organization led by housewives focusing on poverty relief – the first mission having been established in 1966 – and as a way of realizing Buddhist teachings. The promotion of community volunteerism was then started by Master Chengyen in 1996 in Taiwan to encourage members to re-focus their agency on their own residential communities. This reform has transformed the group's structure from a commissioner–member relationship to a geographic-based and functional-based membership (Chiou 2000).

This organizational reform had little impact on Tzu Chi China until fairly recently. Yet, the new formation of 'residential community' (*xiaoqu*) has represented an attempt of state to restructure relationships between the state and urban residents in China. Tzu Chi Shanghai has gradually installed its missions through its 'events' in the residential communities in Shanghai. Urban citizens are attracted to Tzu Chi for its religious and ethnic magnetism. Many local converts report to me that they are attracted to Tzu Chi because of its systematic organization of Buddhist altruism. The Tzu Chi Foundation has given new meaning to social activism for urban Buddhists.

Working for self-cultivation

As a true believer in Tzu Chi, one must work on one's faith by participating in community tasks, such as environmental protection services and visits to needy households. Although the scale of the environmental protection mission in China remains smaller than it is in Taiwan, the mission itself constitutes the major 'karma field' for members to work on self-cultivation in urban areas.

Similar to the Jehovah's Witnesses studied by Beckford, Tzuchians have to work for their faith "by methodical confrontation with intellectual obstacles and by a deliberate program of self-reform" (Beckford 1978: 256). Members must devote themselves to Tzu Chi's mission of social service to prove their piety. Trainees are evaluated on the frequency of their involvement in Tzu Chi's social services as a measurement of their commitment to the faith. Tzu Chi's discourse on environmentalism helps to constitute the ethical body and to form the mind and emotional life of the members it seeks to govern (Weedon 1987: 108).

The emphasis on collective karma

In contrast to traditional Buddhist practices, Tzu Chi teachings focus on the importance of group efforts in self-cultivation. This organizational rationale produces the group's values on individual, organizational, and societal levels. For members, the liberation of self is consistently related to others. How to model one's behavior as a parent, a child, a spouse, a spiritual companion (*dao qin*), and a task force leader (*xiao zuzhang*) are fully illustrated in organizational brochures and videos. The connection of internal and external worlds shapes the emphasis on collective karma, which provides the logics of 'practice' regarding environmental protection and Buddhist communal lives. One can perfect her/his life by acting kindly within the world and transforming those noble intentions and acts into both religious and secular rewards.

Public Buddhist philosophy: civil engagement with this world

In modern society, "religion may enter the public sphere and assume a public form only if it accepts the inviolable right to privacy and sanctity of the principle of freedom of conscience" (Casanova 1994: 58). If this condition is met, Casanova further points out three instances:

1 When religion enters the public sphere to protect not only its own freedom but all modern freedom and rights, and the very right of a democratic civil society to exist against an absolutist, authoritarian state. The active role of the Catholic Church in the process of democratization in Spain, Poland, and Brazil may serve to illustrate this instance.
2 When religion enters the public sphere to question and contest the absolute and lawful autonomy of the secular sphere; in particular its organization in accordance to the principles of functional differentiation yet without regard to extraneous ethical or moral considerations. The pastoral letters of American Catholic bishops questioning the morality of the arms race and of the state's nuclear policies, as well as the justice and inhuman consequences of the capitalist system, exemplify this second instance.
3 When religion enters the public sphere to protect the traditional life-world from administrative or juridical penetration, and in the process opens up issues of norm and will formation to public and collective ethical reflection. The public mobilization of the Moral Majority and the Catholic public stand on abortion in support for "the right to life" are examples of this third instance.

The case of the Tzu Chi Foundation in China presents another instance of a religion entering the world in an undemocratic society. The Tzu Chi Foundation is an associational religion which enters secular society to reform social practices under capitalism, such as mass production, overconsumption, and aggressive development, through introducing Buddhist ethics using secular language. In the process of calling for reform, Tzuchians are not critiquing wrong-doing of the state but of the self. Therefore, the reformed discourse targets the establishment by providing the "collective self-reflection of modern discursive ethics" (Casanova 1994: 58).

The reform starts from the self and extends to the social as the space between household and state. The reform begins by repairing self-karma and transforming it into collective karma. Tzu Chi members believe that benevolent actions cultivate or repair their karma. Demonstrating the Tzu Chi spirit might include visiting the poor, providing disaster relief, or conducting community services. This doctrine provides the basis for mobilizing commissioners and volunteers into becoming involved in a variety of social service activities. Members repeatedly emphasize that it is 'Buddhism in action' that makes Tzu Chi different from other

Buddhist organizations. This is Tzu Chi's way of engaging in publics and societies. Organizational works promote the idea of environmentalism instead of philosophical Buddhist teachings. This Buddhist belief creates a link between religious valuation and moral action. Followers of these teachings cannot isolate their good deeds to certain contexts; they have to reorganize their lives methodically and cultivate themselves through their work in daily life.

As my interviews suggest, these interpretations of karma exchange are fairly common among business people, yet they are expressed differently. Among Taiwanese entrepreneurs, sustainable development and environmental protection have been translated economically into the practice of thrift in the use of electricity and other resources, as well as raw material conservation in manufacturing. Tzu Chi cultivation teaching has been translated into the concept of self-management in order to control questionable excessiveness, if not greed, among employers. As for the rank and file practitioners, there is often a double meaning to their practice of vegetarianism, with both pious and worldly aspects. There is an internal logic in connecting religious and secular aspects, since the earth is seen as the place for the cultivation of the profane body. Furthermore, saving the earth is saving 'the others', which is seen as a mission of compassion in the sense of living in and working for a global community.

Martin Marty (1974, 1981) has argued that when a church reflexively examines and critiques existing social practices and cultural understandings in the light of its deepest religious insights into issues of justice and the good society, it engages in public theology. The Tzu Chi denomination's (*ciji zong*) close predecessor was Taixu's Rensheng Buddhism, a movement to transform the focus from individual cultivation to collective and worldly affairs. In the last century, Tzu Chi continued to develop its public Buddhist philosophy focusing on public virtues.

The concept of 'humanistic Buddhism' has been widely used and promoted among Buddhist communities worldwide. In many of her speeches, Tzu Chi leader Master Chengyen uses the terminology 'humanitarian spirit of the Tzu Chi School' (*ciji zhongmen de renwen jingsheng*). The emphasis on social service in the early 1970s and 1980s generated criticism from other mainstream Buddhist communities in Taiwan. Today, there are no issues categorizing Tzu Chi as socially engaged Buddhism; in fact, since the 1990s, the movement has successfully mainstreamed the practice in Taiwan. In China, the movement eventually received state recognition in 2008, but still faces political challenges due to the government's fear of large-scale social mobilization. The Chinese state has recently adopted the concept of humanistic Buddhism to extend its control over philanthropic funds of Buddhist temples.

One of Tzu Chi's societal imaginaries is to create a peaceful society without calamity (*shehui xianghe, wu zai wu nan*). When facing the increasing frequency of natural disasters in North and Central America, Europe, Africa, South Asia, and China, the organizational rationale is that this increase in disasters can be attributed to human activities, pollution and greenhouse gas emissions.[5] "What can one do about the situation?" Master Chengyen frequently raises this question and urges everybody to reduce their environmental impact by living a simpler life.

By connecting individual cultivation to a change of social practices, she offers three manageable steps: to consume less meat, to use less air conditioning, and to drive less. Followers of these teachings must not isolate their good deeds to certain contexts; they must reorganize their lives methodically and work on their faith in daily life.

Tzu Chi's teachings promote the idea of change in society while never directly challenging the policy or the authority of the hosting states worldwide. The organization, for example, promotes the idea of philosophical Buddhist teachings, such as *compassion, benevolence, happiness,* and *relinquishment*, and translates them into actions, such as mobilizing for disaster relief and providing services for the needy in the community. The organization, in another example, promotes the ideal of mercy through Buddhist environmentalism and extends this to a critique of capitalist society and overconsumption. The organization promotes Buddhist environmentalism, in both individual effort (living frugal, thrifty, and simple lifestyles) and communal effort (recycling in the communities), to deal with the burden of global crises. To live a simple lifestyle is not only a way to cultivate the individual mind to a Bodhisattva path, but also to construct a modern narrative of Buddhist cultivation for collective karma, which is for the care of all beings. These reformed Buddhist teachings have created the linkage between the value of religious tradition and the discourse of ethical actions. In its discourse on a methodical approach to break away from the capitalist system, Tzu Chi challenges the social norms of value, but not policies or political systems.

Conclusion: a new societal imaginary

As Casanova pointed out, "[t]he more a religion wants to transform the world in a religious direction, the more a religion becomes entangled in 'worldly' affairs and is transformed by the world" (Casanova 1994: 49). We have witnessed Tzu Chi's dilemma in the development of its organizational establishment and religious discourse. As Habermas (2005) stresses, religious citizen will have to recognize the secular world and rules and find a way to translate their religious ideas into secular language. Tzuchians have a principled Buddhist morality couched in secular language for secular citizens. A religious citizen, in the case of Tzu Chi, expresses a normative account of political theory by being an ethical citizen. Pious living styles can frame practitioners' daily decisions, including political ones. By focusing the discussion on public religious discourse, I have sought to understand both Tzu Chi's organizational rationale and its practitioners' ethical narratives that shape actions in public space and societal imaginaries regarding public virtue.

Since religious practitioners face many restrictions in China, faith groups cannot openly interact with other institutions, including both religious and non-religious ones. This, however, meant that people could organize at homes or at workplaces if numbers were kept small. The organizational structure of religious groups is thus small by design and flexible. Group leaders can easily coordinate members' participation, quickly move to new locations, or change worship times. Of course, Tzu Chi organization has not adopted these tactics voluntarily. They are conformist tactics that seek to obtain, by submitting to governmental restrictions, a certain degree of autonomy.

Besides becoming community volunteers, Tzuchians are also strongly encouraged to utilize their profession for the public interest. Entrepreneurs should not limit their goals to the pursuit of economic profit. Rank and file members should focus on carbon emissions reduction to pursue sustainable development on earth, which is regarded as a shared responsibility for all human beings. The critical engagement of citizens for the common good and for new communal virtues constitutes an important movement for moral reform in contemporary China. On the organizational level, the Tzu Chi Foundation has positioned its teachings in the currents of the Buddhist reform movement which developed during the last century. When the Tzu Chi Foundation devotes itself to constructing a discursive space for citizen education and the collective cultivation of new moral consciousness, its long-term goal is to change social and cultural practices in larger society.

By focusing on one religious group in this paper, my aim was to show how faith-based conformist groups focus on educating people and creating a social and discursive space in a heavily policed public sphere. It is, maybe counter-intuitively, their political compliance which gains these groups the limited autonomy needed to not only survive but also to aggressively develop in Shanghai. Within its spaces, the Tzu Chi Foundation as a reformed Buddhist group focusing on grassroots education gives practitioners the tools to act in more ethical and politically knowledgeable ways, thereby developing a creative and truly popular politics.

Notes

1 In 2004, Kindopp wrote about the trend that China will become the global center of evangelical Christianity if the growth rate continues. Jason Kindopp's article "Policy Dilemmas in China's Church-State Relation: An Introduction" in *God and Caesar in China: Policy Implications of Church-State Tensions*, ed. Jason Kindopp and Carol Hamrin. Washington DC: Brookings Institution Press. 2004. In *GlobalPlus*, Yang Fenggang (2015) stated the shocking fact that from 1950 to 2010, the number of Christians in China increased from 4 million to 67 million. By 2030, China is projected to have 220 million Protestant Christians alone, a figure similar to the entire Christian population of the United States today.

2 For Christian Protestants in rural China, see Hunter and Chan 1993. For Protestants in urban areas, see F. Yang 2005. For Buddhism in rural areas, see Tam 2006.

3 Article 3 in "Decree of the State Administration for Religious Affairs" No. 1. Rules for the Implementation of the Provisions on the Administration of Religious Activities of Aliens within the Territory of the People's Republic of China.

4 "Four in One" *(siheyi)* is a campaign to promote solidarity among the four tiers of membership.

5 Tzu Chi's offical website. Online at http://tw.tzuchi.org/en/index.php?option=com_content&view=article&id=1123%3Athree-easy-steps-to-save-the-earth&catid=62%3Aenvironmentalprotection&Itemid=186&lang=en, accessed August 20, 2016.

References

Beckford, James A. 1978. Accounting for Conversion. *The British Journal of Sociology* 29(2), pp. 249–262.

Casanova, José. 1994. *Public Religions in the Modern World.* Chicago: University of Chicago Press.

Chan, Shun-hing. 2016. Changing Church-State Relations in Contemporary China: The Case of Wenzhou Diocese. *International Sociology* 31(4), pp. 489–507.

Chiou, D. 2000. *Ciji shequ zhigongong de fazhan ji qi yihan – yi jiayi ciji zuzhi wei li*. Master thesis in the Department of Social Welfare, National Taiwan Chung-cheng University.

Dean, Kenneth and Zheng, Zhenman. 2010. *Ritual Alliances of the Putian Plain*. Leiden: Brill.

Duara, Prasenjit. 2014. *The Crisis of Global Modernity: Asian Traditions and Substainable Future*. Cambridge: Cambridge University Press.

Goffman, Erving. 1959. *The Presentation of Self in Everyday Life*. London: Penguin Random House.

Goffman, Erving. 1963. *Behavior in Public Places*. New York: Free Press of Glencoe.

Habermas, Jürgen. 2005. *Religion in the Public Sphere*. A speech delivered in Holberg Prize Laureate award seremony, November 30.

Hattaway, Paul and Yun, Brother. 2005. *Back to Jerusalem: Three Chinese House Church Leader Share Their Vision to Complete the Great Commission*. Westmont, IL: Biblica.

Huang, Weishan. 2012. Bodhisattva Comes Out of Closet: City, Surveillance, and Doing Religion. *Politics and Religion Journal* 6(2), pp. 199–216.

Hunter, Alan and Chan, Kim. 1993. *Protestantism in Contemporary China*. Cambridge: Cambridge University Press.

Kindopp, Jason and Lee Hamrin, Carol. 2004. *God and Caesar in China*. Washington, DC: Brookings Institution Press.

Laliberté, André and Lanteigne, Marc. 2008. *The Chinese Party-State in the 21st Century*. London: Routledge.

Luckmann, Thomas. 1967. *Invisivible Religion*. New York: Palgrave Macmillan.

Marty, Martin E. 1974. Reinhold Niebuhr: Public Theology and the American Experience. *The Journal of Religion* 54(4), pp. 332–359.

Marty, Martin E. 1981. *The Public Church*. New York: Crossroad.

Potter, Pitman B. 2003. Belief in Control: Regulation of Religion in China. *The China Quarterly* 174, pp. 317–227.

Tam, Wai Lun. 2006. Local Religion in Contemporary China. In: James Miller, ed. *Chinese Religions in Contemporary Societies*. Santa Barbara, CA: ABC-CLIO, pp. 57–83.

Weedon, Chris. 1987. *Feminist Practice and Poststructural Theory*. Oxford: Blackwell.

Weller, Robert. 2001. *Alternate Civilities: Chinese Culture and the Prospects for Democracy*. Boulder, CO: Westview Press.

White, Gordon. 1993. Prospects for Civil Society in China: A Case Study of Xiaoshan City. *The Australian Journal of Chinese Affairs* 29, pp. 63–87.

Yang, Fenggang. 2005. Lost in the Market, Saved at McDonald's: Conversion to Christianity in Urban China. *Journal for the Scientific Study of Religion* 44(4), pp. 423–441.

Yang, Fenggang. 2015. The Other Chinese Miracle: Great Awakening Shifts Growth of Global Christianity to the East. *GlobalPlus, Association of Religion Data Archives*. Online at http://globalplus.thearda.com/globalplus-religion-in-china/ accessed December 1, 2015

Ying, Fuk-Tsang. 2006. New Wine in Old Wineskins: An Appraisal of Religious Legislation in China and the Regulations on Religious Affairs of 2005. *Religion, State & Society* 34(4), pp. 347–373.

Ying, Fuk-Tsang. 2016. Chai zishijia de zhengzi – Zhejiang sheng 'san gai yi chai' yundong de zongjiao yi zhengzhi fenxi. *Daofeng: jidujiao wenhua pinlun* 44, pp. 25–61.

8 Concealing and revealing senses of justice in rural China

Hans Steinmüller

On a sultry summer afternoon in 2006, I sat with Yang Zhuren under the porch roof of the farm house of his brother.[1] After an abundant lunch with the village officials, we had gone over to the house of the brother to sit down in the shade. Smoking cigarettes and cracking sunflower seeds, we talked about common acquaintances in the village. Yang Zhuren was an official in the city government of Enshi, responsible for immigration and foreigners (of which there were about five in the whole prefecture). He had been assigned the task to supervise my stay and became my main point of contact in the prefecture. Yang also happened to come from the same township in which I was doing fieldwork. Having met many times in Enshi city and in Zhongba village where I lived, this was the first time we visited his *laojia*, the place where he had grown up, in one of the more remote villages of the township.

I knew that one of Yang Zhuren's tasks was to monitor the paper trail I left in the hierarchies of the local government, and he probably also contributed his own reports. At the same time I felt sympathy for this man, who had been lucky to become an official after his military service, who kept visiting his parents and young brother on their farm, who worried about his son's education in the city and loved to watch the NBA – Yao Ming, of course – together with his son. It always seemed that Yang also wanted to learn from me, and he often enquired about Germany and the Bavarian countryside where I had grown up. Now our conversation turned from Bavaria back to Bashan, and with some gravitas he asked me what I thought was the most important problem of the local society I had got to know here. I pondered for a while and then tried to express what by then I thought was the crux of China's problems: that there were no abstract and absolute rules and that everything depended on personal relations, on *guanxi*, and that everything was in flux and negotiable. This way people would have no security and confidence, and how could they be asked to belief in the party and the state? This seemed a reasonable answer to Yang Zhuren; he agreed and said, "Chinese society has to move from the rule of men (*renzhi*) towards the rule of law (*fazhi*)." While a lot needs to be done in this respect, he was confident that this was happening already.

I was left with some doubts. While I was heartened by Lao Yang's honesty about current social problems, I was not entirely convinced that actually there was a transition towards the 'rule of law' in the strict sense of the term. What follows are some reflections on the situations and contexts in which the 'rule of law' is invoked in rural China. Lao Yang spoke to me in a very private context; yet at the same time my position (as a foreign researcher) and our relationship (he being the main person in the city government responsible for me) also certainly influenced our choice of words.

In the following I deal with different invocations of the 'rule of law': this includes cases in which the 'rule of law' is presented as congruous or incongruous to conflict mediation; in the latter, the 'rule of law' represented by courts is sometimes explicitly avoided. The ways in which people relate to the discourse of 'rule of law' represent particular senses of justice. I will also deal with other senses of justice that are based on more localized moral frameworks. I focus in particular on the gestures of concealing and revealing such moral frameworks in ordinary social action and talk and argue that the interplay between 'front stage' and 'back stage' recreates "judging publics".

I start my discussion with a brief reference to the classical opposition between Confucian morality and Legalist statecraft. Rather than essentializing Confucianism and Legalism into two fundamental moral frameworks, I take this opposition as an inspiration to think about two aspects of popular law in contemporary China: firstly, the relationship between wider vocabularies of law and of morality – similar to Legalism emphasizing the former, Confucianism the latter. Secondly, this adage also points to the crucial relationship between outside display and off-stage performance.

I will focus in particular on the differences between displays and performances when analysing the interplay between different normative registers in contemporary China. In the following sections I will use moral discourses and conflict mediation in a village in Hubei as examples to demonstrate the varying uses of such normative registers. In their arguments and judgements, people make references to several different vocabularies and grammars available for (semi-) legal justification, similar to what Boltanski and Thevenot (2006) have called "orders of worth", and Hua and Thireau (2001) "registres du juste" (see also introduction to this volume). Shared vocabularies and registers and a shared platform of expression and audience define "judging publics". But some of these vocabularies and registers are not pronounced explicitly; instead actors share them implicitly. In this chapter, I emphasize the moments and gestures of concealing and revealing different normative registers. The situational use of normative registers points towards implicit understandings, and sometimes "communities of complicity" (Steinmüller 2013), which can be crucially important for "judging publics".

From Confucianism and Legalism to the rule of law and men

The opposition between Confucianism and Legalism is perhaps the most important debate in the history of Chinese governance and law (e.g. Qu 1961: 226–46). Confucian scholars promoted a rule of ritual and moral exemplar, which would promote self-cultivation and reward virtue. The followers of Han Fei and Lord Shang, who are commonly called "Legalists", directly opposed the Confucian ideals and suggested using the law to impose order, subdue populations to strict discipline, and if necessary, use manipulation to stay in power.

Some regimes in Chinese history were more obviously one or the other: The first Han emperor Qin Shi Huang's regime, for instance, was founded on the Legalist ideas of his adviser Li Si. Later governors would accord primacy to Confucianism. But in–between, Chinese politics were often "ornamentally Confucian and functionally Legalist" (*ru biao fa li*): rulers pretended to be good-willed Confucians and moral exemplars, whereas in reality they were cold-blooded and power-hungry Legalists.

Even if the rulers and the political system were often "ornamentally Confucian and functionally Legalist", this was so not only to deceive the governed. Surely both in Confucianist- and Legalist-inspired political systems – just like in any system of political order and hierarchy – obedience to rules and the contingencies of human action and thought must be reconciled. One way to do this is by "pretended following" and "pretended rule", or "hypocrisy". The historian Qin Hui points out that hypocrisy in that sense has been crucial for Chinese politics (Qin 2008). In a Confucian-inspired political order, it is vital that people pretend they are good, well-meaning, and polite. Only then can rituals be completed and social order maintained. Yet while rulers 'pretended' to be Confucian, they also sometimes demanded absolute obedience and punished their subjects. This was seen as necessary for cases of grave deviance and offence; but often it was also invoked against the ordinary unruliness of the 'small people'. As Confucian ritual was interlinked with literacy and the art of writing (Zito 1993), the illiterate peasants were potentially incapable of this kind of ethical governance and hence were in need of a strong and unrelenting rule. But if this was a common elite description of ritual and law, the realities were often exactly the other way around: commoners managed their deals according to Confucian propriety, whereas rulers schemed and ruled according to legalist principles.

It is clear that both Confucianism and Legalism are very different from a modern 'rule of law'. Implying that no one is above the law, modern rule of law opposes the arbitrariness of personal rule. Confucianism and Legalism both represent a 'rule of men', be it virtuous philosopher-kings or brutal autocrats. Modern rule of law requires that the law be certain, equal, and known by everyone. The classical texts of the Confucian and Legalist traditions are, however, more dialogical commentaries and mirrors-for-princes than scripted "law". Hence the modern opposition between rule of law and rule of men – *fazhi* and *renzhi* in Chinese – is of a rather different nature than the opposition between Confucianism and Legalism.[2]

In China, just like elsewhere, the rule of law is cause and consequence of political representation, universal citizenship, and nation-state sovereignty. At the same time, 'rule of law' implies independence of the law from state power and social convention. Ideally, law should be separate from both state and society, but obviously it has to emerge from somewhere and be embedded in state and society. This leads to a series of contradictions, which are fundamental to (modern) sovereignty:[3] How can the 'rule of law' be guaranteed and protected by a sovereign, and to what extent can the sovereign itself be subject to the 'rule of law'? How can abstract law be made to address concrete moral practices? In China, these contradictions of the foundation and social embeddedness of the law have a lot to do with the previous Confucian and Legalist heritage: these were the intellectual and moral resources that had to be negotiated in the creation of modern sovereignty and law.

Qin Hui goes as far as saying that the expression "ornamentally Confucian and functionally Legalist" (*ru biao fa li*) embodies the single most important problem of contemporary Chinese society (Qin 2010). Qin extends the meaning of the phrase to a general opposition between moral talk and immoral action, or people "talking about justice and virtue, while behaving like thieves and prostitutes" (ibid.). While I do recognize that contemporary legal practices in China cannot be described in terms of some unchanging essences of Confucianism or Legalism, I think that the opposition of "Confucian outside" and "Legalist inside" still has important implications now: if mandarins and rulers appropriately showed Confucian propriety and concealed Legalist manipulation, villagers and officials in contemporary China sometimes declare 'rule by law' (*fazhi*) and conceal the 'rule of men' (*renzhi*). Or, at other times, they pronounce the 'rule of law' irrelevant and reveal some kind of 'rule of men'. My suggestion is that such creative practices of display and concealment might bear important insights into popular senses of justice in contemporary China.

Philip Huang, in a recent overview article on Chinese legal practices (2015), identifies a long-lasting preference of substantive over procedural justice, concrete over abstract reasoning, and altogether emphasizes the influence of what he calls "Confucian familism" and "practical moralism" in Chinese law. Huang also makes the points that the history of the relationship between Confucianism and Legalism in Chinese thinking and practice should not be seen as a binary opposite, but rather as a symbiotic and corollary relationship (2015: 28). So 'Confucianism outside, Legalism inside' does not have to mean that both frameworks exclude each other, but rather have to be constantly related. By concealing and revealing different moral frameworks in ordinary social action, people relate to and recreate "judging publics". This is the core point that I want to explicate with some examples from everyday moral/legal disputes and discourse.

A dispute in the village

During my fieldwork in Bashan Township in the southwest of Hubei province, I only rarely encountered "the law".[4] Obviously there were conflicts between villagers or between villagers and government officials: conflicts over land rights, for instance, and over the land appropriations by local government for a small land development district near the market town of Bashan. But only in the most exceptional circumstances were these conflicts resolved by involving lawyers or bringing the case in front of local courts. Much more commonly, people sought to find informal agreements by involving mediators, typically men of high standing in the local community who were respected by both sides. More than once, people told me about their complaints and conflicts and sometimes they tried to involve me as a witness, if not as a mediator.

Walking home from the market town up the road to the village of Zhongba one afternoon in autumn 2006, for instance, a man of the Liao family called me over and invited me for a meal at his house. I had only met him two or three times before in other people's houses and didn't know him well, so I was slightly surprised at his invitation and politely refused to stay for dinner. But I accepted the cigarette he offered, and he immediately started telling me about a recent fight in which he had been involved. My neighbours had already told me that he had been involved in a very bad fight on the road to Zhongba.

Liao told me that a nephew of his, Deng, had been driving his cargo trike down the road to Bashan when a child of the Yang family ran into the vehicle and was hurt badly. The men of the Yang family ran after him and they caught Deng just next to Liao's house. The argument and yelling alerted Liao, who came over to mediate, he said. After a few words, fists were flying. Liao said that they started beating him, and when the blood was already running down his face, he got really angry, and started beating around, not paying attention whom he was hitting. "I would have beaten them to death if necessary, because they started it," he concluded. Even though Liao insisted that the Yang brothers had started it, at the end he and Deng got away with some bruises, while the two Yang brothers were now in the hospital of the prefecture with severe injuries.

They are not "reasonable" (*tamen mei you daoli*) and he is ready to "go to court" (*da guansi*), Liao said. He had already called up some of his friends and relatives in the township of Bashan and in the city of Enshi, and tomorrow he would go again to Enshi to meet a relative of his who works in the city government. The neighbours, and especially the people from the Yang family, painted a very different picture when I asked them later: Liao is known as a hooligan and he really started the beating, several others said. Over the following days both parties negotiated and threatened each other with a court case. At several occasions members of the Liao and Yang families publicly stated that they were not afraid of going to court.

Finally the issue was resolved through the mediation of an official who was a distant relative of both families. I met Liao some time later on the bus, where he told me that in the end he had agreed to pay 15,000 RMB for the treatment and hospital stay of the Yang brothers – even though they had started the fight, he insisted. The same payment had been suggested by the intermediary, and ultimately Liao agreed to pay. He insisted defiantly that he paid while at the same time strongly implying that it was not actually his fault.

In this case, then, the two groups were able to settle their conflict without the involvement of formal law. Yet the threat that the other party would "go to court" (*da guansi*) played an important role in the negotiations: Liao confidently claimed that he wasn't afraid to do so; but probably he conceded and paid the indemnity because his chances to win the case if it would have gone to court were minimal.

Such a case is surely not unusual in rural China; it is broadly in line with the accounts of dispute resolution and popular justice that scholars such as Zhu Suli and Zhao Xudong have given: a situation in which formal legal processes are often not followed (Zhu 2000) or are one possible source of authority amongst a number of others (Zhao 1997, 2003). Conflict resolution in such a context includes references to a diversity of normative references: moral principles of reciprocity and hierarchical standing in local communities, kinship relations, and the 'rule of law' represented by courts. Liao referred to "reason" (*daoli*), and tried to mobilise his network and appropriate mediators (including me). His opponents did the same, and they also emphasized strongly the bad moral standing that Liao had in the community as a known troublemaker.

Ultimately, successful mediation needs for people to agree on the same normative framework, or at least the authority of the mediator. In this case, I had the impression that Liao did actually not agree that he was guilty, but he wanted to avoid further trouble, and so agreed on the suggestion of the mediator to avoid further trouble – and especially, to avoid going to court.

Another important aspect is the timing and context in which different claims are made and different normative registers are invoked. Liao was very direct towards me, giving himself the appearance that he had nothing to hide, but at the same time he tried to involve me in his case in one way or the other. This was quite different from the sensitivity and secrecy that surround other cases of disputes: especially local officials tried hard not to reveal too much about local conflicts in my presence. Timing and context, then, are crucial for the judgement within local communities, and ultimately for conflict resolution.

The 'rule of law' was barely invoked in this case, if only as a potential threat – to "go to court" (*da guansi*). But even for ordinary people in Bashan, the 'rule of law' represents also a larger, ultimate morality. Somewhat contrary to the importance of personal relations in these conflict resolutions, some people in Bashan also expressed the view that actually, conflicts *should* be resolved by recourse to "the law", "as in Western countries and in the cities". My neighbour Wang Wei, for instance, had spent about eight years working in Shanghai. When I asked him about the difference of life in Shanghai and Bashan, he included the following criterion: In Shanghai, he said, people do not fight with their hands, but they resolve conflicts by resource to the law.

Such statements are similar to the official discourse about "spreading the law" (*pufa*) and "legal consciousness" (*falü yishi*) (e.g. Chu 2007; Trevaskes 2007: 33 ff.). Ordinary people like my neighbour Wang Wei, or Yang Zhuren (mentioned at the beginning of the article) sometimes also expressed similar views – that the 'rule of law' was already more prevalent in Chinese cities, corresponding to the higher degrees of economic development and the level of "population quality" (*renkou suzhi*) in urban China.

One might see in such cases of dispute resolution elements of a popular Neo-Confucian morality in opposition to modern formal law. But in popular discourse there are also hints towards ideas of law and order and the 'rule of men' that are much more akin to Legalist ideas.

The rule of great men

When talking about the law in farmers' households in Bashan, one thing that drew my attention various times was the unanimity in which people consented to harsh sentences and capital punishment. I do not remember hearing anyone in Bashan speaking out against the death penalty, for instance. Common reasons given for the death penalty are that it exists to "protect society", "because there are so many people in China", etc. What is more, many adults have also seen executions in their lifetime; and they are commonly reported in the local news.

Such discourses, to my mind, do not speak of the rule of law or the rule of virtue, but of the 'rule of men', based on threatened and actual violence. This opposition, however, is barely noticed in either official or private discourse: the 'rule of men' is generally used only in the negative sense, and drastic measures, such as the death penalty, are represented as part of the 'rule of law' – in many ways not too different from the death penalty elsewhere, including the United States. Such a discursive combination could be seen in the Legalist tradition, or in contemporary China in the tradition of modern policing – towards dangerous criminals and enemies of the revolution 'justice' has to be meted out, and without recourse to formal law, let alone Confucian rule of virtue. The state of exception – when measures outside formal law have to be applied – has to be decided by single actors. And such a Schmittian perspective can certainly be applied to many features of Chinese political and legal history: for instance internal party policing,[5] extra-legal detention, and spontaneous interrogation and detention.[6] In such cases, one might speak about the 'rule of men' within the 'rule of law'.

More than once I had long conversations in Zhongba about Hitler. One occasion I recall vividly was a dinner with a man from the city of Enshi who came to invest in some local tea factories. At the invitation of a neighbour who was thinking about renting his tea factory to him, we had a lavish dinner and long conversation. While the boss was world-savvy and a good talker, he seemed also very aggressive to me. He wanted to know what my plans were and found it ridiculous that I would not want to be rich and famous. Who were the highest officials I knew in the city and provincial government? And here too he found my answer disappointing. The conversation really turned a little bit antagonistic when he started telling me about Hitler – a tremendous military leader and a great man, really a source of pride for all the German people. I tried to explain that most German people, including myself, did not think highly of Hitler; if anything, we thought he was a disgrace and a catastrophe for German history. But the boss did not want to believe that and went on insisting on the greatness of Hitler.

That sense of the 'great men' who are 'tremendous' (E. *xiong*, P. *lihai*) links up with the revolutionary tradition of violence. The communist armies often recruited soldiers and leaders from armies and warlords. And Mao himself famously said that the "revolution is not a dinner party". With its roots in guerrilla warfare, the Communist Party's early leadership was based both on political affiliation and personal allegiance (Chen 1986). A leader such as Mao is commanding respect not only because of his intelligence and charisma, but also because of the fear he inspires. As one of my friends in Zhongba put it, "the Chinese like leaders who are a little evil" (*you dian huai*).

There was also a very widespread admiration, especially amongst young men, for local gangsters. I heard many stories about a local man of the Kang family who was a small gangster and had spent several years in prison in the 1990s, before he settled in the market town. Several young men in the neighbourhood, who had spent years in the cities, would often say to me that they also knew some men like Kang – actually, men who were even more powerful than Kang. When talking to Kang himself about his deeds in his youth, he would sometimes say to me that when they were young "they had no notion of the law" (*meiyou falü de gainian*).

At least regarding Hitler and Mao, private discourses often blatantly contradict the official discourses about the same historical figures: Hitler and fascism are condemned in official history writing, and so is the personality cult of Mao. But the respect for great leaders is sometimes expressed too, and especially in more private surroundings.

I want to emphasize here that the principles that are invoked in conflict mediation – including local moral frameworks and the 'rule of law' – depend on the occasion and situations in which they take place. The 'rule of law' and the 'rule of men' have undergone substantive transformations in China's modern history and they can refer to many different things now.

In the following I will look at different invocations of the 'rule of law' and relate them to emerging senses of localized 'publics' at the village level. The cases I have dealt with so far were about local discourses and conflict mediation. Now I will present two cases from Enshi that made it into national news, and compare the local events with the national reporting on the same cases. I will try to show how the combination of normative repertoires is remarkably different in local and national discourse. While government propaganda and official media largely represent the party-state itself as the source both of socialist morality and the 'rule of law', this particular combination is frequently contested, in particular in more private and intimate surroundings.

The Bashan nail house

In August 2014, a report about a "nail house" in Bashan appeared in national news, including on the very popular newsfeed of Tengxun (the company that operates the social media service QQ). In the last decade, a number of "nail houses" (*dingzihu*), whose owners were refusing to yield to large-scale developments, have become topics of national debate (Erie 2012). Homeowners who resisted forced eviction could sometimes take advantage of broad support, especially on social media. That was not the case in Bashan, however, where the report of the nail house was a showcase for a successful solution by local government of such a case. Entitled "A 'nailhouse' in Hubei that occupied a schoolyard for 56 years finally moved", the report told the story of a farmhouse on the schoolyard of the primary school. The Gong family that lived there had originally refused to move when the school was built in the 1950s; but now, persuaded by one very diligent official of the township government, they had finally agreed to move. The report in the national media pointed out the repeated efforts of the local government that only met with the stubborn resistance of the Gong family:

> For 56 years, every new generation of officials in the local government and the Education Departments, and more than ten headmasters in the school, tried to mobilize and convince Gong Houzhi and his family to move out of the schoolyard, so as to improve the study environment for the students; and the government promised to help him to build a new house not far from the school. But Gong Houzhi kept the last will of his parents: 'You mustn't lose the land of your ancestors'.

The report went on to describe the kind of problems the house of the Gong family caused for the school:

> The house of Gong Houzhi covers a surface area of about 500 square meters, it is a traditional wooden two-story structure. Around the house, there are some vegetable plots and fruit orchards, and Gong keeps some pigs and chickens. So when you enter the schoolyard, it smells of fowl. One teacher told this reporter that sometimes when the students did exercises in the schoolyard, a few hens were running back and forth between the students. The students' dormitory is right next to Gong Houzhi's house, and so the sounds of pigs and chickens would wake up the students early in the morning.

Finally, in 2014, the government planned an extension of the school and here the Gong family home caused further problems:

> In early 2014, an extension of the schoolyard was in the planning phase, and there was also a problem regarding the security standards: Gong Houzhi and his relatives always had to enter through the main gate of the school [to reach their house], and that was harmful to the security of the school. At the same time, the further construction and extension of the schoolyard was impossible, if Gong Houzhi wouldn't move.

At this point, an official from the township government, Tan Dalun, took up the case:

> For more than half a year, the 42-year-old Tan Dalun exhausted his brains in this task, more than ten times he visited, to chat about all the small and big things that mattered to Gong; no matter big or small, everything that Gong Houzhi needed, Tan Dalun willingly took it over and helped him.

The article goes on to describe how the official Tan helped the farmer Gong with paperwork for his pension, and other things. In this way they became close, and then the official took the opportunity to slowly convince Gong that he should move his house from the school. After all, having the farmhouse in the schoolyard did not only disrupt the teaching there, but also was not that convenient for Gong either. And having a new house elsewhere would be also much better for Gong himself, etc. The article even gives a verbatim quote of what the official said to the farmer:

> "You just have to agree to move, and I, Tan Dalun, promise you I take care of everything, you can choose the place for yourself, I take responsibility of all the paperwork." Gong heard Tan Dalun's guarantee, he discussed it with his wife, son, and daughter-in-law, and everyone thought that what Tan Dalun had said was reasonable (*you daoli*).

And so, finally in August 2014, Gong Houzhi signed an agreement with the local government; the local government, and the official Tan would help him and arrange the building work, and give subsidies. The building work had already started, and:

> At the end of the interview, Gong Houzhi said with a big smile, he is just waiting until Tan Dalun will have finished the new house, and he will move.
> (Tengxun 2014)

This article was widely circulated on the internet. One clear message was that Tan Dalun was a good official who had resolved a complicated situation. In comments on social media, some observers remained a little skeptical whether the report didn't exaggerate the benevolence of Tan Dalun and the local government. Friends from Bashan confirmed that the Gong family had actually received appropriate reimbursements for their new house and that the township government had helped them in particular with any necessary paperwork for the new house. They also emphasized, however, that the media attention had been particularly fortunate for Tan's career in local government.

The article represents a harmonious solution of various potentially conflicting discourses – including the stereotypes of selfish farmers (who don't see the public good) and corrupt officials who do not pay attention to the plight of poor farmers. Similar to official pronouncements on conflict mediation and the 'rule of law', the potential conflicts between different registers are downplayed in the official news report.

The case of this "nail house" contrasted broadly with a large-scale local development project that took place in the immediate vicinity of the school: on the paddy fields between the school and the market town more than 200 houses were built from 2008 to 2010, effectively doubling the area and reach of the market town. During my fieldwork in 2007, and during a revisit in 2012, there was a lot of talk about the corruption of local officials who had enriched themselves in the process. Yet nothing of these complaints ever reached the news, let alone national news. This is perhaps what typically happens during many forced evictions and development projects in contemporary China.

In the above case, the local official Tan Dalun was ultimately represented as the source of reason and morality. Against the odds, he convinced the 'unruly' farmer to move his house. Yet surely the newspaper report, as part of official discourse, is also in some way a shared production that relies at least also on the cooperation of ordinary people. In other cases, legal conflict has been more substantially shaped by public opinion. One famous case – that of Deng Yujiao – took place not very far from Bashan township.

Public opinion: the case of Deng Yujiao

In another county of Enshi prefecture, an incident took place in 2009 that became a national cause célèbre. On 10 May 2009, Deng Yujiao, a 21-year old pedicure worker in a hotel in Badong County, refused the advances of Deng Guida (no relation), the director of the local township business promotions committee. Deng Guida had come to the hotel together with colleagues, looking for sexual services. When he didn't respond to Deng Yujiao's refusals, she stabbed him repeatedly with knife, and he bled to death at the scene. Following the incident, Deng Yujiao was charged by the local police and put under arrest.

The case caused a stir in chatrooms and bulletin boards on the internet. Deng Yujiao was widely seen as a symbol of ordinary people's defense against corrupt officials. Following public pressure, the case came to national attention. Consequently, reporting on the case was censored to some extent, but the public discussion of the case also influenced the court proceedings to some extent. On 16 June 2009, the Criminal Court of Badong County announced Deng Yujiao's sentence as "intentional assault based on self-defense" and she left the court as a free person.

In the aftermath of the court decision, the case led to a minor earthquake in local government. The various officials who had been at the scene of the stabbing were all demoted – one of them, who apparently had supported the victim Deng Guida, was expelled from the party. A number of officials in the police and propaganda departments also lost their positions – some of them without any proven wrong-doing, merely because their names were tainted by having been involved in this famous case. The plight of the Director of the Public Security Bureau of Badong is of particular interest. He had given an interview to *Southern Metropolis Daily*, defending the initial arrest of Deng Yujiao for "intentional murder".[7] Even though he had done nothing wrong, the case severely damaged his career, and he was put in a quiet position in the Enshi City government with no hope for further promotion. A good friend of his in the Prefectural Government described his case in the following words to me:

> It is really a shame, my brother, the director was at the wrong place at the wrong time, Deng Yujiao's case caught up with him and was his downfall, now he is spending his days as a small official in Enshi. Of course, Deng's case is already decided, and there is an explanatory post on Baidu [the Chinese equivalent of Wikipedia], so I don't want to say much about that. But

> what I want to say is that when he was in office a murder happened; so certainly first you have to arrest the suspect, and that's still not too late to presume innocence. Any person in his right mind would understand this, and you don't need to have any particular legal training, because this is common sense knowledge. But exactly because of this decision, which was 1,000 percent correct, he lost his position. Higher officials, who had to deal with the challenge of public opinion, and the lawyers from Beijing who came to Enshi and didn't want to leave, all of them called again and again for justice for the underprivileged. In this hostile environment, he became a victim of this case. Later on, I asked some friends in the legal profession about the case, and they said that given the particular situation in which both [the perpetrator and the victim] had been, the lightest punishment should have been to pronounce her guilty, end the litigation without indictment and release Deng. There is no doubt that Deng was a weak girl, it is highly probable that her self-defense was excessive; society can provide support through certain ways, but if there is too much [support], that means to disrespect the law, and to trample on the principle of rule of law (*fazhi*). I don't know whether those Beijing lawyers just wanted to step into the limelight, or whether they acted for social justice (*shehui zhengyi*) and the rule of law (*fazhi gongping*). I think if this happened today, when the state promotes 'using the law to govern the country' (*yi fa zhi guo*), this director wouldn't encounter so much misfortune.

The case of Deng Yujiao shows other emergent publics forming around certain senses of justice. There was a large-scale popular movement, in particular on the internet, concerned with this case: numerous netizens read on the internet about this case and wrote commentaries on blogs and BBS [Bulletin Board System]. In public opinion, Deng Yuqiao became a personification of the fight of poor citizens against the corruption of party officials. The fact that she was a young woman who refused to prostitute herself made her into an icon of popular resistance.

My friend's comments are particularly interesting because his opinion points to the potential conflicts in the promotion of the rule of law. He says that there is already an official interpretation of the case, which is available to everyone on Baidu – and he does not want to be contentious with this explanation. What he wants to point out, however, is that in the process, his friend, the director, lost his job and any chance for promotion. What might be presented as a success of the rule of law has, in his opinion, also led to some consequences that blatantly contradict the rule of law: the fact that the director, who had done nothing wrong, lost his position.

But what is also crucial in this case is the context and situation – a private conversation – in which my friend voiced this opinion. The situation itself marks the relative powerlessness of this opinion, and as my friend insisted, he does not want to dispute the official decision about Deng Yujiao, which can be found on the internet.

Conclusion

Various contributors to this volume have emphasized the combination of different registers, orders of worth, or "registres du juste". This corresponds to what anthropologists of law have described as the use of various "normative repertoires" in conflict resolution (Comaroff and Roberts 1981). I have tried to show the combination of such registers, including local moral frameworks, Communist equality, and the 'rule of law', in various Chinese cases: in conflict mediation following an accident, in the case of state acquisition of land, and in the public case of Deng Yuqiao. Concrete arguments and mediation always involve shifting between these registers – for instance, between local ideas of kinship and the letter of the law.

A successful mediation must reach a point where both parties agree on one register; submit to the authority of the mediator; or at least one party either doesn't have the stamina to continue arguing or agrees otherwise on sufficient reimbursement. The latter might have been the case in the example of the man who agreed to pay for the hospital costs of the family he had had a fight with.

In recent years, mediation has also been promoted explicitly by the Chinese government. National and provincial authorities prescribe regulations for conflict mediation, including by village authorities. This promotion is explicitly supported by some legal scholars (e.g. Zhu 2000; Zhao 2003). But, as Pia (2015) points out, the local moral frameworks invoked in these mediation processes do not always 'harmonise' with the 'rule of law', but instead are often locally perceived as contradicting the law. During fieldwork in Bashan, even though the township government had officially appointed "conflict mediators" in the village government, these official points of contact were in fact barely, if ever, sought out by villagers. The general situation was similar to my first case: locals preferred to deal with conflicts informally and often used the threat of "going to court" (*da guansi*).

The larger point I would like to make here is about the loci of conflict, mediation, and agreement. The official discourse in the PRC promotes both the rule of law and local mediation; and affirms that there is no tension or contradiction between the two. Yet locally, in vernacular discourse, the conflict between the two is often pointed out. Not only is "national law" (*guojia falü*) used and abused by many different actors. But often 'the law' is conspicuously ignored, or 'downplayed', as when young men in my presence admired 'tough' and 'tremendous' leaders, and then also admitted that 'they didn't have a notion of the law'. That generally happens in more private contexts. In the public – even the local public of village level discourse – universal standards are more frequently invoked.

This is especially the case in official newspaper reports, such as those that deal with the Deng Yuqiao case, and with the Bashan nail house. The local meanings of such cases (e.g. that the head of the Badong police lost his job, that reporting about the nail house was very fortunate for Tan Dalun's promotion in the government hierarchy) must remain local. In the sense in which they point towards relatively particularistic and selfish aims, they are also potentially embarrassing, compared with the larger meaning of the "law". Speaking out in those (more localized) senses would produce an immediate loss of authority – you cannot produce a public on the basis of hidden values. In that sense, perhaps, the emerging 'new publics' are often built on implicit and local understandings.

Notes

1 Many thanks to the participants of the workshop on popular justice at the University of Oslo and Susanne Brandtstädter for helpful comments.
2 For an overview of early debates about the 'rule of law' and the 'rule of men' in early republican China, see Jenco 2010.
3 Gilmartin and Ocko (2009) frame their very insightful comparison of the rule of law in China and India exactly along these contradictions.
4 I did eighteen months of participant observation based in a village that I call Zhongba, in Bashan Township, in the southwest of Hubei Province between 2005 and 2007, and visited again in 2012. All names of people and places below the prefecture are pseudonyms.
5 In *Policing Chinese Politics* (2005), Michael Dutton proposes an insightful perspective on Maoist policies and politics. Noting the striking parallel between Carl Schmitt's definition of the political – the distinction of friend and enemy – and a core sentence of Mao's collected works ('Who are our enemies, who are our friends?'), Dutton analyses the passion and violence of Maoism in terms of this binary opposition.
6 Flora Sapio (2010) suggests that a similar Schmittian perspective might help us to understand the place of lawlessness within contemporary Chinese law. She focuses on practices such as *shuanggui* (extra-legal detention by party disciplinary bodies), labour re-education, spontaneous interrogation and detention. All of these practices are clearly outside the law, and Sapio suggests looking at them as 'areas of lawlessness' and 'zones of exception', which are organically articulated with the workings of the law in China.
7 See 'Interview with Yang Liyong, Badong public security bureau director. May 22, 2009', online at http://zonaeuropa.com/200905c.brief.htm#011.

References

Boltanski, Luc and Thévenot, Laurent. 2006 [1991]. *On Justification: Economies of Worth*. Princeton, NJ: Princeton University Press.

Chen, Yung-fa. 1986. *Making Revolution: The Communist Movement in Eastern and Central China, 1937–1945*. Berkeley: University of California Press.

Chu, Yingchi. 2007. Legal Report: Citizenship Education Through a Television Documentary. In: Vanessa L. Fong and Rachel Murphy, eds. *Chinese Citizenship: Views From the Margins*. London: Routledge, pp. 68–95.

Comaroff, John L. and Roberts, Simon. 1981. *Rules and Processes: The Cultural Logic of Dispute in an African Context*. Chicago: University of Chicago Press.

Dutton, Michael. 2005. *Policing Chinese Politics: A History*. Durham and London: Duke University Press.

Erie, Matthew S. 2012. Property Rights, Legal Consciousness and the New Media in China: The Hard Case of the "Toughest Nail-House in History." *China Information* 26(1), pp. 35–59.

Hua, Linshan and Thireau, Isabelle. 2001. Le sens du juste en Chine: En quête d'un nouveau droit du travail. *Annales HSS* 6, pp. 1283–1312.

Huang, Philip C. C. 2015. Morality and Law in China, Past and Present. *Modern China* 41(1), pp. 3–39.

Jenco, Leigh K. 2010. "Rule by Man" and "Rule by Law" in Early Republican China: Contributions to a Theoretical Debate. *The Journal of Asian Studies* 69(1), pp. 181–203.

Pia, Andrea. 2015. "We Follow Reason, Not the Law:" Disavowing the Law in Rural China. *PoLAR*. Online at http://eprints.lse.ac.uk/64113/1/Reason_law.pdf.

Ocko, Jonathan K. and Gilmartin, David. 2009. State, Sovereignty, and the People: A Comparison of the "'Rule of Law" in China and India. *The Journal of Asian Studies* 68(1), pp. 55–100.

Qin, Hui. 2008. Wei shan shi shehui hen zhongyao de gongneng (Hypocrisy Is a Very Important Social Function). Online at http://blog.sina.com.cn/s/blog_532cf03501009lt6.html, accessed 3rd March 2017.

Qin, Hui. 2010. Zhongguo wenhua zui da de wenti shi ru biao fa li (The Biggest Problem of Chinese Culture Is Being "Confucian Outside and Legalist Inside"). Online at: http://blog.sina.com.cn/s/blog_1309645640102w58l.html, accessed 3rd March 2017.

Qu, Tongzu [T'ung-Tsu Ch'ü]. 1961. *Law and Society in Traditional China*. Hague: Mouton.

Sapio, Flora. 2010. *Sovereign Power and the Law in China*. Leiden: Brill.

Steinmüller, Hans. 2013. *Communities of Complicity. Everyday Ethics in Rural China*. New York: Berghahn.

Tengxun News 2014. Hubei "dingzihu" zhanju xiaoyuan 56 nian zhong qianchu' (A "Nail-house" in Hubei That Occupied a Schoolyard for 56 Years Finally Moved). *Tengcun News*, August 27, 2014. Online at http://news.qq.com/a/20140827/064988.htm, accessed April 5, 2015.

Trevaskes, Susan. 2007. *Courts and Criminal Justice in Contemporary China*. Lanham, MD: Lexington Books.

Zhao, Xudong. 2003. *Quanli yu gongzheng: Xiangtu shehui de jiufen jiejue yu quanwei duoyuan (Power and Justice: Conflict Resolution and the Plurality of Authority in Rural Society)*. Tianjin: Tianjin Guji Chubanshe.

Zhu, Suli. 2000. *Song fa xiaxiang: Zhongguo jiceng sifazhidu yanjiu (Sending Law to the Countryside: Research on China's Basic-Level Judicial System)*. Beijing: Zhongguo Zhengfa Daxue Chubanshe.

Zito, Angela. 1993. Ritualizing Li: Implications for Studying Power and Gender. *Positions* 1(2), pp. 321–348.

A brief afterword

Isabelle Thireau

The nine fascinating papers of this volume present a groundbreaking contribution to our understanding of 'popular politics' in contemporary China and the 'quest for justice' manifested by a diversity of publics. After Susanne Brandtstädter's brilliant introduction, the studies gathered yield illuminating and important conclusions while describing a variety of empirical objects and thus making possible comparison across different situations, contexts, realms. The topics explored range indeed from local to national issues. They focus on urban and rural settings, religious groups, labor relationships, internet forums or discussions held regarding national regulations such as the *hukou.* They are anchored in a multiplicity of communicating spaces, encompassing both horizontal and vertical links. They unravel episodes of tension or rupture but also moments of persuasion or education. Such a diversity of places, events and social actors allows for a broad understanding of the issues at stake but also for a systematic confrontation of the situations explored, each contribution being a carefully carved study of its own while engaging in a discussion with the others. The similarity of the perspectives adopted, the relatedness of the questions raised, the readings and discussions shared account for the robustness, the complexity and the originality of the conclusions provided. In reading these pages, a few comments arouse. I will mention them briefly and in a rather disorderly manner just to highlight the significance of this collective endeavor.

The authors of this volume rightly stress the importance of judgements, that is, of the acts of judging, through which individuals or groups try to make sense – or to make a new sense – of the situations faced: residents opposing unexpected housing constructions, individuals and groups involved in political activities in Chinese cyberspace, land losing farmers contesting local development projects, religious groups attempting to accommodate state regulations, a variety of publics discussing citizenship, villagers critical of the idea of "rightful management" advanced by the local government, to name but some of the situations analyzed in this book. Hannah Arendt is frequently quoted and we can further rely on her work to point out that the faculty of judging is even more justified when the measuring rod of judgement has disappeared, or is blurred (Arendt 1982). Such indeed is the situation observed nowadays in China, although the factors accounting for it are too complex to be developed here. One may simply underline that the reasons for the current normative uncertainty are not to be found only in the rise of antagonistic interests observed after economic reforms were launched more than thirty years ago, as it is often claimed. Such uncertainty seems to me more deeply anchored in the Maoist era, characterized by an exclusive language to name and evaluate social reality, a language often possessing distorted relationships with reality while establishing blurred links between the descriptions of particular persons and events and their normative qualification. Moreover, not only were such descriptions and assessments often imposed upon social actors and social actions as if taken for granted, without proper justification, but the validity and relevance of the moral and ideological principles in which they were grounded could not be publicly debated or discussed, that is, they could not be publicly tested, experimented, denied or confirmed. In other words – and to be very brief on a problem that would require much longer and detailed developments – judgement, as a specific action during which a particular, be it an individual, an event or a situation, is connected with general descriptive categories and normative principles, was largely made to disappear. As a consequence, not only normative principles became unclear and uncertain, but a crisis of social reality emerged, that is, a crisis of the capacity of society members to name and appraise with a certain level of certainty the particulars their environment was filled with; or to say with a certain amount of accuracy "who is who for whom", to use C. Lefort's (1981) expression in his discussion of processes of "de-institution of the real". The economic reforms have thus been launched on a very fragile normative base which has not been recognized as such and has not been given the public space required to be renewed, transformed, consolidated. Indeed, not only was the crisis of social reality observed at the end of the Maoist era ignored but it has been further complicated by its official denial. In the meantime, rapid social and economic transformations ended in a deep rupture of experience for many China citizens.

Today not only the space for judgement has enlarged but judgement is very much needed in order for individuals and groups to assign a meaning, even tentatively and often through the confrontation of multiple perspectives, to the diversity of situations they are embedded in. In this sense, the moments and forms of judgements analyzed in this collective volume are of fundamental importance to seize the ongoing process of reconstitution of a normative realm. They show how particular events, actions or situations are opened to the investigation of individuals and groups attempting to link these events, actions and situations to general norms, rules or principles in order to assess their meaning as well as their normative orientation. Should, for instance, the 'rule of law' or the 'rule of virtue' or the 'rule of men' prevail to interpret and settle a specific village dispute? More precisely, the persons observed do not deal with pure particulars – that is, particulars that they do not try to sort and rank – nor do they deal with mere abstract general or political principles: it is the relationship established between both which matters. Of course, their choices are not disconnected from their own interests and strategies, as shown for instance in a paper analyzing how the 'corporate social responsibility' ethos is used by Chinese and international NGOs. However, whatever their objectives and strategies, those observed in this book are brought to use that specific political ability that consists in trying to assign a meaning to a particular experience by referring it to shared norms, that is to a common world whose existence is then assumed, tested and consolidated. In other words, judgements allow them to “place what they judge into the field of what makes sense to men”, as Ronald Beiner (1991) beautifully puts it. Of course, not all normative expectations need to be formulated. In this sense, if the social scientist needs to localize and describe the evaluations expressed by those he is investigating – and thus incidentally shuts away from his own evaluation patterns – he must also discover the implicit norms they take for granted. It is perhaps for such a reason that many contributions focus on situations in which persons and groups face normative disillusions and are thus brought to identify and formulate the principles or regulations they believe have been transgressed and that would otherwise remain unformulated.

> Empiricism maintains that knowledge depends on experience. This contention, although true enough, may be misleading. For it neglects to mention that the dependence goes both ways – that experience likewise depends on knowledge. Our expectations and beliefs about a situation affect the character of our experiences concerning it. They guide our investigation and structure our perceptual field. This is not to say that our expectations are always borne out or our beliefs always confirmed. Plainly they are not. But what attracts our attention is most often what defeats or fulfills a hope or a fear or violates a complacent assumption. What is routine often goes unnoticed.
>
> (Goodman and Elgin 1988: 5)

Accordingly, it is important to understand: When do the persons investigated resort, for instance, to law, to public commitments, to moral principles or to social usages in order to protect what they value? It is also important to grasp the specific goods and interests at stake. However, it is even more important to understand how they articulate the particular situations they pay attention to with broader norms and principles. To put it another way, we should avoid stressing only one of the two components – the particular interest at stake or the general forms used – inasmuch as we should avoid considering *a priori* the rules, norms and principles mentioned as mere determining constraints or instrumental strategies. We can borrow here from Ludwig Wittgenstein, who considers that a word only makes sense as part of a language game, which itself is part of a common form of life. He also indicates that in the explanation of meaning and judgements, sentences or propositions take priority over concepts or words (Glock 2003). More simply put, as far as the act of judging is concerned, the analysis needs to focus not on the vocabulary used but on the whole unit made up by the concrete case at stake and the general forms, norms or principles conjured. Within such a unit, a specific interpretation of the situation considered goes hand in hand with a specific interpretation of the rule referred to. At least, the connection made between the two – a connection revealing the knowledge and imagination of those who take the floor – cannot be ignored.

Using such an approach, this volume provides many examples of the diversity of connections made, expected or unexpected, such as when residents of Chaoyang district in Beijing link their fight for preserving a green space in their neighborhood to the defense of public health and to the SARS crisis, or when NGOs understand the situations faced by migrant workers in terms of law violations or in terms of their unfortunate backwardness and low quality. It shows how rules and norms, sometimes imported from abroad, are articulated to concrete situations in an unanticipated way or been put to multiple and sometimes contradictory uses. It illustrates how, if recourse to official regulations and public commitments may seem appropriate for many to express legitimate expectations, using them does not mean using them in an anticipated, predefined, ready-to-use fashion, as already noted by Kevin O'Brien and Li Lianjiang (2006; O'Brien 1996). A correct use of an official rule or public pledge, as far as the grammar of action is concerned, can indeed also be a new, unexpected or even transgressive use. The same is true for moral principles or social usages. The situations depicted here are even more complex that individuals and groups often resort not to one but to as many rules or principles as possible. They try to demonstrate that the injustice experienced goes against a plurality of norms. Such a move rules out the idea of merely obeying an exclusive rule or complying with it. Most accounts show indeed that, as a diversity of common references are conjured up, the meaning of each of them is altered by their mutual coexistence and their intricacy. Put together, they create a specific normative framework stemming from the way they are organized into a hierarchy and combined.

Many situations or events examined in this volume are characterized not only by acts of judging but also by some form of publicity. The judgements expressed are indeed often public: they can be heard by many although they enjoy varying forms and degrees of publicity. As a consequence, the analysis of 'what is publicly judged?' – and in the meantime of 'what is not publicly judged?' – as well as that of 'how it is publicly judged?' allows us to explore the emergence of new social realities in contemporary China. At least this is so if we agree that what appears in public acquires in the same movement some consistency as a social reality. The answers to these questions provide clues regarding not 'values' but processes of 'valuation' as part of the investigation made by individuals and groups.

> The conclusions [. . .] do, however, state the conditions within such a theory [of valuation] must satisfy. [. . .] The undertaking can be carried out only by regulated guidance of the formation of interests and purposes in the concrete. The prime condition of this undertaking [. . .] is recognition that desire and interest are not given ready-made at the outset [. . .] for desire always emerge[s] within a prior system of activities or interrelated energies. It arises within a *field* when the field is disrupted or is menaced with disruption [. . .].
> (Dewey 1939: 239)

The existence of varying forms and degrees of publicity – and not of a simple dichotomy between the private and the public – calls also for the systematic comparison of the answers given, *in situ*, to the following questions: 'who is speaking, of what, to whom, in front of whom?' More pointedly, how do those investigated take into account different modes of visibility and interaction in order to choose among potentially relevant norms and principles? How do they undertake successive processes of reformulation in order to be heard and to strengthen their legitimacy in different settings? How are given judgements transported and translated in a diversity of more or less institutionalized environments? In other words, the context of enunciation matters a lot and we are here provided with a fine spectrum of situations allowing for a more thorough and systematic comparison.

If investigation and valuation are public but also dynamic processes, temporality has to be taken into consideration and the different temporalities depicted in this book cannot be ignored. As far as this issue is concerned, it could be useful, as French sociologist Alain Cottereau invites us to do, to distinguish more clearly between the interpretations and judgements expressed while action is still ongoing (and its outcome undecided) and those expressed after action has come to an end. In their fascinating book on the household budget of a Moroccan migrant family living in Spain, *Une famille andalouse. Ethnocompabilité d'une économie invisible*, a study in which they 'count all that counts' for this family, Cottereau and Marzok (2012) suggest indeed to use the word 'valuation' for ongoing action and the word 'evaluation' when action is reported afterwards. He rightly stresses that 'valuation' is often made in a context of doubt, indecision and uncertainty that disappears when the event is recalled. In this sense, 'valuation' is a process of experiments, of trial and error moments, of internal discussions and debates embedded in a landscape of power relationships and normative possibilities that vanishes when the choice finally made is reminded afterwards.

Another element proves to be central in the studies gathered in this volume: the relationship established by those in 'quest for justice' between themselves and those they are directly or indirectly addressing. Indeed, many authors in the book stress how those who take the floor position themselves differently according to the circumstances. Such variations appear to be linked with the main interlocutor their words and actions are intended for. To take just one example, designating oneself as *qunzhong* (群众) brings to light an interlocutor, close or distant, responsible for the well-being of 'the masses'. It brings also to light, including to a public of observers and commentators, the legitimate principles presumed to be shared by the "masses" as well as by those who rule them.

I could not but correlate these remarks with the analysis of the written accounts sent to the Letters and Visits Administration (Thireau and Hua 2006, 2010; Thireau 2012). The relationship established between the complainants and their addressees is indeed growingly at their core and influences the argumentation developed, as shown for instance in these two excerpts:

> Dear and respected President Hu Jintao,
>
> My name is Wang An. It has now been two years since I have become some sort of fugitive forced into hiding from both the authorities in the city of Yulin who want to arrest me and the hoards of those who have lent me

money and who can no longer contain their anger. I do not know how much longer I will remain on the run, nor do I know how this will end. Originally I was a lowly farmer who kept to his place and who chose to spend all his energy taking the risk of trying to exploit the oil wells in Yulin in the north of Shaanxi province. I had signed a contract with the local authorities and then suddenly, two years ago, the police, the public prosecutor's department and the courts rallied together and came armed to seize my oil wells. (. . .) President Hu, I do not have enormous experience of the world, but I know what rules should be respected. A government which forcibly takes possession of the property of the people, whatever the dynasty or era, is clearly wrong. We have committed no crime, no matter how small, but nevertheless, the local authorities want to arrest me to prevent me from lodging a complaint. They are ready to do anything to find me and at one time there were several hundred people looking for me. At the present time, many like me have suffered terribly for wanting to complain against the Yulin government. I cannot continue to live in this situation. I am Chinese and you are the President of the Chinese. What would you have done in my place? I hope that you can help me! (. . .)

(Gao 2006)

Dear respected Mayor,

I hope you are well. My son Ma Wei wrote to you at the beginning of June to bring to your attention and to challenge the fact that the Overseas Chinese Residence has started to consider as its own a passageway that has always been a public right of way. They have installed barriers and have imposed the necessity of buying a ticket on those who wish to use it, thereby preventing the locals from moving around as they have always been able to. Today, two officials from the resident committee X came to see my son to give him a document that the Residence had written in response to questions asked by the local legal services about this case. In reading this document, I had some thoughts that I wish to submit to you in this letter. (. . .)

The document states that "there would be security problems if idle individuals with no clear position were allowed to wander freely through the passageway." This claim cannot constitute a justification for the closure of this passageway or for the introduction of a ticket system.

The so-called "idle individuals with no clear position" are also citizens of our country. They have the right to come and go as they wish. As far as I know, there are no national directives forbidding "idle individuals with no clear position" from using public passageways in certain residences, areas or towns. Preventing these "idle individuals with no clear position" as well as other locals from using a public passage is therefore against the law. If the State spends money maintaining public rights of way, it is indeed so that people may use them. People are not discriminated against whether they are from North or South or young or old. Everyone has the right to walk around the town. In acting as it has, the Residence is violating people's right of

> movement – which is a fundamental right of human persons – and acting in a way that is contrary to reason (. . .).
>
> (Letter collected by the author, written in Beijing in 2007 by Ma Lina)

The authors of these letters raise questions, confront their interlocutors – here political authorities at different levels of the hierarchy – with contrasting interpretations of a given situation and ask them to choose among them. They do so in a situation where they are the ones who took the initiative to speak, whether in an oral or written form. Their address is indeed an action – A writing to B – that, in this specific context, means also that a 'ruled' is writing to a 'ruler'. A relationship between rulers and ruled, between 'I' (or 'we') and 'you' is thus developed at the initiative of those who speak out. Such relationship is important not only to understand "who is speaking in front of whom" but because it highlights the relational dimension of the sense of justice expressed. "The continuities between the parties and the whole are also encompassed in the Chinese thoughts about the relationship. This one is not understood as a simple link being established between pre-existing entities, but it is constitutive of the beings in their existence and their future", writes A. Cheng (1997). Such assertion embedded in the history of Chinese thought could be considered as irrelevant to interpret present situations. However, it bears some resemblance with H. Arendt's (1958) words when she understands power as a relation rather than something that can be acquired, and action as mainly the start of something new in human relations. It reminds me also of a discussion about the upcoming presidential elections in France in Tianjin, on March 30, 2012, with a second-hand bookseller. Mentioning the absence of such elections in China, he concluded: "As I cannot vote for those who lead me, I am not a citizen of this country". Rather than claiming that his basic rights as a citizen had been denied as voting was not a possibility, as others elsewhere would have promptly done, he focused on the relationship (or lack of it) of "a citizen voting for his President" in order to reinterpret his status as a citizen.

In the corpus of letters currently under study, the expected, presumed relationship between rulers and ruled as disclosed by petitioners thus reveals how they perceive and envision their power over each other. More pointedly, a relationship between the complainants and those they are addressing is posited by the first ones, enabling them to assign a specific position and specific obligations to both parties in the relationship. This expected relationship cannot be controlled, or contested, beforehand. As Wang An says in the above letter: "I am Chinese and you are the President of the Chinese". However, both the positions and the relationship depicted are not merely factual; they rely on specific interpretations of what should be versus what should not be. In other words, they encompass duties and responsibilities. They are described in terms of legitimacy and illegitimacy. Saying how you envision yourself in given circumstances thus allows you indeed to take the initiative to designate the related opposite party as well as the related legitimate normative principles. Such an emphasis put on the relationship established between the various parties at stake seems to lead to an emphasis on mutually binding normative principles, that is, on familiar and legitimate principles rather than on conflicting ones.

However, to come back to the first lines of this brief afterword, general principles are interpreted by individuals and groups in diverse and contrasted manners when connected to the particular situations at stake. In other words, the sense of injustice expressed in these letters (public commitments, laws and regulations, moral principles, social usages) is grounded in shared legitimate arguments which as such compel one party in the relationship while nonetheless being re-interpreted and eventually assigned a new meaning by the other party. The second party having reassessed the shared normative principles – after having been reinterpreted when connected to particular situations – it leaves the first one with the possibility either to agree with the judgement expressed and act accordingly or to take responsibility for publicly moving away from shared normative principles. In other words, rather than dismissing what separates them from the State and Party representatives, complainants put forward the links that mutually bind them in spite of their dissimilar positions. Rather than challenging official measures and directives, they strive to reduce current normative uncertainties by selecting and reinterpreting laws and official pledges as promises whose meaning they nonetheless contribute to establish.

By sharing these brief comments, I hope to have demonstrated that the present volume, by the diversity and the quality of the studies gathered, offers an unprecedented opportunity to study ‘popular politics’ as varying forms of interplay between judgement, publicity and situated or imagined relationships among citizens as well as among citizens and their rulers.

References

Arendt, Hannah. 1958. *The Human Condition*. Chicago: Chicago University Press.

Arendt, Hannah. 1982. *Lectures on Kant's Political Philosophy*. Chicago: University of Chicago Press.

Beiner, Ronald. 1991. Hannah Arendt et la faculté de juger. In: Hannah Arendt, ed. *Juger ou la philosophie politique de Kant*. Paris: Editions du Seuil, pp. 13–221.

Cheng, Anne. 1997. *Histoire de la pensée chinoise*. Paris: Editions du Seuil, p. 41.

Cottereau, Alain and Marzok, Mokhtar Mohatar. 2012. *Une famille andalouse. Ethnocompatbilité d'une économie invisible*. Paris: Editions Bouchène.

Dewey, John. 1939. *Theory of Valuation*. Chicago: Chicago University Press.

Gao, Zhisheng. 2006. *Zhongguo minqi weiquan di yi an* (The First Case of Rights' Protection Movement of Chinese Private Entrepreneurs). Taipei: Taipei Broad press International.

Glock, Hans-Johann. 2003. *Dictionnaire Wittgenstein*. Translated by Hélène Roudier de Lara and Philippe de Lara. Paris: Gallimard.

Goodman, Nelson and Elgin, Catherine Z. 1988. *Reconceptions in Philosophy and Other Arts and Sciences*. Indianapolis and Cambridge: Hackett Publishing Company.

Lefort, Claude. 1981. *L'invention démocratique*. Paris: Fayard.

O'Brien, Kevin. 1996. Rightful Resistance. *World Politics* 49(1), pp. 31–35.

O'Brien, Kevin and Li, Lianjiang. 2006. *Rightful Resistance in Rural China*. Cambridge: Cambridge University Press.

Thireau, Isabelle. 2012. Les déboires du Pasteur Lin: une dénonciation venue des masses à Shanghai au début des années 1950. *Le Mouvement Social* 239, pp. 61–90.
Thireau, Isabelle and Hua, Linshan. 2006. The Critical Competence of Chinese Citizens: From Lodging Complaints to Assessing Social Reality and Public Institutions. In: Katsuji Nakagane and Tomoyuki Kojima, eds. *Restructuring China: Party, State and Society After the Reforms and Open Door Policy*. Tokyo: Toyo Bunko, pp. 96–126.
Thireau, Isabelle and Hua, Linshan. 2010. *Les Ruses de la démocratie: Protester en Chine contemporain*. Paris: Editions du Seuil.

Index

For Product Safety Concerns and Information please contact our EU
representative GPSR@taylorandfrancis.com
Taylor & Francis Verlag GmbH, Kaufingerstraße 24, 80331 München, Germany

www.ingramcontent.com/pod-product-compliance
Ingram Content Group UK Ltd.
Pitfield, Milton Keynes, MK11 3LW, UK
UKHW022124190926
475702UK00013B/1632